**Dancing with digital natives : staying in ste**
302.23 DAN 20        *31201200070*

Manafy, Michelle
Butler Community College

DEMCO

# Dancing With
## Digital Natives

# Advance Praise

"In a competitive world filled with new technologies and constantly evolving tastes, *Dancing With Digital Natives* serves as a brilliant roadmap for connecting with the elusive teen and young-adult consumer. Read this book!"

—R. Lee Fleming, Jr., screenwriter,
*One Tree Hill*, *Friends*, and *She's All That*

"I love this book. The digital native generation doesn't want to be talked to; young people want to interact, engage, and effect change. And *Dancing With Digital Natives* shows you how to make that real connection happen."

—Lou Frillman, chairman, Unity Fund, and multiple leadership roles, Barack Obama 2008 Presidential Campaign

"With *Dancing With Digital Natives*, you'll get to know the next generation of consumers so that you can create products and strategies that appeal and engage."

—Sam Ades, vice president,
Digital Web Group, Warner Bros Animation

"Audiences today are not interested in one-way communication. In *Dancing With Digital Natives*, you'll learn how to start a genuine conversation with your audience so that you can create real engagement and better entertainment."

—Ed Marinaro, actor, *Blue Mountain State* (Spike TV)

"Tomorrow's historians and social scientists may very well look back on *Dancing With Digital Natives* as one of the seminal works describing the ongoing community-building imperative in this new epoch of information."

—Hugh McKellar, editor-in-chief, *KMWorld*

"*Dancing With Digital Natives* shows how our next generation of consumers expects us to know them well, by engaging them every step of the way. This engagement is both an imperative and a great opportunity. And this book lays out an incredible roadmap for doing great things with that opportunity."

—Andrew Panay, producer, *Wedding Crashers*

# Dancing With Digital Natives

### STAYING IN STEP
WITH THE
### GENERATION
THAT'S TRANSFORMING
THE WAY BUSINESS
IS DONE

## Michelle Manafy and Heidi Gautschi

CyberAge Books

**Information Today, Inc.**
**Medford, New Jersey**

First Printing, 2011

*Dancing With Digital Natives: Staying in Step With the Generation That's Transforming the Way Business Is Done*

**Publisher's Note:** The authors and publisher have taken care in the preparation of this book but make no expressed or implied warranty of any kind and assume no responsibility for errors or omissions. No liability is assumed for incidental or consequential damages in connection with or arising out of the use of the information or programs contained herein.

Many of the designations used by manufacturers and sellers to distinguish their products are claimed as trademarks. Where those designations appear in this book and Information Today, Inc. was aware of a trademark claim, the designations have been printed with initial capital letters.

**Library of Congress Cataloging-in-Publication Data**

Dancing with digital natives : staying in step with the generation that's transforming the way business is done / edited by Michelle Manafy and Heidi Gautschi.
    p. cm.
    ISBN 978-0-910965-87-3
    1. Generation Y. 2. Technology and youth. 3. Young consumers. 4. Information technology--Social aspects. 5. Information technology--Economic aspects. 6. Diffusion of innovations. I. Manafy, Michelle, 1967- II. Gautschi, Heidi, 1972-
    HQ799.5.D36 2011
    302.23'10842--dc22

                                                                    2011003709

Printed and bound in the United States of America

President and CEO: Thomas H. Hogan, Sr.
Editor-in-Chief and Publisher: John B. Bryans
Managing Editor: Amy M. Reeve
VP Graphics and Production: M. Heide Dengler
Book Designer: Kara Mia Jalkowski
Cover Designer: Laura Hegyi

# Contents

Acknowledgments ................................. ix

Introduction ..................................... xi

*Michelle Manafy and Heidi Gautschi*


PART ONE: THE DIGITAL NATIVE GOES TO WORK

Chapter 1: When Facebook Comes to Work: Understanding
    the Work Practice of the Digital Native ............. 3

*Brynn Evans*

Chapter 2: Thinking Outside the Cubicle: Examining the
    Changing Shape of Today's Workspace ............. 19

*Susan Evans*

Chapter 3: The Dis-Organization of Invention ................ 39

*Carolina M. Reid*

Chapter 4: Native in Blue: Understanding the Challenges and
    Opportunities in Managing Today's Police Officers ... 61

*Christa M. Miller and Lt. David Hubbard*

Chapter 5: I'm With the Brand: How Generation Y Will
         Transform Hiring Through Personal Branding ........ 81
    *Dan Schawbel*

PART TWO: MARKETING AND SELLING TO THE DIGITAL NATIVE
Chapter 6: With, Not To: The Value of Social CRM ............ 97
    *Marshall Lager*

Chapter 7: Inspired Interaction: Youth Marketing on Mobile .... 115
    *Peggy Anne Salz*

Chapter 8: Adapting Old-Fashioned Marketing Values to
         the Needs of the Digital Native ................. 133
    *Michael P. Russell*

Chapter 9: The Social Media Imperative: Learning to Engage
         Digital Natives Where They Live ................ 153
    *Shashi Bellamkonda*

Chapter 10: Social Capitalism and the Reputation Economy .... 173
    *Michelle Manafy*

PART THREE: ENTERTAINING THE DIGITAL NATIVE
Chapter 11: The Digital Natives *Are* the Entertainment! ....... 191
    *Richard Hull*

Chapter 12: Ethics, Technology, and the Net Generation:
          Rethinking IP Law .......................... 211
    *Albert M. Erisman*

Chapter 13: The Old News and the Good News: Engaging
          Emerging Readers Through Social Interaction ..... 227
    *Michelle Manafy*

Chapter 14: T'écoutes quoi ti? Digital Natives as Music
        Consumers in Lille, France . . . . . . . . . . . . . . . . . . . 249
        *Heidi Gautschi and Emilie Moreau*

PART FOUR: EDUCATING THE DIGITAL NATIVE

Chapter 15: Making the Grade: Standards and Promoting
        Achievement Through Technology . . . . . . . . . . . . . . 269
        *Sarah Bryans Bongey*

Chapter 16: Quest to Learn: A Public School for Today's
        Digital Kids . . . . . . . . . . . . . . . . . . . . . . . . . . . . . . 291
        *Robert J. Torres, Rebecca Rufo-Tepper, and Arana Shapiro*

Chapter 17: Teaching Digital Literacy Digitally:
        A Collaborative Approach . . . . . . . . . . . . . . . . . . . . 315
        *Jami L. Carlacio and Lance Heidig*

Chapter 18: French Lessons: How France Is Educating Its
        Digital Natives . . . . . . . . . . . . . . . . . . . . . . . . . . . . 333
        *Heidi Gautschi*

Chapter 19: Native Knowledge: Knowing What They Know—
        and Learning How to Teach Them the Rest . . . . . . . 351
        *Mary Ann Bell*

About the Editors . . . . . . . . . . . . . . . . . . . . . . . . . . . . 373

Index . . . . . . . . . . . . . . . . . . . . . . . . . . . . . . . . . . . . . . 375

# Acknowledgments

That we were able to complete this project with our sanity and friendship still intact owes much to the advice, help, and support of our friends, family, colleagues, and contributors. To list all of these people here would be a book in itself, but please know that we value your support.

Heidi would like to thank Michelle for embarking on this adventure with her. Michelle is incredibly well organized and a fabulous editor, and these abilities certainly raised the likelihood of completing this project. Heidi, however, is even more grateful for Michelle's intelligence, thoughtfulness, sense of humor, and love of Yahtzee. Heidi would also like to thank Marc Dupont, David and Adelle Gautschi, and Lisa Gautschi for their love and steadfast belief in her, as well as Fatma Ramdani, Sabine Lesenne, Emilie Moreau, and Olivier Cornille for their support and help. She would also like to thank her students at the University of Lille 3 for giving her the opportunity to observe digital natives in action.

Michelle would like to thank Heidi for knowing her as well as she does and still choosing to undertake this project as partners. The work here benefits greatly from the added perspective of Heidi's distinct world view. Michelle benefits greatly from Heidi's steady calm, sense of fun, and fearless honesty. Michelle would also like to thank Daniel and Harlequin Sullivan for their unending patience, love, and support; Tom and Claire Sullivan for their belief in her; and Anita Kemmy for instilling in her a lifelong love of learning and literature. Michelle is also lucky to have had the daily influence of the team at *EContent* magazine for inspiration while putting this project together, and the support of Ron Miller, Nancy Davis Kho, and David Meerman Scott in particular for pushing her to get out of her comfort zone.

Without doubt, we are both deeply grateful to all of our contributors for their expertise, hard work, and patience. This project would not have been possible without them and owes its strength to their breadth of knowledge, openness of mind, and willingness to do the hard work it takes to create a contributed volume like this one. We are also grateful for the support we received from the team at Information Today, Inc., especially Amy Reeve and John Bryans.

Lastly, we thank all the digital natives out there using digital technology in creative new ways. You are our inspiration. We're counting on you to tell us what we got right and where we went wrong. We can't wait to get your feedback.

Heidi Gautschi
Sains du Nord, France

Michelle Manafy
New Preston, Connecticut

# Introduction

Michelle Manafy and Heidi Gautschi

It is always tricky to make generalizations about generations. For every conclusion drawn about the behavioral habits of people in an age group, there will be a seemingly endless number of individuals who refuse to toe the line that analysts have so precipitously drawn. Certainly there are those any label would fail to fit. Hard to say, though, whether this is why generational labels themselves have grown fuzzy around the edges: Generation X, Generation Y, Millennial. These certainly don't bear the same strong stereotyping stamp as generational monikers such as Baby Boomer, Greatest Generation, or Lost Generation.

Today, however, we are witnessing the emergence of a fully loaded generational epithet: digital native. So named by Marc Prensky in 2001, this generation encompasses all those who have grown up with ubiquitous digital technology. While lacking a hard-and-fast start date, it most often refers to those born since 1984. As with all of the preceding generational profiles, there are those who will not fall neatly into line with the assumptions made about the generation of digital natives. Many factors contribute to variations—from homes in which computer use is discouraged and those in which financial circumstances result in less technological exposure to the vast individuality of the people who fall into this (or any) age group.

Despite the challenges and limitations in applying assumptions to a whole generation, generalizations can be explored and applied in order to better understand the characteristics of its members. These days, we find ourselves in great need of this sort of understanding because, while members of every generation may find themselves muttering about "kids today," with the generation of digital natives, some face what looks like an unbridgeable gap.

Consider the way in which digital natives can, themselves, respond to what is said about them. These days, young people who don't see themselves accurately reflected in pundits' descriptions of their generation can—and do—make their disdain very publicly known online. These very actions are what make digital natives just that: natives of a digital world. They take the tools at their disposal and modify them to meet their personal, evolving needs. With natural ease, they have staked out their territory on the web and made it into a network of communication, where they can carry on a tangle of never-ending conversations.

Those of us born before the inception of the internet, before the proliferation of cell phones, who remember the first time we saw—much less used—a computer will never assimilate digital communication tools in the same way as natives. Many of those in older generations find it baffling to witness a generation living such a social life publicly online: a nonstop sharing of ideas via text messages, feeds, and networks. Of course, these differences flow both ways: Just as a member of Generation X can't understand her grandparents' obsession with having a fully stocked pantry because she didn't live through the Great Depression, natives will never be able to fully appreciate older generations' knowledge hoarding or privacy concerns.

As generation gaps are not unique to the Western world, the ubiquity of digital technologies is becoming an increasingly global phenomenon. From using Facebook to sharing videos of protest in Tunisia to cell phone novelists in South Korea, innovative personalized use of communication technology applications is spreading worldwide. While previous generational labels did not often cross international borders, digital natives are not restricted by locale.

Arguably, they aren't truly limited to one generation either. "Digital nativity" depends on early exposure to digital technologies. However, while digital immigrants may have taken part in the creation of these digital technologies, the key distinction is that natives have never known a world without them. Certainly, there are many out there who are extremely adept adopters of digital technologies, toying with them as they emerge and even developing a mastery of them. However, as with any adopted culture or second language, these digital immigrants may never be able to intuit social mores or subtle inferences.

Certainly, there is no small irony in calling people immigrants in a world they helped create. Yet, with technology there is often a schism between the innovator's initial vision and actual use. It is doubtful that Arpanet engineers envisioned that the Pirate Bay Party would one day be represented in the EU Parliament. And cell phone engineers probably didn't anticipate that kids would use their cell phones as 21st-century boom boxes or that texting would be more popular than talking on the phone.

These twists and turns, this appropriation, modification, and re-appropriation are what everyone faces when a new technological development goes through. Even as we seek to understand digital natives and create strategies and solutions aimed at them, we must accept that once our ideas are in their hands, this generation will make of them what they choose.

For better or for worse, today we all live together in this digital world. We are connected to and must tap into this generation as we educate them and work with them, and as they become the dominant consuming force. These three aspects are intimately linked. We must understand how their lifelong immersion in digital technologies colors every aspect of their behavior, so that we can maximize their effectiveness in the workplace and understand their buying behaviors. However, just because this generation has grown up in a digital world does not necessarily mean that they are expert users of digital technology, nor does it mean they always know best how to apply these tools to achieve their goals. Educating this sometimes superficially tech-savvy generation means giving them a head start in their professional success, as well as helping them become discerning and engaged consumers. To this end, this book offers a snapshot of current thought on the digital native culture, which will certainly grow and change as more and more digital natives reach adulthood and longitudinal data starts to become available.

We solicited contributions from many different sectors in order to provide a broad overview of this first generation of digital natives. Contributors come from both the business and the academic worlds, and some have a foot in both. Their generations range from Baby Boomers to the natives themselves.

We chose to divide this book into four sections: Part One: The Digital Native Goes to Work; Part Two: Marketing and Selling to the Digital Native; Part Three: Entertaining the Digital Native; and Part Four: Educating the Digital Native. Each part includes four or five chapters, each of which offers a unique viewpoint. Thus, contributors may sometimes contradict conclusions drawn in other chapters. However, this is representative of the point we're trying to make: Digital natives have a common experience—growing up in a digital world—but how they assimilate that experience is up to each individual.

That said, after reading these collected essays, we hope you will be equipped with tools and ideas that will allow you to better navigate this digital world and understand just what makes its natives tick. You might find yourself focused on one particular section that seems to fit best with your immediate needs or perhaps might jump around to chapters that address pressing concerns, or you may choose to read the book from start to finish. No matter. Here we offer a range of interconnected ideas that provide new insight into this generation of digital natives that will empower those of us working with them to make the most of these interactions, to drive education, business, and innovation forward in the digital age.

# Part One

# The Digital Native
# Goes to Work

CHAPTER **1**

# When Facebook Comes to Work: Understanding the Work Practice of the Digital Native

Brynn Evans

The most valuable thing I learned in graduate school is that progress is not linear. It would take me 10 days of hard work before a big insight would come along and give me the equivalent of a week's worth of progress. Although I'm talking in the past tense here, this simple life lesson is true of my current work too—and of the work style of many so-called knowledge workers.

This pattern reveals itself in other domains as well. Imagine that a soccer game is coming down to the wire, tied at 0–0. From an absolute perspective, each team has made zero "progress." Of course, both teams have played a full game—they're exhausted—but nothing quantifiably distinguishes them from each other. Yet, at the last possible moment, either team could orchestrate a single clever play and score the tie-breaking shot. The game would technically end with a winner and a loser, although a score of one to nothing hardly reflects the deliberate work

3

that both teams put in throughout the match. Still, what matters is that the winning team finally pulled through.

This perspective is important to keep in mind as you read this chapter. Although digital natives may conduct their work differently, they still recognize the need to pull through and meet the same deadlines. Even if they appear to be progressing slowly, be aware that, in their work too, progress is not linear.

## Work as a Practice

This chapter is about the way that digital natives approach work—something that I'll refer to as their *work practice*. We all have a work practice that's unique to us; but if you've been employed in an office setting for more than 10 years, chances are that your work practice revolves around the office. When you're at work, you're working. When you're home, you're not working. This is a mindset (and perhaps a coping strategy) that many people adopt in order to lead a balanced life. Yet it's a work practice that is likely absent among the digital natives at your company, even if you still work in a traditional office environment.

What exactly is a work practice? It's not a matter of what work gets done but rather how it gets done. It's the doing of the work; it's the process of producing; it's a frame of mind for dealing with the mundane as well as the urgent. Included in this frame of mind are habits, standards, expectations, and social norms. For example, a familiar standard is the one-hour lunch break. Additionally, there are certain workplace expectations, which may vary within enterprises (e.g., how quickly to respond to a coworker's email). Finally, basic social norms apply regardless of company culture (e.g., it's rude to be on Facebook during a client meeting).

However, digital natives have a different set of habits, standards, expectations, and social norms that stem from being raised in a culture deeply immersed in technology. While their differences may not always clash with non-natives, their work practice is unique and demands patience and compromise from non-natives to understand it and make the most of it. It certainly matters that your employees—from whatever generation—get their work done: Business is business. However, if you have a greater appreciation for digital natives' attitudes about working, you will learn better how to coexist productively and appreciate the perspectives and techniques that help them succeed.

## The Life and Times of a Digital Native

The following account depicts a young woman, Robin, whose childhood was filled with digital technologies, which were used for both work and play. Today, her behaviors reflect the attributes of a digital native, quite distinct from the attributes of workers from previous generations. As you read the following story, consider how Robin's upbringing might affect her current work practices:

> Robin is a 25-year-old technical project manager at Intuit. Growing up in a large family, she needed to jockey for attention with her three younger brothers. She took to video games as a way to compete with them, spending hours on gaming consoles and on the family computer late into the night. She was a natural with computers and even won a programming contest in high school. However, her intellectual passions were history and English.
>
> Her parents sent her to college with a personal laptop. It became her life. She used it for taking notes during class, researching material for writing assignments, and doing homework. It was with her in the dorm, on the front steps of the cafeteria, in the noisy student center, and in off-campus cafes. She never hesitated to call upon the trustworthy machine in the middle of a conversation (even once with the dean of her university) if she thought that Google or

Wikipedia could resolve some pressing issue or embellish an important point.

Her laptop was also her social lifeline. She kept Facebook a click away in an ever-present tab in her web browser. She'd check it during class and when stress caused her to wake up in the middle of the night. Now, only a few years out of college, Robin has more than 1,500 friends on Facebook, from high school, college, and various extracurricular activities. She hasn't spoken directly with many of them in years, but instead maintains a semi-complete awareness of their whereabouts and activities through continuous partial attention to their streams. It's a convenient, lightweight way to stay in touch.

Today, Robin is always connected, always online. It's a fast-paced lifestyle—no longer about gaming and programming but still deeply connected to technology. It's second nature to her. She doesn't know another life.

Unfortunately, her managers at Intuit aren't aware of these past experiences and are often confused by her work practice. She's not at her desk when they walk by at 9 AM on their way to get coffee. She always grabs her iPhone when she steps away from her desk. And she often sends emails to the team very late at night, though she does consistently produce good work on time. In recent months, her managers have noticed some exciting new technical ideas coming from her—not something they expected from a history major. Thus, they have resolved to put up with her "idiosyncrasies," even if they don't really "get" her.

What appear to Robin's managers as idiosyncrasies are actually the habits and practices of a digital native. This is her work practice, and it's something that she shares with other digital natives across the industry: Her work comes with her anywhere (and everywhere) she goes, and social activities play a central role in her life. This shouldn't come as too much of a surprise if you think about her day-to-day experiences in college: Robin worked wherever her laptop was (and her laptop was always with her), and she was always connected to her friends.

The next section will elaborate on the anywhere–everywhere nature of work and the type of social activities that digital natives engage in to give you an idea of how these approaches help digital natives succeed in their work.

## The Anywhere–Everywhere Nature of Work

The nature of "work" has changed a lot over the course of the past few centuries. This is most striking if we think about how our ancestors spent their waking hours just trying to meet their basic needs: finding food, making clothing, securing shelter. Significantly, much of today's work force performs information-based tasks, or knowledge work. Uday Apte and Hiranya Nath noted in their article, "Size, Structure and Growth of the U.S. Information Economy" (*Annals of Information Systems*, vol. 1, 2007: 1–28), that this type of work accounts for almost 70 percent of the U.S. labor force.

What's more, many types of knowledge work can now be done from anywhere and everywhere—across devices and across locations. Robin, for example, checks email on her iPhone first thing every morning. She uses this time to take care of urgent requests, provide her team and managers with status updates, and prepare herself for what's to come during the rest of the day. By starting her workday at home, she gets a head start on her projects, though she inevitably arrives "late" to the office.

Perhaps digital natives embrace this anywhere–everywhere mentality because they treat technology as a trusted partner in life rather than as an irritating mother-in-law. And yet, it's largely simple communication and networking technologies that make possible a distributed workplace. Laptops and netbooks, mobile phones, instant messenger (IM),

Skype, virtual private network (VPN), Gmail, and cloud computing resources like Google Docs all support this networked lifestyle.

One of the characteristics of this work style is what Anne Zelenka from the blog Web Worker Daily calls "bursty work." Instead of working in four-hour continuous blocks, digital natives work in smaller chunks. Dawn Foster writes that she intentionally splits her day into chunks so that she "can be productive for longer periods of time" ("How I Work in Chunks," posted September 5, 2009, bit.ly/hiuGke). Although this sounds counterintuitive, there is a rationale and structure behind her segmented work blocks.

Since meetings greatly disrupt her day, Foster has learned to set aside Mondays for meetings so that the rest of the week goes uninterrupted. When this isn't possible, she makes sure to leave a few solid hours in the morning before her first meeting, in order to complete her important client work first. She further batches her client work into smaller chunks, saving a number of client-related tasks for a continuous block of time, reporting that this "helps to avoid getting projects confused by jumping too quickly between clients."

On another blog, Paul Graham discusses the difference between a "maker's schedule" and a "manager's schedule" ("Maker's Schedule, Manager's Schedule," posted July 2009, bit.ly/eVtDkI). As they are younger employees, most digital natives in the work force today are not yet managers. Instead, as makers, they are expected to produce: by making sales, writing code, or submitting deliverables on time. However, their style of work tends to coincide with the "manager's schedule" of chunking the day into hour-long blocks (although managers often use this time for meetings). What's critically different, however, is that frequent interruptions and scheduled meetings tend to reduce the maker's productivity. Thus, even if it appears that digital natives' work style outwardly conforms to their managers', makers might do better with a certain amount of autonomy regarding their schedules to find their own balance and accomplish their work.

It's important to note that bursty work is not the same as multitasking. Digital natives who break their work into smaller segments are not performing multiple tasks simultaneously. They're doing more focused work for smaller periods of time. I expect that we've all experienced this at some point, where one hour of dedicated work can be more productive than a workday full of interruptions.

It appears that research supports this notion as well. Joshua Rubinstein, David Meyer, and Jeffrey Evans report in their article, "Executive Control of Cognitive Processes in Task Switching" (*Journal of Experimental Psychology: Human Perception and Performance*, vol. 27, no. 4, 2001), that goal shifting carries a high cognitive burden, especially when shifting to tasks that are novel or unfamiliar. Concentration and cognitive capacity may actually be at their highest during short periods of focused, familiar work.

Other research has found that a certain level of task switching is optimal for productivity in the workplace. In one study of information workers, Sinan Aral, Erik Brynjolfsson, and Marshall Van Alstyne report that employees who have a high capacity for managing several simultaneous projects at once—accomplished only by deliberate and tactful task switching—have greater outputs and year-end revenues. This report, titled "Information, Technology and Information Worker Productivity" (NBER Working Paper No. 13172, 2007), notes that this outcome is not the result of working faster. Sometimes projects last longer than originally projected but result in better quality outcomes in the end.

Furthermore, project-based work benefits the most from bursty work practices, largely because demanding projects often require attention in the "off hours." People are better equipped to deal with an unexpected crisis or a bug in the codebase that can't wait until morning when they have an anywhere–everywhere attitude toward work. In large, distributed organizations, it is becoming more common to coordinate meeting schedules with international team members very late at night or early in the morning in order to synchronize the project work.

Additionally, time away from a problem often sheds new light on puzzling issues. Workers who segment their work into smaller chunks have the advantage of perspective when they return to a task at a later time. First, the pre-coffee morning perspective is different from the afternoon one. And second, related information may be brought to their attention during those moments when they aren't specifically working on the task. Here is an example:

> Daniella is an intern at Microsoft. Most recently, she's been trying to incorporate Flash technologies into Silverlight (a project aimed at creating interoperability between competing products). She successfully drafted an initial proposal for her manager but then felt stuck. Over the next week, she spoke casually with her friends about her project and someone happened to point her to a relevant blog. When she later had a moment to review the blog, she realized that it contained information that was critical for the project. She was able to re-draft her proposal and point her manager to the information resources that she'd discovered in the meantime.

Despite how it may sound, having a bursty work practice with an anywhere–everywhere mindset does not mean that digital natives are constantly working. Leisure time is taken in bursts as well. Digital natives log more hours at their computer (in total) but switch between work and leisure tasks in one sitting. Andrei, a 19-year-old programmer, engages in this very practice:

> Andrei's primary task is writing code. He spends most of his time in a debugging tool, but when he gets stuck on a problem, he switches to his web browser to read articles. He does this to take a mental break—something we've all been

known to do when we're stumped. For him, this means checking in with friends on Twitter and Facebook who frequently share interesting articles and tidbits. After he's done snacking on information, he has usually re-worked the problem in his head so that he can tackle it with motivation and a fresh perspective.

Now, you might be wondering why he doesn't just go for a walk or brainstorm his idea on a whiteboard. Walking and whiteboards are common strategies for those in previous generations. Digital natives see technology as a tool that enables them to work or play, which results in their leisure time activities taking place via digital technologies. You're more likely to see them texting, IMing, Facebooking, or browsing the web at their computers in the middle of the workday than see them step out for coffee or take a walk around the block.

There are benefits to taking digital breaks. Dr. Brent Coker from the University of Melbourne observes that "people who surf the internet for fun at work—within a reasonable limit of less than 20 percent of their total time in the office—are more productive by about 9 percent than those who don't" ("Freedom to Surf: Workers More Productive if Allowed to Use the Internet for Leisure," posted April 2, 2009, bit.ly/dFRJOH). Of course, leisure activities must take place in moderation, but they can lead to increased productivity because short breaks help us "zone out" for a while, so that we can return to our tasks with greater concentration afterward. Another benefit to digital breaks is that if your concentration returns or inspiration strikes in the midst of leisure time, you're already at the keyboard ready to capture your insights.

In sum, distributed networking technologies are creating an anywhere–everywhere work practice, leading to bursty work and digital leisure time. Digital natives take advantage of these opportunities to get a head start on their workday, to segment their time into meaningful chunks, and to gain perspective and reset their concentration after time away from a task.

## Social Permeance

Having continuous connectivity with digital devices has both advantages and disadvantages. Receiving a phone call at 5 AM from someone in a different time zone is terribly inopportune. However, texting someone when you're running late for an appointment is wonderfully convenient.

What's really happening here is that these digital devices are creating a type of "social permeance"—an expression that conveys how social activities are beginning to permeate our everyday lives. Daily affairs as mundane as grocery shopping are steeped in social interactions, as the digitally equipped text their friends, tweet about what's happening, and broadcast the GPS coordinates of their locations. And their friends communicate back within minutes, if not seconds. Most of us feel that this trend makes it increasingly hard to separate out the professional from the personal. Digital natives don't think in these terms; instead, they find distinct advantages to this social culture.

Some of the same enablers of the anywhere–everywhere work mentality—advanced networking and mobile technologies—also support the social permeance trend. On social networking sites, people forge and strengthen connections with family and friends as well as acquaintances they've only met once. Texting, IMing, and video chatting with Skype are other popular ways for staying in touch throughout the day. A level of social continuity is maintained; it's this ongoing connection that provides unique benefits.

My former roommate, Angela, demonstrates how this is possible:

> Angela is one of the most diligent, hard-working students in her PhD cohort. Upon first impression, she might not even strike you as very social; she rarely goes out to dinner, parties,

or gatherings. Yet she often has as many as eight active IM conversations going on simultaneously; she texts her friends on the bus on the way to school; and she passively, yet continuously, monitors their updates on Facebook. It turns out that her life is filled with momentary, yet frequent, social interactions, which she manages with what Linda Stone calls "continuous partial attention" (bit.ly/e7hgyF).

Those digital breaks mentioned earlier are part of what makes continuous partial attention possible today. This is a very common habit and expectation of digital natives, and they don't consider it to be socially superficial or fake. Instead, it creates just enough of a connection that people begin to feel a sense of ambient intimacy. Clive Thompson of the *New York Times* writes about the significance of this in his article, "Brave New World of Digital Intimacy" (September 5, 2008):

> Each little update—each individual bit of social information—is insignificant on its own, even supremely mundane. But taken together, over time, the little snippets coalesce into a surprisingly sophisticated portrait of your friends' and family members' lives, like thousands of dots making a pointillist painting. This was never before possible, because in the real world, no friend would bother to call you up and detail the sandwiches she was eating. The ambient information becomes like "a type of E.S.P."

Many non-natives would question the value in maintaining semi-complete accounts of the thousands of friends you've ever met. However, it is important to understand that, for the native, it's not just about the numbers—friends aren't like collectible trading cards. It's all about diversity—friends are more like the olive in a martini, infusing your environment with their distinctly flavored perspectives. Having a wide, diverse set of active ties is where the critical advantage lies.

Research has shown that workers with large, diverse social networks who are active in nonoverlapping social groups have more measurable outputs, earn more money, and advance faster in their careers. The simple reason for this is that they are privy to nonredundant information. In other words, these workers bridge so-called structural holes in a communication network. Ron Burt explains this in his book, *Structural Holes: The Social Structure of Competition* (Harvard University Press, 1992). According to Burt, individuals who form "bridges" to neighboring networks connect to people who may have very different ideas from their own. They then absorb these ideas, which gives them access to alternative perspectives and, at times, exclusive knowledge that may only exist in some tangential domain. What they do with this knowledge is up to them, but it often comes in handy down the line, often at unexpected moments. This advantage is illustrated in the following anecdote:

> Nathan is particularly social and works full-time as a consultant. He is constantly working but spends a lot of time passively engaged in social media—much like the other digital natives portrayed in this chapter. This usually makes him the first person to have heard about a new study, fact, or website, and at times, these discoveries are highly relevant to a client project. A notable example occurred in October 2008 when he attended an informal conference called BarCamp San Diego—a gathering of social peers rather than a gathering of professionals. He was interested in a session I was leading on "lifetracking," a method for recording personal data as a way to gain insights about yourself. He attended my session and we spoke at length about it afterwards.
>
> A full nine months later, Nathan received a request from a client to help start a lifetracking project. Although my session never caused him personally to adopt lifetracking, he

remembered many things from that day in San Diego and was able to draft a proposal for his client. Immediately afterwards, he privately asked me for additional tips. We hadn't seen each other face-to-face since BarCamp, but we remained peripherally connected through Twitter and Facebook in that period. I recalled his interest in my session and replied to him immediately.

Digital natives, like Nathan and Angela, who attend social events and hang out with friends online are doing more than just socializing. They are establishing a remarkably diverse set of social peers, which brings value to them—and indirectly to their companies and managers—in at least three distinct ways.

First, it is the network of social ties from different industries, backgrounds, interests, and life stages that confers the nonredundant information advantage. Having a large network of professional contacts is not the same, since professionals within a single industry tend to flock together. In contrast, our first protagonist, Robin, keeps up with friends from high school, college, and beyond nearly every day. Even 15 years and a thousand new colleagues from now, her world will be composed largely of social ties.

Second, it's the act of socializing that helps spread ideas. Anyone can collect a thousand trading cards, but good things only come by actually playing those cards. Knowledge only gets transferred by keeping relationships active and having conversations. At that point, social ties represent both people resources and information resources. For example, Nathan-the-consultant had absorbed enough information from my BarCamp session to draft a lifetracking proposal for his client. Yet, I was also a direct "people" resource in his network, as he turned to me to get additional information.

Third, social interactions may actually improve our cognition. Dr. Oscar Ybarra and colleagues report as much in their article, "Mental

Exercising Through Simple Socializing: Social Interaction Promotes General Cognitive Functioning" (*Personality and Social Psychology Bulletin*, vol. 34, no. 2, 2008). Their study was simple: 1) Subjects were divided into three groups; (2) each group performed a different, initial exercise; and 3) everyone was then given the same set of standard cognitive tests. The first group initially did a passive social exercise: Subjects sat silently watching an episode of *Seinfeld* (seated next to another subject). The second group did an active social exercise: Two subjects had a conversation together about privacy protection. The third group did an intellectual exercise: Subjects had to solve a crossword puzzle, perform mental rotations, and answer questions about a written passage.

Surprisingly, the researchers found that subjects who began with the active social exercise did just as well on the later cognitive tests as subjects who started with reading comprehension and crossword puzzles. Even more surprising was that merely observing passive social interactions did not improve cognitive performance. These findings suggest that interacting with friends may help us in more ways than one. Their knowledge is infectious and socializing may actually prime parts of our brains to help us with intellectual tasks.

In sum, social permeance is creating a culture of social continuity, in which digital natives maintain large, active networks with a diverse set of social peers. As a result, daily interactions create a sense of ambient intimacy and condition the mind, and represent people and information resources that can prove valuable in the future.

## Conclusion

So, how are digital natives transforming the way business is done? It's not just their hip iPhones and contemporary slang ("Facebook me!") that marks this as a new era. Their work practice is fundamentally changing as they live and breathe this culture of distributed networking and social technologies. It may never be a practice that managers and previous generations wish to embrace personally—and that's fine. They will, however, need to recognize and understand this emerging work practice if they wish to maximize the digital native work force. The goal of this chapter is to describe this emerging work style and highlight the role it plays in digital natives' success. An anywhere–everywhere mindset means that work is done in chunks, intermixed with leisure time. Leisure activities are often social: staying in touch with old friends and new acquaintances, and sharing intimate tidbits and interesting news stories. These social interactions help to spread ideas and improve problem-solving ability. The end result is that the digital technologies enabling this shift in work practice may actually be imparting a critical cognitive advantage to your employees and simultaneously driving innovation and creativity in your enterprise.

## About the Contributor

**Brynn Evans** is obsessed with the intersection of social networks and human behavior. At first she shunned social psychology, finding joy in neuroscience and dissecting brains. But after a 6-year stint as a neuropsychologist, she began studying how people interact with and use technology. Three years later, she completed the graduate program in cognitive science at University of California San Diego and moved on to more practical applications of user experience and interaction design. Since then, she's been a freelance consultant, social interaction designer, and gamestorming facilitator. Today, she's the chief experience officer at a stealth tech startup in San Francisco.

Brynn is an active speaker and writer, and is involved in community events such as hackathons, workshops, and conferences that bring together designers, developers, and entrepreneurs. She's also a board member of the Awesome Foundation in San Francisco, which gives out mini-grants to "awesome" local projects every month. Her website is brynnevans.com.

## Recommended Reading

Burt, Ronald S., and Don Ronchi. "Teaching Executives to See Social Capital: Results from a Field Experiment." *Social Science Research* 36 (2007): 1156–1183. bit.ly/hchIAl (accessed October 18, 2010).

Graham, Paul. "Maker's Schedule, Manager's Schedule." PaulGraham.com, July 2009. bit.ly/eVtDkI (accessed October 18, 2010).

The University of Melbourne. "Freedom to Surf: Workers More Productive if Allowed to Use the Internet for Leisure." The Voice, April 2, 2009. bit.ly/dFRJOH (accessed October 18, 2010).

CHAPTER 2

# Thinking Outside the Cubicle: Examining the Changing Shape of Today's Workspace

Susan Evans

The definition of *office* is being rewritten in response to the digital age. While web-based collaboration has had an impact on office workers of all kinds, it has distinctly shaped the work style and expectations of digital natives—who have never known work without the flexibility of always-on connectivity.

Digital natives are not bound by location. Armed with a laptop and a cell phone, they are emerging as a breed of nomadic workers who can get the job done from anywhere: their homes, the airport, local coffee shops, and yes, even in an office.

Digital natives—and those influenced by the digital age—shift work to suit their lifestyles in ways that allow them to work when their focus is sharpest. They tip the scales of work–life balance in ways that may baffle traditional managers. However, if understood and properly channeled, the digital native may transform the workspace for the better—for us all.

With the influx of digital natives into the work force, companies are beginning to realize that, to meet the needs of this new breed of worker, office environments must be transformed from monochromic cubicle farms to varied spaces that can accommodate myriad work styles. Companies both large and small recognize that they can attract the best of this burgeoning work force, and keep employees happier and more productive, by allowing them more freedom, rather than trying to mold employees to conform to an outdated system of policy and procedures.

Simultaneously with the influx of digital natives into the office-based work force, organizations of all types are increasingly relying on contractors, freelancers, and consultants. In many ways, this work option—which may make previous generations as uncomfortable in its uncertainty—suits the digital native's flextime work style and may increase its prevalence going forward.

As the tools to get work done evolve, so do the physical spaces in which work happens. The number of mobile workers increases each year (Reuters, "Remote Workers Aren't Going Anywhere—Literally," August 26, 2009, reut.rs/dLQUvs). Yet, being freed from the confines of an office will not automatically maximize a native's productivity. Left adrift on their own sofas, not all workers feel more comfortable than they would in a traditional office setting.

Hybrid spaces, shared office environments, and coworking spaces have emerged to meet the demands of a growing population of virtual workers who find themselves unable to put together a productive work day in their living room. These office options have gained popularity in recent years because they overcome some of the key challenges faced by remote workers of all kinds: finding affordably priced spaces, overcoming social isolation, establishing a professional setting, and fulfilling the desire for collaboration.

This chapter will explore offices and workspaces that have responded successfully to the emergence of the digital native, as well as the spaces to which digital natives are naturally attracted.

## Where Does a Digital Native Want to Work?

Where the digital native *can* work and where the digital native *wants* to work may still be quite different as the market adjusts to meet the needs of these employees. Drab monochrome offices will probably never disappear, and cube farms will persist. However, as the market catches up to nomadic workers, it is doing so by adjusting to their diverse and distinct needs.

In this chapter, we will stroll through the offices that delight digital natives: places where their talents are harnessed, encouraged, and supported in ways that old-fashioned offices may not offer. What shines through in all examples of the digital native's ideal space is that successfully reimagining the office means keeping *diversity* in mind. Our expanding understanding of the way that individuals learn (for example, Howard Gardener's *multiple intelligences*) can and should be expanded and applied to how we work. There is no single model for the ideal work environment. Successful spaces can house multiple work environments, allow employees to go off on their own to find their ideal workspace, or provide some combination of the two.

The offices used as examples in this chapter are not your average offices. These examples are spaces that speak to the eight "norms of the net gen" as laid out by Don Tapscott in *Grown Up Digital* (McGraw-Hill, 2009): freedom, customization, scrutiny, integrity, collaboration, entertainment, speed, and innovation. These norms will be referenced throughout this chapter as ways in which specific workspaces speak to the digital native. Spaces that enable, enhance, and support these qualities will allow digital natives to flourish and to deliver their best work to the organizations that employ them.

## "Office Space" Revisited

There still are, and always will be, companies that choose to have their employees come into an office and work a standard 9-to-5, five-day-a-week schedule. These offices range in size, scale, and appearance, but all generally provide employees with workstations and shared office resources. We'll look at several companies of various sizes, reviewing how they serve the needs of their employees in general, and digital natives in particular, either by providing personalization in centralized offices or by allowing employees the freedom to find their own workspaces.

Going to work for a traditional employer no longer has to mean being shackled to one of an endless row of identical desks. Companies today are doing what they can to accommodate a multitude of work styles and personalities, driven in part by the emergence of the digital native. As noted by Robert J. Grossman, paying attention to office design and layout can help improve employee productivity, retention, and job satisfaction ("Space, Another HR Frontier," *HR Magazine*, September 2002, bit.ly/1HGyNV). What companies, both large and small, choose to provide in terms of office amenities can have an immense impact on employee culture and productivity.

According to a 2008 Gensler survey, companies that emphasize collaboration, learning, and socialization see some key benefits in comparison to companies that focus solely on productivity. Specifically, "companies providing workplaces that are more effective for knowledge work are seeing higher levels of employee engagement, brand equity and profit, with profit growth up to 14 percentage points greater than those with less effective work environments" ("Gensler Survey Measures Connection Between Workplace Design and Business Performance," October 23, 2008, bit.ly/1Xlx4f). Beyond benefits to the individual employees, thoughtful office design strategies can provide considerable benefits to the company.

Let's consider some examples. Google's offices, currently more than 60 worldwide, are commonly referenced to show a company that truly puts the focus on providing for its employees. From free lunches and nap rooms to laptop lounges, Google does what it can to enable its employees to live their lives at work. To really get a sense of its workspaces, take a tour of the Googleplex (its main campus in California) via YouTube (bit.ly/ejZJLV). When watching the video, one nearly forgets that the Google employees are there to actually *work*— they seem to do everything but. A look at the Googleplex offers a glimpse into the corporate culture of Google, one of the most successful companies in the world.

What Google's offices exemplify is a large-scale shift in workplace mentality. The company wins awards for its offices not just because it provides mouth-watering perks, but because it fosters worker creativity in ways cubicle farms simply cannot. However, Google and other companies that provide this sort of whole-life workspace do not do so for purely altruistic reasons. Google would not likely continue to provide this environment if it did not see an increase in productivity from employees. Google's success only reinforces that assumption: The company's net income was $1.97 billion in the three months ending at December 31, 2009, compared with $382.4 million in the year-earlier period (Alexei Oreskovic, "Google Profit Rises, Revenue Misses Some Forecasts," Reuters, January 22, 2010, reut.rs/e2fX0l).

Google is not the only organization that takes great pains to enable employees to create a new type of work–life balance. Looking at a smaller-sized example of creative office design, we see that office space perks can be tailored specifically to the needs of individuals when a company only has a handful of employees.

Maycreate is an "idea group" in Chattanooga, Tennessee. The online studio tour of its current office space (bit.ly/1ZHOP1) provides a look at the originality reflected throughout. Vibrant colors, quirky additions (a large swing in the middle of the workspace is a highlight), and comfortable furniture abound. By filling the space with creative décor and developing a distinctive layout, companies like Maycreate fuel the creativity of their employees and give them an ideal space in which to create the best ideas. It's working for them: Maycreate was chosen as Chattanooga, Tennessee's YP 2009 Friendly Business of the Year, and the company wins a great many awards for its logo, website, and branding design. Currently, Maycreate is in the process of building a new studio to house its employees, with a creative layout and design that will undoubtedly excite and entice the digital native (see the photos at Maycreate's Flickr page, www.flickr.com/photos/maycreate).

The benefits of workspaces constructed with employee satisfaction in mind are many: The space is comfortable, opportunities to collaborate are increased, and the office is tailored to personal productivity, rather than leaving employees to squeeze their work style into a one-size-fits-all desk. The digital native is a clear winner in these scenarios because, as Tapscott points out, customization is a key marker of the native's nature. Natives work better and thrive in spaces that allow them to be who they are and not who the company wants them to be.

There are, of course, drawbacks to these types of setups. Companies that provide above-and-beyond perks do raise eyebrows. Critics cry out "High overhead!" and "Leave the fun at home!" Matt Labash touches on the extreme lengths some companies go to cater to their employees in an article titled "Are We Having Fun Yet?" (*Utne Reader*, March–April 2008, bit.ly/OEzY). The article argues that, in focusing so much on the extras of a job, employees sometimes forget to actually focus on the work at hand. Dubbing the phenomenon "the infantization of corporate America," Labash wonders whether the reason we are now so focused on fun is because we're less concerned with the actual work that needs to get done.

Without doubt, there is a learning curve when it comes to mastering this new workspace culture. During this time of transition, it is easy to confuse a desire to "make work fun" with the digital native's true needs, such as freedom, customization, collaboration, and innovation. These values are not radical; they just play out differently in the highly connected world in which natives flourish.

It is important to recognize that this is not a generation that expects to play instead of work, nor does it need every aspect of life to be entertaining. However, the concept of "office space" does need to evolve to accommodate the increasingly blurred line between work and private life—something Google demonstrates in its office complex. Smart companies will strive for a new flexibility that allows digital natives to feel that the balance between work and life is maintained—all day, every day, from anywhere at any time. The silver lining here is that reorganizing, even just slightly, to diversify the office doesn't have to cost a company millions in overhead.

## Going Virtual

According to WorldatWork's "Telework Trendlines 2009," there are more than 17 million full-time employees in America today who work remotely at least once a month, up 39 percent from 2006 to 2008 (February 2009, bit.ly/HJVF6). Add to this the number of government employees who are encouraged to telecommute at least one day per week (bit.ly/g2WkRX) and the large number of independent one-person businesses, and you have a veritable tribe of nomadic workers emerging in the marketplace.

Virtuality is a key factor shaping today's workplace: It has begun to segregate workers from traditional offices to some extent and to allow the growth of an entirely new range of office models. These will be discussed in greater detail when we look at the self-employment track for digital nomads, but the virtual option for work also pertains to those who work for large companies.

Certain industries, such as customer service companies and travel booking agents, have carved out a niche by employing entire work forces that are based out of their own homes. Not only can jobs in these sectors be done from anywhere, but dispersing employees across a wide variety of time zones enables companies to do an even better job of providing 24/7 services to their clients.

We are seeing evidence that working virtually is beneficial not only for some sectors of business but for the employees themselves. According to a survey by Cisco of 2,000 employees, "a majority of those surveyed experienced a significant increase in work–life flexibility, productivity and overall satisfaction as a result of their ability to work remotely" (Jennifer LaClaire, "Telecommuting Linked to Job Satisfaction, Employee Productivity," June 29, 2009, bit.ly/QlB8I).

Alpine Access, a customer service company, reports that one of the benefits of having a completely remote work force is the minimal impact it makes on the environment. As Alpine claims on its website (www.alpineaccess.com), it is "an eco-friendly, socially responsible business model that reduces your costs and increases revenue." By studying the impact of its employees working from home as opposed to commuting to and from an office, Alpine claims to cut out 7,275 commutes every day. "That translates into real savings—2,827,500 gallons of gas and 70,687,500 vehicle miles traveled in one year" ("Eco-Friendly Customer Care," bit.ly/4cWVES). So not only can telecommuting provide a slimmed-down company profile and reduce overhead, but it can apparently be good for the planet too ("Environmental Benefits of Telecommuting," The Environmental Blog, July 31, 2009, bit.ly/IWfAe).

A completely virtual work force isn't just smart business for large customer service-related operations; it can be deployed by smaller companies to keep overhead low and employee satisfaction high. Consider Newstex, a content syndication company, which has no centralized office and employs nearly 50 contractors who work remotely. Other than a single one-hour virtual meeting each week, Newstex staff work with minimal management and on their own schedules.

According to president Larry Schwartz, employees who can succeed in this model are those who are technologically savvy, independent, and don't require much day-to-day direction. When asked whether his model was best-suited to younger employees, he replied simply,

"Younger is an attitude, not an age." The Newstex staff, half of which is under the age of 30, works on a flexible, technology-assisted schedule. "Just last night around 2 AM, there were several of us all online working on the same project," Schwartz describes. "We wound up having an impromptu conference call on Skype to hash out some of the details." Newstex employees are also always "on" for projects.

Schwartz believes that the no-overhead model he has created with Newstex is not only successful, but it is also replicable. His business mantra—"No assets"—has worked incredibly well for him: Employees use their own workspace and their own equipment, and therefore do not place any ownership burden upon the company itself. This allows the company to be nimble and grow quickly. In order to be a replicable organizational model, Schwartz says that it requires companies that have a great deal of trust in employees. "Large companies tend to throw a lot of energy into middle-management in order to ensure that their other employees are being productive." Instead of adding the burden of a management department, Schwartz simply makes sure that he hires employees who are not only smart and well suited for the job but who do not require very much day-to-day direction. "If there isn't corporate trust, it doesn't work."

Many companies cannot go fully virtual for one reason or another. However, some can and do encourage employees to telecommute regularly or to flex their schedule in such a way that they can create a three- or four-day workweek. U.S. government programs encourage telecommuting for a variety of government branches, and some local governments encourage companies in their states to do the same. Washington State has a Commute Trip Reduction Program (www.ws dot.wa.gov/TDM/CTR) that affects companies with 100 or more full-time employees at a single worksite.

As we look toward the rise of digital natives as the predominant work force and consider their habits, expectations, and abilities, it will be increasingly important that employers examine the potential gains in offering at least some opportunities for working remotely. Completely remote companies may not become the norm, but it is clear that some level of remote working opportunities can benefit a variety of organizations.

## Self-Employment: The Nomadic Life

Not everyone wants to work for someone else—be it in an office space or not. The independent spirit is alive and well, and digital natives realize that they can weave together a patchwork pattern of clients and enjoy life "doing their own thing." Digital natives, typically embracing freedom in their work, often eschew traditional employment models and create their own. In her book, *The Anti 9-to-5 Guide* (Seal Press, 2007), author and freelancer Michelle Goodman writes about the transition many digital natives and other telecommuters go through when deciding to escape the traditional cubicle: "We've all had those Dilbert moments when we realize something's got to give. If you find yourself slapping your forehead repeatedly as the CEO delivers yet another unintelligible, acronym-riddled speech, it's probably time you gave your day job a much-needed face-lift" (p. 194). As with the general population, certain digital natives simply can't manage to fit themselves into a traditional employment setup and instead prefer to work on their own.

For the ever-expanding pool of remote workers, there are a growing number of options for where work can get done. This section will examine the current options, ranging from working at home and hybrid workspaces to shared offices and coworking spaces. Each option provides concrete benefits and drawbacks, and the variety of working arrangements speaks to the different types of workers who exist today. With the emergence of the digital native, we will see an even greater number of options that cater to their work needs specifically. This is no surprise, as customization and individualization are so critical to the lifestyle of a digital native.

## Home Offices

For many independents and telecommuters, working from home is the ideal lifestyle: They can set their own schedule, create a perfect workspace, and cut the dreadful commute out of the day entirely. For digital natives, home offices provide the freedom to work any day, any hour, in an environment they can carve out on their own. Working in a home office can enable a digital native to work on their own terms, breaking when they want to and working when they're feeling at their most productive. Compared to previous generations of home workers, digital natives may be exceptionally well suited to working from home. As Nicole Hemsoth notes on her blog, Remote Revolution, "This generation of digital natives understands the inherent value of technology and will be likely far more capable of 'handling' remote work simply because of an increased ability to multitask" ("Why Digital Natives Will Usher in the Remote Revolution," April 8, 2009, bit.ly/4wITw). As one digital native, Terry Phillips, 28, of Delicious Monster, notes of her remote work, "The kinds of jobs that are conducive to this type of work environment require, in my opinion, a higher level of discipline than, say, a typical 9-to-5 job. We work until the job is done, not until 5 PM rolls around. In fact, I can't remember the last time I finished work for the day at 5 PM—that seems ridiculously early to me. But then, I think I'm part of a different generation."

Karrie Kohlhaas, 38, owner of ThoughtShot Consulting in Seattle, is one such worker. She says, "First of all, let's get one thing clear, I do not love my home office just so I can work in my pajamas ... Working from home I have this sense that I can use my space and time exactly how it suits me. The only rules here are the ones I make. Working out of my home is a statement." Independence is critical to Kohlhaas's success as a young business owner; not being on a set schedule or having to work from another location enables her to best express her work style to her clients. For Kohlhaas, as with many other home-based workers, working from home is an expression of individuality. It is one way to work on one's own terms.

Home offices come in many shapes and sizes. For some, the kitchen table might suffice as a productive workspace. For others, separate loft spaces might be the answer (some have gone so far as to put "office pods" in their backyards; see www.officepod.co.uk). Particularly for workers who thrive in quiet, controlled environments, working from home can be an incredibly rewarding experience.

However, others face significant challenges with this option. If left to their own devices, some who try to work from home might find that "do the laundry" regularly moves up the to-do list above "make sales calls." Productivity can quickly tank when distractions abound, as demonstrated in the video "'Procastination' Tales of Mere Existence" by Lev Yilmaz (bit.ly/3wUUzi). Reconciling home and work life in one location can be a significant challenge for those who are not highly self-motivated. It requires the ability to pivot between work responsibilities and those of a domestic nature on a dime.

Historically, there was generally a healthy separation between work and home, allowing our minds to make a critical shift when entering our homes after a workday. The always-connected digital native, who works and plays at all hours, will change that dynamic and thereby create a host of new balance issues: how to get work done when not in an "office," how to allow home to still be a place of rest and recuperation, and how to deal with the isolation of working alone instead of in an office community.

### Hybrid Spaces

Humans are innovative, social animals. This means our creativity comes out when we are faced with challenges—and usually the marketplace responds in kind. When working at home alone poses hurdles, some workers seek out alternatives. Today's culture has provided a few quick go-to places in the form of what we'll call *hybrid spaces*. These are locations that are not designed as work environments but, with free Wi-Fi, become impromptu offices for independent workers who crave a working landscape that includes other people.

Workers who flock to cafés or other Wi-Fi-equipped locations are drawn not just by the free internet connection but also by the desire to be around people. Whether a restaurant, a coffee shop, or a branch of the public library, these spaces often attract independent workers not just because they offer a change in scenery, but because the new scenery includes other people. At Stumptown Coffee on Pine Street in Seattle, one nearly always encounters more 20-somethings on laptops than casual coffee drinkers. Digital natives in cities are flocking to local cafés as an escape from the doldrums of being isolated at home.

Delicious Monster, a small software company based in San Francisco, does all of its business from local coffee and sandwich shops. Why cafés? For employee Jessica Char, 23, coffee shops provide an energetic, dynamic environment compared to a regular office. "Instead of your 7 x 7′ beige cube with fluorescent ceiling lights, you can sit in a colorful café with good music and an endless supply of lattes … When most people, to-go cup in hand, run out the door to make it to the office on time, I get to just stay at the café. It's like pausing at the happiest part of my day and remaining there for 8 hours." For the Delicious Monster team, the right coffee shop becomes the ideal workspace without the unfriendly overhead of having to keep the office running. To make up for their all-day presence, the team is sure to tip heavily and create solid relationships with the crews behind the espresso bars.

For some workers, hybrid spaces can even help bring a boost to business. For Ryan Salva, 32, principal of Capitol Media, working out of coffee shops brought some new business to his doorstep when he first started his web design firm. "Coffee shops were quite valuable," Salva says. "I once got a TV interview because I was working out of a café and a news crew came through to talk to folks about how working in cafés was in terms of our company's privacy issues. It was great publicity for us." Hybrid spaces support the needs of digital natives because they incorporate aspects of collaboration, even if the collaboration is not intentional. Casual interactions can lead to new business contacts, and onlookers in line for espresso may see a new product or design on the screen of a mobile worker that intrigues them enough to inquire about it.

Not all hybrid spaces are keen on having remote workers plop down and work all day. Some coffee shops combat the nomadic work force with one-drink-per-hour rules, intentionally loud music, and even having a manager stop by and ask laptop jockeys to move on. Some turn off their Wi-Fi all together to save themselves the hassle (Laura Copeland, "Downtown Coffee Shops Pulls Plug on Power-Hungry Patrons," *Santa Cruz Sentinel*, October 19, 2009, bit.ly/IjYdh).

Like home offices, hybrid workspaces are a great solution for some natives who work remotely. They provide a low-cost, nimble, semi-social environment in which to work and get work done. For others, though, hybrid spaces still do not provide adequate office space for their needs. "I envy those people who don't have to lug their computer everywhere with them," says Phillips of Delicious Monster. "All their stuff is there, at their desk. They have a phone, office supplies, light … consistency." For her, sometimes the challenges of café-based work stack up. "You can't turn the lights up more or the heat or change the music, although you can cancel it out by blaring your own through headphones. Sure, you don't have annoying office mates—instead you have the general public: baby clubs, domestics, and people playing World of Warcraft and hogging all the bandwidth, making the internet painfully slow." As the *intention* of these hybrid spaces is not to be a working environment, it is no surprise that for some remote workers, hybrid spaces just don't cut it.

## Shared Office Spaces

Shared office spaces can provide many of the advantages of private offices, with lower overhead and increased opportunities for social interaction. Shared spaces come in a wide variety of formats, from several small companies banding together to share one large office space to a large company subletting a small section of their offices to another company that wants to share resources. Often, shared office scenarios enable multiple companies to share key office supplies and resources such as printers, internet connections, and phones. The level of collaboration and connection between organizations is fully dependent on the organizations themselves.

Re-Vision Labs, a Seattle-based consulting firm, moved into a vacated space in another company's offices. Founding partner Gabriel Scheer, 33, was excited about the move. "It was a great fit for us because it provided furnished office space at a rate we could afford, and we liked the idea of sharing a space rather than isolating ourselves. As a startup, all of that was important for us." Although the majority of the tangible benefits of the scenario are financial, Scheer also spoke of the intangible benefits of a strategically shared space. "Mithun is highly inspiring," he says of his office mates. "They have great projects all over the place, and their space is inspiring as well."

During the recent economic downturn and commercial real estate slump, a number of websites were created to foster the sharing of commercial properties. Particularly for larger companies that had to go through significant job cuts, finding new tenants to use the available space tied to their current leases provided a significant administrative challenge. So rather than taking care of it all in-house, companies turned to sites like Open Office Space (openofficespace.com), Ready Offices (readyoffices.com), and SuiteMatch (suitematch.com). These sites demonstrate a new market being carved out to ensure the economic viability of current buildings in major U.S. cities as well as smaller towns all across the country.

Of course, as with other workspace options, not all shared office scenarios are ideal. Unless the relationship is truly sought out to be collaborative from the start, there is a risk that new parties in an office environment will feel more like office squatters than part of a dynamic community. When asked about any drawbacks to his shared office environment, Scheer only had one: "The collaborative element is not particularly extant." Even though their work scenario is beneficial to both parties, unless intentionally entered into, collaboration is not guaranteed.

### Coworking Spaces

As the rise of nomadic workers continues, the market continues to respond with new, innovative ideas to address the needs of those workers. Coworking spaces, the market's newest addition to workspace innovation, evolved from groups of independent workers, mostly digital natives, who were dissatisfied with the isolation of working from home and who did not find the type of social interaction they desired in hybrid spaces like coffee shops.

In 2005, digital native Brad Neuberg, then 24, coined the term *coworking* when he came upon an idea that would give him the structure and community of an office, while at the same time allowing him the independence and self-direction he desired in a solo career as a software developer. In an initial blog post about the idea, Neuberg wrote: "In coworking, independent writers, programmers, and creators come together in community a few days a week. Coworking provides the office of a traditional corporate job, but in a very unique way" ("Coworking—Community for Developers Who Work From Home," Coding in Paradise, August 9, 2005, bit.ly/6LacQX). By creating Spiral Muse, his first coworking space in the Bay Area, and spreading the word about what he was doing via his personal blog, Coding in Paradise (codinginparadise.org), Neuberg started a movement.

Since Neuberg's original coining of the term coworking in 2005, more than 150 coworking spaces have been established worldwide, in dense urban centers as well as in more rural areas (wiki.coworking.info/w/page/29303049/Directory). Regardless of location, the idea is the same: Coworking spaces exist to allow independent workers—

entrepreneurs, telecommuters, students, and others—professional office space that also serves as a community in which they can thrive. Coworking spaces are designed to speak to the digital native directly: They encourage collaboration, support independence, and enable workers to get work done on their own schedule but alongside other like-minded folks.

Coworking is an open-source, community-based business model. From its origins, it was never conceived of as a big money-making scheme. It was designed to provide community where it was needed. Coworking space owners collect and share ideas and challenges in online forums, and have banded together to offer shared benefits to their members, such as the Coworking Visa program (wiki.coworking. info/CoworkingVisa), which allows members of one space to drop in and use another space free of charge.

Robyn Welch, 29, is an urban planner for a company in New Jersey and currently works remotely from Office Nomads, a coworking space in Seattle. When her husband was accepted to a medical residency at a hospital in Seattle, they relocated and Welch was able to continue on at her firm as a remote employee. For her first months working remotely, she did what most do: She stayed at home. "I was so isolated when I never left the house ... Office Nomads has given me a good social network," Welch says of her time in a coworking space. For Welch, having a coworking space is valuable not only as a place to be productive, but it also has a social value. For many self-employed or telecommuting natives, the loss of a professional social network is a detriment. Coworking spaces, inherently social in makeup, enable independent workers to remain independent, yet not alone.

The draw of a coworking space to a digital native is strong; many spaces provide access to the office 24/7, meaning members can set their own schedule and ensure they are the most productive during their "on" hours. As opposed to coffee shops or other hybrid spaces, coworking spaces are built with the *intention* of being an office space. In addition, coworking spaces speak to the values held by digital natives. The "tenets" of coworking are made clear on the Coworking Google Group: "Everyone is welcome, no matter what their interests (corporate, personal, community, etc.), but do remember that coworking is rooted in strong values: Collaboration, Openness, Community and Sustainability" (groups.google.com/group/coworking).

The collaboration value of coworking spaces is one that is of particularly strong interest for digital natives. Solo workers who need recommendations, advice, feedback, or even partners on a project no longer have to only seek out help online—they can ask the coworker sitting next to them. Coworking spaces create "accelerated serendipity." It's simple: You get more ideas and have your ideas come to fruition faster when working among other eager, driven workers than you are likely to when working alongside your cat.

The fact that these spaces only began arriving on the scene within the last five years or so is a clear indicator that the digital native has had a hand in creating them. Many coworking space owners are young entrepreneurial workers who were inspired to create these spaces in order to finally have the type of workspaces they desired.

## The Shape of Office (Space) to Come

Without a doubt, office space formats have been transformed from the once-uniform setting in which business-attired employees sat behind identical desks arranged neatly in rows or isolated in vast cubicle farms. Today's workers may find masseurs, ping-pong tables, and swings interspersed with a variety of shared tables and glass-enclosed concentration rooms. Or they may simply find a more diversified offering of desks to entice them, such as closed-door offices for those who need privacy, and collected shared-space areas for those who work best among the hustle-and-bustle of others.

The most critical shift occurring in office space today is the emergence of diversified workspaces. The digital native has not only introduced new styles and patterns of getting work done but has also helped to normalize work styles that in the past may have been considered radical or somehow "alternative." Digital natives are poised to truly transform the expectations of their fellow coworkers, managers, and bosses by continuing to reinforce what we have known for years: We are not at our best in monocultures. Employers who encourage individual workers to create their best work environments not only attract digital natives but also see increased productivity and employee satisfaction in their business.

## About the Contributor

**Susan Evans**, the co-founder and owner of Office Nomads, discovered the coworking concept before she ever heard the word. Her dreams of neighborhood work centers, where anyone with the ability to work outside the confines of a standard office could come and work alongside others, grew from her desire to give more Seattle residents the ability to walk to work instead of drive. She saw this as a way to help people win back the time they waste commuting and spend it better: with their families, their friends, outdoors, and in their community. From that initial dream grew Office Nomads, a coworking space in Seattle's Capitol Hill neighborhood. As the person responsible for the growth, maintenance, and cultivation of Office Nomads and the community it fosters, Susan has gained experience in nearly every aspect of running a business, from constructing furniture and devising organizational budgets to crafting events designed to foster collaboration and education among coworking members. With a professional background in environmental education and outreach, Susan believes coworking spaces are a key aspect of a truly sustainable urban environment and hopes to inspire and support more coworking spaces locally in the Northwest. Like any good Seattleite, Susan also spent several years behind an espresso bar slinging shots and crafting designer foam. Susan earned her degree in sociology from Boston College in 2003.

## Recommended Reading

### *Books and Articles*

Goodman, Michelle. *The Anti 9-to-5 Guide: Practical Career Advice for Women Who Think Outside the Cube.* Emeryville, CA: Seal Press, 2007.

Jones, Drew, Todd Sunsted, and Tony Bacigalupo. *I'm Outta Here! How Coworking Is Making the Office Obsolete.* Not an MBA Press, 2009.

Tapscott, Don. *Grown Up Digital: How the Net Generation is Changing Your World.* New York: McGraw-Hill, 2009.

### *Websites*

Biznik, biznik.com

Coworking Community Blog, blog.coworking.info

Coworking Google Group, groups.google.com/group/coworking

Coworking Wiki, wiki.coworking.info

Office Design Blog, www.officedesignblog.com

Office Nomads Blog, www.officenomads.com/blog

Office Snapshots Blog, www.officesnapshots.com

Remote Revolution, www.remoterevolution.com

Web Worker Daily, gigaom.com/collaboration

CHAPTER 3

# The Dis-Organization
# of Invention

Carolina M. Reid

Long before today's digital natives drew breath, there were those who used technology to share their work and ideas with surprising openness, believing fervently in the greater good that comes from many minds coming together. Comprised mainly of scientists and technologists, these communities spanned the globe, acquiesced to English as their primary language for sharing information and agreed upon the technical protocols, such as URLs and http:// for sharing data without the need for proprietary software to decode it.

Tim Berners-Lee, then a researcher at the Swiss nuclear research laboratory CERN (Conseil Européen pour la Recherche Nucléaire), is credited with inventing the World Wide Web (aka, WWW). Berners-Lee's motivation was to reflect the way people in the physical sciences research community shared data and then to further expand this community to include new communities in a more open network.

Yet, true to form as an inventor of modern collaboration, he exclaims: "I can't emphasize too often that I didn't invent the internet!" He goes on to say that it was another collaborator, "Vint Cerf and his colleagues who realized that a computer connected to more than one network could act as a kind of postal sorting office." However, ask Cerf and he too will place the credit elsewhere. What he noticed was that while there were many networks in existence, "the paths between them were very long." As a culture, we make heroes of these people who, in their own minds, merely built a tool to further their work as scientists and researchers. For these inventors, innovation was a means to a common goal, not a quest for fame.

What these men left to the digital natives is a large and important legacy. They took a culture of sharing and gave it form. As they laid the foundation for the internet, their fundamental beliefs in access to any piece of data on it, through any path, have made it a place that resists any form of hierarchy. Hence, one of the greatest gifts in the form of the internet came to the digital native from the government and scientific institutions. In receipt of an essentially subsidized set of tools designed by people whose primary goals were not so much economic advancement as holistic information exchange, the digital native has been able to create a subculture of innovation that has existed alongside the mainstream business culture with very little overlap.

Even as open source culture continues to develop and to add corporate feature sets to its free tools, traditional Fortune 1000 companies partake very little in the culture or its products. In one example, Dolibarr, an open source financial enterprise resource planning (ERP) and customer relationship management (CRM) package, is used entirely by small- to medium-sized companies and foundations, though it has a number of features similar to those found in the Oracle ERP or CRM systems. There is little likelihood it will grow to rival the likes of Oracle, a $23 billion company with thousands of clients. Even so, Oracles finds it useful to provide the ability to connect to open source systems and confirmed this with its 2006 purchase of a Berkeley University-based open source company called Sleepycat Software. So while it is making inroads into corporations, in large part, open source is viewed as a feature, not a framework; it is still seen as a curiosity. In a sense, open source software is a corporate IT version of graffiti art, something that cannot be owned or hung in a museum, so it has no value.

With the coming of age of an entire generation of digital natives reared in a culture of free content and free software, we are at a historical crossroads in which the open source world, with its tradition of free sharing and collaborative creation, is colliding with the corporate mentality of guarding information and ideas for profit. Today, we see a generation of digital natives who have grown up never knowing a world without the internet, with all of its free or ad-subsidized tools, and this has profoundly shaped their expectations. Their emergent code of behavior—that of a highly connected knowledge worker who feels compelled to contribute to these open source projects as a way of participating in the exchange of answers to all sorts of questions—is shaping innovation on a larger scale, inside corporations and far beyond the boundaries of cubicle walls.

Thanks to the entry of these digital natives into the ranks of corporations, as well as their hive-minded work outside of organizational strictures, the very nature of innovation is becoming broadly collaborative. The lone tinkerer or the top-secret corporate research and development (R&D) center is being out-maneuvered as a generation migrates toward the more fertile ground of networked collaboration.

## The Hero Inventor

Historically, we have sought to attach individual names and faces to inventions. (Think of the origins of the word *history*, as in *his story*.) We were once raised to think of inventors as mavericks or eccentrics who work in solitude braving adversity until they had something to show for it: Alexander Graham Bell, Ben Franklin, Eli Whitney, and Guglielmo Marconi. We honor these independent heroes and are a little uneasy with the idea of a mass of unknown people coming up with something together. Despite the highly distributed and collaborative nature of its invention, if you ask a handful of traditionally educated people in the U.S. about the origins of electricity, the top cited event will be Ben Franklin standing outside in a lightning storm holding a kite with a piece of metal dangling from it. Even if people know this is probably an urban legend and that Franklin didn't invent electricity, the image of curious Ben out there braving the elements dominates the imagination. However, the open source paradigm—embraced by this generation raised on the web—runs counter to this lone-wolf mentality. Today we do not think of lone tinkerers, we think, instead, of crowdsourcing: solving problems using the web to access the ideas and work of thousands of people at once.

To track the pace of innovation today, organizations may have to explore the uncertain path of openness even as they worry that it may threaten their returns on investment in innovation or weaken their competitive advantage. It may help to keep in mind that at some point, most corporate innovation is released as a product or service in the marketplace and today the feedback loop is nearly instantaneous. Today's digitally savvy consumers are out on the internet using the tools and communities at their disposal to shape the success or failure of products in the marketplace. According to semantic search company TextWise, currently 4 percent of the tweets on Twitter are about products, in the form of either recommendations or complaints; not an astounding percentage, but a great deal of data if you consider that Twitter is logging more than 50 million tweets a day (bit.ly/hVzdD2). In addition to the dominant social networks, there are product-based community sites for every type of interest, be it technology, heavy equipment, pharmaceuticals, sailboats, vacuum cleaners, or automobiles. Consumers seldom make a purchase today without first taking a look at the vast array of online commentary.

## The Rise of the Consumer

It is the digital native's natural inclination to flit about the internet debunking theories, correcting information, and contributing to projects without upfront pay agreements. This works because of the speed and transparency of the medium, helped in large part by social media websites such as Twitter, Facebook, or Digg, which encourage communities to form and news to spread from one network of individuals to the next. The need to monitor and participate in the constant buzz online about corporations and their products or services has propelled businesses in several directions. Like bears running from a swarm of bees, companies find themselves in a race to stay ahead of their virtual reputations. The smart ones take action by dedicating resources to monitoring what is being said about them in social media networks and industry blogs. Companies that fail to monitor a wide array of digital venues have what digital native marketing advisor Lisa Whelan dubbed "selective hearing" on her blog Socialize Mobilize (socializemobilize.com).

Undoubtedly, one of the biggest effects the social web has had on organizations is through the influence of user reviews on purchasing behavior. Some 58 percent of all Americans say they have used the internet for product-related research, up from 9 percent in February 2004, based on findings from a Pew Internet study ("Online Product Research," September 29, 2010, bit.ly/a51IXq). Consumers use the web to research products and also rely upon customer inputs to help them cut through the clutter of same-sounding communications, reading the commentary and reviews on everything from software to soda. Another Pew study, "Trends in Online Shopping" (February 13, 2008, bit.ly/i81NBR), assesses this process of weighing in: "With respect to ratings, 32 percent of internet users have rated a product, service, or person using an online ratings system," pointing out that this act of rating products skews to younger people.

Without a doubt, customer-driven rating systems have become very important. Frank Eliason, a customer service manager who founded Comcast Cares, a Twitter-based service group (twitter.com/comcastcares), says, "Once a product is launched, consumer feedback is imperative." He states, "Follow new products on Amazon. Poor reviews [and] they will not be around long."

Examples of the impact of user comments are not hard to find: During the Christmas 2009 shopping cycle, the Hamilton Beach Set 'n Forget Programmable Slow Cooker, a product unheralded by mainstream media, quietly climbed to the top of the ranks in the cooking product area of Amazon. The reason was that the ratings and comments on the product were very favorable and were widely read, as evidenced by how many people voted on the helpfulness of various customer reviews.

This community groundswell did more than drive sales on Amazon. The high ratings on that site actually provided a level of credibility that caused the product to be featured in a segment about healthy cooking on *The Today Show*.

On Amazon, consumers' product reviews can be rated by other shoppers as helpful or not, and the number of highly rated positive remarks drives the list order of the product. The comments ranked as "Most Helpful" for this product date back to December 2008, when a reviewer commented that the Set 'n Forget was the top-rated slow cooker from *Consumer Reports* and went on to share a way of cooking potatoes for Thanksgiving. That trickle started a flood of comments, with one review from a self-described "Seeker of Quality Products" getting almost 200 votes from other shoppers. The overall number of votes for all the comments for this single product is in the thousands. The mere fact that customers do more than comment, but also vote on others' comments, signals that there is a strong involvement on the part of the shoppers and that the comments themselves foster a feeling of community.

Beyond sales and marketing, however, this sense of involvement in products has other ramifications for organizations that are listening. The day-to-day collaborative, interactive relationship formed by today's consumers around the products and services they use may well shape future iterations of these products, and even the process of innovation itself.

## Corporate Snail Race

The generally accepted view of how innovation occurs—or should occur—is changing because of the rise of web-based collaboration. While feedback and ratings are the most visible form of how the digital native as a social consumer will increasingly impact business, there is another significant direction forward-thinking companies are taking in response to the growing power of the social web: They are listening and responding to the voices of their communities to fuel innovation. Consider how the social web can allow organizations to gather rapid input on products. One example is UBS in Switzerland, which hosted a contest called Web 2.0 @ UBS. In a post on a talent and ideas website called Starmind (www.starmind.com), UBS invited entrants to suggest ways to integrate Web 2.0 technology into the UBS business, taking a first step toward engaging with its customers by engaging with an online community who was most likely not already customers. One of the winners recommended the use of collaborative filtering as a "Driver to enable clients to explore, share experience and build recommendations for Product and Service."

The Starmind website is a global marketplace for knowhow where business and science problems, as well as "daily challenges," are answered by a swarm of independent, yet connected knowledge workers. Starmind accelerates research and innovation "by motivating brilliant minds and talents around the globe to solve challenges." Topics range from the phenomenon of consciousness to quantum mechanics to how long food stays in your stomach.

In another example, LG Mobile Phones has partnered with 3D-design company Autodesk and crowdSPRING, a crowdsourced, creative marketplace, to hold a competition aimed at defining the future of mobile communications. In this case, the customer is the designer and strategist. At crowdSPRING, designers are only paid if their finalized design is selected. This setup would seem unfathomable to the old-school designer used to being paid by the hour regardless of outcome.

But digital natives—who believe that their ratings and exposure (their clout) will quickly rise with the amount of highly (and publicly) valued "free" work they do—see their contributions as a form of currency that gives them access to increasingly better projects.

However, despite emerging examples of companies engaging users to fuel innovation, the overwhelming reality is that most invention inside corporations and institutions is done in a very orderly and conservative way. Hence, much of what companies invent is incremental improvement, hardly invention at all in some cases. Because companies have a massive investment in people, knowledge, and infrastructure, they are looking to make a solid business case with predictable returns, and incremental improvements are the only kind of "inventions" that stand up to such analysis, as Stanford law professor Lawrence Lessig explains in his book *Remix: Making Art and Commerce Thrive in the Hybrid Economy* (Penguin, 2008). Given the need for a precedents-based ROI analysis, the tried-and-true commercial model is at odds with the disruptive innovation economy, comprised of products and applications that may be completely new and therefore hard to prove.

In his investment blog Seeking Alpha (seekingalpha.com), Sean Maher writes about the challenges to innovation: "The key fundamental drivers of sustainable prosperity are technical innovation and productivity growth, and their interaction over time ... It may seem strange in our world of ever sleeker wireless gadgets and broadband connectivity to question the pace of technical innovation, but in fact, R&D productivity has been slumping across many industrial sectors in the past couple of decades" ("Has Stagnating Innovation Led to This Economic Crisis?" bit.ly/h3NxG5).

The good news is that the increasing sense of customer engagement, and the use of crowdsourcing and scout missions outside corporate compounds, can be leveraged to compensate. In the last five years, the concept of "re-mixed" products—ideas found elsewhere then shined up and brought into mass distribution—has not only gained acceptance as a management philosophy but is now touted as a strength.

One remarkable example is a program at Procter & Gamble (P&G), informally called Proudly Found Elsewhere, that set out to make adopting ideas from other inventors or companies into solid business practice. As the *Harvard Business Review* reported in its case study, "Connect and Develop, Inside Procter & Gamble's New Model for Innovation," it became a simple matter of mathematics, in that the company could tap into "200 smart engineers who did not work for P&G for every one that did" (March 2006, bit.ly/fEBqh1).

This program brought consumers a raft of new products, including the wildly popular Mr. Clean Magic Eraser. While there are varying stories of the exact route the product took to American grocery shelves, the original product was a melamine resin foam called Basotect used for soundproofing and insulation in the construction and automotive industries, manufactured by German chemical company BASF. A small Tokyo-based consumer-products company somehow figured out (the stories vary as to how) that Basotect foam could be used as a household sponge and began to sell it under the name Cleenpro. In 2001, a "technology entrepreneur" with P&G found the product in an Osaka grocery store and vetted it, and this discovery ultimately led to collaboration between P&G and BASF to make and market the enhanced product, the Magic Eraser Duo.

This process of outside-in innovation is openly showcased in P&G's Connect + Develop website (www.pgconnectdevelop.com), which provides a marketplace for submissions of ideas and solutions to some of P&G's current R&D issues:

> It's our version of open innovation: the practice of accessing externally developed intellectual property in your own business and allowing your internally developed assets and

> know-how to be used by others. … We now embrace open
> innovation, and we call our approach "Connect + Develop."

Connect + Develop features about 50 current needs and invites anyone to browse the list and and submit ideas. The problems to be solved
include things like "All day facial beauty without shine" and "Food sea-
soning or ingredient that imparts the flavor and/or aroma of fried potato
… with high-impact." Connect + Develop is contributing to the company's bottom line; the *Harvard Business Review* article stated that 50
percent of P&G's lines of business that generate more than $1 billion in
revenues came from innovations outside of the company, and 35 percent
of products overall were found outside the company.

The reality is that internally driven corporate innovation is, for the
most part, a game of inches. Company's staff inventors are not mad scientists or special, creative people who get brightly colored office suites
and toys to play with while at work. The corporate inventor type is
much more likely to be the type of person content to achieve steady
incremental improvement.

In 2009, Intel actually went public with this reality, with its humor-
ous look at the real world of the R&D worker. First, the campaign chose
to glamorize its decidedly unglamorous processes of development and
invention. Intel's biggest advertising campaign in three years, a wonderful effort, is called Rock Star (intel.ly/9EkCI7). In it, we are treated to
music-video-style vignettes of pocket-protector-wearing nerds making
their coworkers swoon to accompanying guitar riffs.

However, peeling away the layers of corporate communication, we
see something interesting going on here; rather than focus on "original
breakthroughs," through its Rock Star Gallery website and campaign—
which has since been mimicked by Intel Sponsors of Tomorrow
(www.intel.com/consumer/tomorrow/index.htm)—Intel  showcases
people whose jobs are largely to partner with outside companies, in a
manner very much like P&G's Connect + Develop program. In these

profiles, the Intel inventors speak poetically of a changed world, of things like patient-driven healthcare or an oil-independent world. We grow misty over these decent and modest-sounding people dreaming of a better world (enabled by myriad applications of Intel chips).

What Intel rightly saw when it approved this campaign is that the world still wants inventor rock stars, so it "invented" some by taking some typical R&D employees and shining a spotlight on them. At the same time, the Intel Rock Star campaign puts "everyman's" face on these inventors. We like it, and even if we laugh at our own folly, we can imagine ourselves in the limelight.

The fact is that some of the greatest inventions don't really have inventors—and there is something sort of unsatisfying about this. To name one: the mountain bike. Charles Leadbeater, former editor at the *Financial Times*, and author of *We Think: Mass Innovation, Not Mass Production* (Profile, 2008), points out that the mountain bike was "invented" by a group of bike enthusiasts who assembled and adapted parts of disparate bikes.

The mountain bike actually represents a pre-web version of community-based remix culture. Taking existing bikes and altering them to fit their needs, this group of bike enthusiasts built a new kind of bike that eventually led to the birth of a major new segment within the industry. However, it took at least 15 years before *any* major bike company began to commercialize the mountain bike. Today's mountain bike industry is worth $58 billion and represents 65 percent of all bicycles sold—yet no one in the bicycle industry thought of it.

This kind of populist invention will come naturally to digital natives. They would not hesitate to dissect and reconstruct a product to make it better suit their needs. And, when we consider how they are reshaping innovation, it is important to remember that digital natives are a group of people defined not only by their age and access to technology but also by a sense of entitlement: Note the wobbly attempts by major news outlets to make their online versions into paid subscription sites, or the music industry's many battles to stem the tide of illegal music distribution, and you can see how hard it is to go against the tide of free content online. Digital natives expect free access to nearly any piece of information or digital asset (music, pictures, videos); assume that they have the right—or even the obligation—to comment on or contribute to the topics they follow; and have a sense of being part of a large group of virtually connected people. Digital natives work creatively by building upon things they find online. They discover things—music, video, text, and ideas—and then rework them and release them again into the community.

## The Customer Manages Us

Today, organizations that fully leverage customer-facing collaborative technologies can discover sooner whether their products can be reworked to their advantage. And, while many of us may wish there was a lone tinkerer who built a mountain bike to deliver mail in his hillside village, the cool stories today are about the emergence of collaborative invention and the sheer scale of its power. Today, inventors have tools for collaborating that stretch far beyond putting notes up on the local bike shop bulletin board, and these tools and strategies are being taken up by some of the most successful businesses on Earth.

One of the best-known examples of using the social web for customer relationship comes from cable television provider Comcast. The company's former director of digital care, Frank Eliason (mentioned earlier), spearheaded an initiative called Comcast Cares, in which a team answers customer service concerns in real time on Twitter. However, in addition to being responsive to customer issues, he thinks the new culture of openness in social networking provides an enormous creative resource for businesses.

Eliason says, "The Consumer is now front and center for product development. In the past it was usually more centered on the design team. Then as it moved to the development cycle Customers might get a view and share thoughts. Now the ideas come directly from Customers and there is real time feedback." He says that the worst sticking point for a corporation engaging in an open dialogue on Twitter is, "Competitors obtaining insights prior to launch." The second, he adds, is, "Sifting through the noise in social media." Despite the clutter, there are a growing number of people who are well versed in mining the social web to find what they are looking for—including competitor information.

With the rise of Web 2.0 authoring tools, digital natives have developed into a connected, collaborative population realizing the vision of their scientist forefathers. Consider the innovation community Quirky, founded by a "23-year-old entrepreneur-in-chief, Ben" (full name, Ben Kaufman). Quirky was the digital native entrepreneur's third startup, motivated by his perception that customers need to be directly involved in the product design and development process. Founded in 2009, the self-described "social product development" company enables inventors to submit new ideas, solve questions submitted by others, or influence ideas in the process of being solved. The following are examples of successful products launched from the site: an iPod case with a built-in light named the Beamer; a nicely designed solution to messy power cords named the PowerCurl; and a "portable camera tripod and keychain with attitude" named the Digidude.

## Open Source Enterprises

While this public development cycle might be anathema to the closed-door R&D of previous generations today, there are companies out there that have decided that they not only can survive but can thrive by letting it all hang out there on the web for all to see. Saul Griffith, a TED Talks speaker on invention, created a forum called Instructables (www.instructables.com). It is described as an open source company (yes, those words together may seem like an oxymoron) that designs and distributes simple engineering instructions as well as a few ready-made products. All of the instructions on the site are free, and the topics covered range from toys for kids to toys for grown-ups.

One of the products that emerged from the Instructables sphere is called Howtoons (www.howtoons.com). Griffith says that Howtoons is all about empowering kids. Turning the hero theme on its ear, Griffith says, "Howtoons is about how to get children to be their own heroes." He also adds, "It's about teaching them how to hack the hackers of tomorrow." Every demonstration of an experiment on Howtoons shows several failed attempts, such as rockets that do not take off on the first try. "We want to teach children how to persist through failures," Griffith explains.

Another Instructables offering is a procedure for making beautiful-looking furniture entirely from plastic oil drums (bit.ly/fqnHaF). A co-collaborator named Bas Van Alen, comments that he made 55 of these chairs for the Instructables Restaurant in the Netherlands. Mind you, in keeping with the philosophy of the company, this restaurant is not a franchise in the traditional sense. This was the open source version of expansion, which credits the Instructables name. Van Alen says that not only the inspiration and name came from Instructables, but also most of the food served came from recipes on the Instructables website. Restaurant visitors are encouraged to contribute their own recipes, which will be attributed in the manner defined by Creative Commons (creativecommons.org).

## Co-opting Open Source Culture

Clearly, open source culture is making inroads into businesses all over the globe. Consider the online gaming company Shanda Enterprises, located in a country aggressively set on reinventing itself: China. According to a white paper issued by the Chinese government in January 2010, Tencent was the top Chinese online game operator, followed by Shanda, and

NetEase; these three companies account for 52.9 percent of China's total online game market.

Shanda's growth makes it a rising star. Ranked No. 7 of *Fortune's* fastest growing companies in 2009, Shanda had more than $522 million in sales in 2008 (the last full year reported), and the company is growing at more than 18 percent a year. In January 2010, Shanda Games Ltd. acquired U.S. online game network Mochi Media in a deal valued at $80 million.

What is astounding about Shanda in terms of innovation is that its employees do not actually create most of the content on its network. Company founder and CEO Tianqiao Chen provides his customers with a platform, some clear rules, and tools, and the company orchestrates the action in their virtual worlds. It is the users themselves who create the content.

The personal investment of these consumer-creators is immense. According to Leadbeater, who interviewed Chen in 2008, if a user's virtual character has a problem, usually violating a rule of some sort or failing to pay, he must pay $600 and show up in person to reclaim his or her character, or pay $100 and create a new character and start all over. According to Leadbeater, every morning there are 600 people lined up outside the Shanda main offices to reclaim their lost, virtual characters.

This model demonstrates the sense of dedication that can arise from being part of a community that creates something. Some estimate the user base of Shanda to be more than 250 million in 45 countries. Yet the company employs just over 1,400 people. Clearly Shanda cannot keep up with all of these users all the time. The trick is that it does not have to. Given the right tools, rules, and a common purpose, the community essentially takes care of itself (Shanda Company Overview, ir.shandagames.com/overview.cfm).

Certainly, gaming seems to lend itself to leveraging the groundswell of the digital natives' collaborative and community tendencies. However, there are other examples of leading organizations leveraging this emerging model of innovation. One company that continuously captures innovative mindshare is Google. Google is known for fostering creative culture within the organization; however, it also recognizes the opportunity offered by the open innovation model.

Mark Pilgrim is a developer advocate for Google. In a video describing his work (code.google.com/doctype), Pilgrim discusses GoogleDoctype, an "open encyclopedia and reference library written by web developers, for web developers."

GoogleDoctype, Pilgrim's brainchild, takes the form of a wiki, and any Google user is invited to log in with his or her Google account and "Click the Edit link on any page." Pilgrim describes GoogleDoctype as a "Hitchhiker's guide to the web." He explains that it draws on the experience of Google developers to provide specific snippets of code and solutions to problems to developers anywhere. The killer app of GoogleDoctype is that code is available uncompiled and searchable on the database. This is of much greater use to developers than compiled code. In a sense, one is like looking at the framing of an unfinished house with the electrical and plumbing exposed as opposed to trying to tear down the walls to understand—and improve—what's going on inside.

Pilgrim says it is part of a "Broader push within Google to ... have more of a developer relations ecosystem." He also points out that Google wants to target the entire open web. He points out that *open web* does not mean *open source*. He defines it more broadly as applications that run in a lot of places on devices, like Gmail and Google Earth, to name a few. He also is quick to point out that all the content on GoogleDoctype is protected by Creative Commons.

Another Google example comes via David Pablo Cohn, a senior research scientist with Google Labs. Cohn believes that having clear laws that govern ownership of ideas and information is crucial to the ongoing success of the emerging digital native culture influencing innovation on the web. During a conversation I had with Cohn on Facebook, he said, "A few years ago, I got to talk with the founders of Second Life. Their thesis was that, in order to create a successful (virtual) society they didn't need to get the rendering/UI/gadgets or any of that perfect, but they *did* need to get the virtual property rights perfect. If they did that, they reasoned, people would stake claims in this virtual frontier and build it themselves. And the past few years seem to demonstrate that they were absolutely right." Cohn picks up where Pilgrim left off in terms of rights and ownership as key to open source sharing of ideas.

Cohn believes that the biggest contribution of digital natives and their culture of collaboration will be "new models of owning and sharing information." Cohn notes that, "historically, information has been valued, but privately, and primarily as a means of arbitrage: If you were privy to some special information about shipping, troop movements, gold strikes, etc., you could use that for your personal advantage before it became broadly known. Mechanisms for that sort of information have been well developed for centuries."

However, he says, "What I'm talking about here is more along the lines of copyright and patent—the mechanisms for other people to make use of Bach's compositions was slow diffusion. Similarly for Watt's steam engine. With the explosion of connections, and technological abilities now anyone can make use of intellectual property, but our culture and laws haven't kept up. The open software industry, with its new licenses (GPL, Creative Commons, etc.) has been pioneering new models of how people assert and share property rights."

While Cohn and Pilgrim are not involved in each other's work at Google, they share some common threads that are woven into the culture of collaborative innovation: Both refer to Creative Commons intellectual property rules and are working to enable collaboration and remixing. The goal is to provide a framework for the continuous sharing of content that deals with credit or ownership in a way that does not impede the pace of this progress.

Another thing they have in common is a free-form style that implies they are not so much working off of a corporate script as from their own creative judgment. This may not jibe with many traditionalists to whom today's digital native inventors seem to live and work primarily in a nameless, faceless cloud, driven purely by their own whims and intentions. This image is disturbing to some who wonder how profit can be derived in this free-flowing culture. Yet clearly, if a company with the global success exhibited by Google is not only developing tools to enable collaborative innovation but also fostering this culture for its own growth, there is a successful business model at work here: By creating an open library of software code, Google is actually making it easier to avoid the issues of interoperability that plague developers. For instance, why does Flash, which is used on many websites, not work on the iPhone? Why does the script software programming on ecommerce site Amazon often cause errors for users of the Safari web browser, placing the wrong number of items in the checkout basket? These are just a few examples of how even the most high-tech of businesses and products can be improved by efforts like the Google Doctype library, so that users do not stumble on odd roadblocks on the web.

## Dis-Affiliation

The culture of openness that is so fully embraced by digital natives will certainly have an impact on organizations as these younger employees join the corporate ranks. However, this form of innovation also relies on openness with those outside a company's walls, which will challenge the current thinking of many corporate leaders.

Business executives who have flourished under the old rules of innovation—incremental and internal—are uneasy with the open source culture for some fundamental reasons. Foremost is the fact that it threatens their way of doing business. Today's corporate culture may actually be geared against any mold-breaking innovation, if for no other reason than that a corporation cannot commit the resources of a couple hundred to a thousand people, voluntarily working away all over the planet, to solve a particular problem. Yet this phenomenon occurs daily in the open source community.

The second major issue faced by traditional organizations is abandoning product testing methods and embracing open, communal ones. The traditional view is that consumers are a passive group at whom companies lob products over the wall. Sure, some traditional companies might opt to pay a handful of consumers $150 each to sit in a room behind a two-way mirror and try to talk about a product. However, today's consumers are intensely interactive. They expect real-time feedback loops for existing products, and many will want to be involved in future products as well. Forward-thinking companies will need to raise the drawbridge, and, yes, risk having competitors get a peek inside as well. The future of innovation does not lie in having more structure and more protection. It lies in having less.

Remember that the people who emerged to collaborate on the innovation of the internet were not formally affiliated. They came from nuclear research, defense, and technology organizations from all over the globe. In the case of the collaborators who created the early browsers (Mosaic /Netscape), their philosophy was based not on selling products but on expanding the network of users. The logic went like this: If we want to build a new way for people to engage with the world, we must give our systems away so as many people as possible will use them. If we are going to give them away, we cannot spend millions to build them behind closed doors. Instead we will tap into a community of collaborators who will offer us their talents in exchange for free tools. And this very logic still lies at the core of open source technology.

As digital natives—who grew up steeped in this culture of openness—increase in numbers and importance as workers and consumers, companies will need to think harder and better about how to engage with them and, more importantly, how to learn from their inventions and their collaborative culture of innovation. The rock star inventor of tomorrow will actually be a chorus.

Leadbeater calls for "new kinds of organization." He asks, "How do we organize ourselves without organization, for instance to achieve large and complex tasks, like new software programs?" The answer lies in rethinking intellectual property theory and even the law itself. With this foundation in place, open source can organically organize in the non-organized manner that has caused it to flourish. There is a new breed of inventors, with an infinite number of faces, who want to join the team. To work with them, we need to open up in terms of research and development—and in terms of corporate culture.

Open source culture must find its way into the corporate world. But to open up the company and its projects fully, to invite input and criticism from outside, is not how companies do things. It's risky, certainly. It's anti-competitive, we surmise. Therefore, it's probably a waste of time, we conclude.

Maybe it's time to rethink.

## About the Contributor

**Carolina Madeleine Reid** is a technology writer who runs an interactive marketing advisory service (www.inagrain.com) that increases sales for new products, new books, and new services using social media tools. She has worked in internationally based jobs at both a big consulting firm, Ernst and Young, and a big corporation, General Electric, where she handled the numbers-oriented rigors well and was also labeled as highly creative, which sometimes felt like a bad thing, depending on the day. Later, she immersed herself in cultures of creativity at a few high-tech startups, where, ironically, she earned the reputation of being the reasonable, analysis-driven one. Carolina grew up in Peru and in the U.S. with a mother who was a journalist at the Voice of America and a father who was Prime Minister of Peru, as well as a fund manager and an investment banker, back when those creatures roamed the Earth. Now, she has a husband who runs an enterprise software startup and three adorable children, and she lives in Connecticut. She is very glad the internet was invented because it is almost large enough to contain the ever-flowing fount of ideas she likes to play with, and she can't wait to see what is coming next in its ever shifting tides.

## Recommended Reading

### *Books and Articles*

Abbate, Jane. *Inventing the Internet.* Cambridge, MA: MIT Press, 2000.

Fried, Jason and Hanson Heinemeir. *Rework.* New York: Crown Business, 2010.

Huston, Larry and Nabil Sakkab. "Connect and Develop: Inside Procter & Gamble's New Model for Innovation." *Harvard Business Review* 84, no. 3 (March 2006).

Leadbeater, Charles. *We Think: Mass Innovation, Not Mass Production.* London: Profile, 2008.

Lessig, Lawrence. *Remix: Making Art and Commerce Thrive in the Hybrid Economy.* New York: Penguin, 2008.

### *Websites*

Seeking Alpha, seekingalpha.com

Socialize Mobilize, socializemobilize.com

"Technology, Education and Design," TED Talks, www.ted.com/talks

# Native in Blue: Understanding the Challenges and Opportunities in Managing Today's Police Officers

Christa M. Miller and Lt. David Hubbard

Law enforcement may seem a natural choice for the civic-minded digital native. After all, high tech has become as much a part of police work as cruisers, two-way radios, and—yes—guns.

In-car computers let cops type reports and get real-time video of crimes in progress. Case management and intelligence software allow detectives instantly to see connections among people, places, and items. And social networking applied to community relations enables easier, clearer two-way communication between police and the public without media or other filters.

It would seem, on the surface, that this is an age in which digital natives will step smoothly into the law enforcement fray, translating their natural comfort with and mastery of digital technologies into an ability to effectively combat crime. Yet despite technological advancements in crime fighting, old problems persist: Digital natives struggle to convince administrators that the benefits of these technologies for police work outweigh the costs. And civilians, thanks to TV and movies, continue to perceive police and police work as different from reality.

In the real world, police departments are underfunded, lacking the training, equipment, and personnel to keep up with technological advances. Some problems, such as cybercrimes, are not well understood in either their scope or the methods required to combat them.

In addition, human resources simply do not exist on the scale that TV suggests. Police officers in small towns wear many hats. A patrol officer may double as a crime scene investigator or computer forensic examiner or even a deputy coroner. A lieutenant may also be city prosecutor. Administrators of these agencies seek out technological "force multipliers," which can make everyone more efficient, yet despite the advantages such technologies offer, many departments are not able to afford them.

And the ultimate truth about police work remains the same: The street is still the street—the most dangerous place for a cop. Shift work and long stretches of physical inactivity, punctuated by intense activity such as a foot chase, have always been physically taxing. The inability to help every victim of crime, or to put every criminal behind bars, is emotionally wrenching. And dealing with the worst of the worst in society— child molesters, murderers, chronic abusers—is spiritually draining.

Digital natives enter this landscape influenced by media-driven perceptions, as well as their belief in technology's ability to solve the world's problems (as evidenced by youth-driven protest movements in Iran in 2009 and in other countries over recent years).

Digital natives are both savvy and naïve with regard to the demands that law enforcement will place on them. Their task is to learn how to leverage their unique perspectives on the job, both to solve problems and to avoid being sucked into the reactive mindset of policing that has existed for so many generations.

In turn, their managers must learn how to help them navigate the realities of law enforcement without discounting or restricting their use of the very tools that could make them the most effective crime-fighters ever to hit the streets.

## The Digital Native Joins the Force

Whether recruits are hired first and then sent through the police academy, or go through the academy and then apply to law enforcement agencies, the academy is by and large their starting point in law enforcement. Academy training traditionally features a mix of "book learning," boot camp-style physical exercises, and specific training on defensive tactics, building searches, traffic stops, and so on. This initial training is built upon over the years with in-service training for sworn officers.

However, research suggests that digital natives learn differently because their brains are structured differently from digital immigrants' brains. They are simply not able to learn in the same ways that previous generations did (Marc Prensky, "Do They Really *Think* Differently?" 2001).

### *Training the Digital Native Using Real-World and Digital Innovations*

Some educators have learned to adapt. For instance, an August 2009 Nurse.com article reported that the Student Health Awareness Center in New Jersey built the Michelle and Jennifer Tobias Adventure to Health Museum, which contains about 19 interactive exhibits. These use as many of the five senses as possible to teach digital natives, trying to make health and healthy decision-making fun. And the program curricula are not scripted. Instead, teachers work with general guidelines and use "teachable moments" as they come up (Rita Marie Barsella, "CentraState RNs Use High-Tech Health Education to Engage Children," Nurse.com, tinyurl.com/yg5sp6h).

Similarly, in law enforcement, some trainers have begun to move toward "reality-based" training, during which both recruits and in-service officers qualify with their guns not on a static firing range, but in a dynamic interactive environment, complete with weather changes, the sounds of gunfire and screaming, light and dark, and other real-world elements. (Hogan's Alley at the FBI Academy is perhaps the best example.)

These environments put officers under stress and demand that they make the kind of split-second decisions they would on the street. The best trainers record everyone's performance and use the videos to teach. The advent of both dashboard and body-worn cameras provides additional perspectives from the officer's point of view.

In a 2008 report for the Law Enforcement Executive Forum, "A Survey of the Research on Human Factors Related to Lethal Force Encounters" (bit.ly/hPvIEN), Audrey Honig and William Lewinski discussed how this kind of regular training changes an officer's performance under stress by "short-circuiting the adrenaline response." In essence, it reprogrammed the brain to make the right decisions despite a suspect's verbal and nonverbal aggressive hostility.

A real-time environment is not necessary for such training, however. The U.S. military has found that digital simulation in the form of video gaming works, too. According to Prensky, "Practice—time spent on learning—*works*. Kids don't like to practice. Games capture their attention and make it happen. And of course they must be practicing the right things, so *design* is important." Referring to military training, he added that not only do commanders recognize games' importance to digital native learning; they have seen it work in the field.

Although budget troubles make it unlikely that many police academies will be able to invest in the kind of multimillion-dollar simulators the military owns, they *can* properly balance existing digital resources with real-world reality-based training.

The Second Life Blog reported in October 2009 that its web-based virtual reality application had been used to train doctors. While the online world can never replicate distracting sights and sounds or verbal and physical cues that intimidate, it can help to school officers in proper procedure without distraction or hazards.

For example, Second Life could be used to train officers for felony stops, active shooter situations, and use of the incident command system. A June 2009 post on the New World Notes (bit.ly/OaVWa) blog reported that a private consulting firm used the application to develop a virtual methamphetamine lab, where it trained officers to identify and respond to these hazardous environments.

In such contexts, police could use Second Life or similar virtual reality tools as a sort of 3D-tabletop exercise—to train with officers and teams from other agencies, learning from the different tweaks each organization puts on universal protocols. Collaborative cloud-based real-time environments such as Novell Pulse could also work for this purpose.

Use of such tools doesn't have to be limited to critical incidents, of course. Game-based learning could be used to engage and train digital natives for a variety of skills, from the mundane to the tactical. These skills include not only proper traffic stop procedures but also figuring out the lowest level of force needed to get a subject to comply with orders.

### Training for Officer and Public Safety

Technology can be used in many ways to capture the imagination of digital natives and to better engage them in training activities. However, specific attention must also be paid to teaching them the appropriate use of technology. Digital natives must understand how technology affects the most basic law enforcement principle: officer safety. For example, most law enforcement agencies have installed laptop computers in their patrol vehicles. This technology enables officers to work on reports, get more detail on calls via computer-aided dispatch, and perform other tasks without leaving the street to work at a desk back at the station.

However, late at night, officers working on reports or messaging each other on personal mobile devices compromise their own safety. The bright screen shows the location of the parked cruiser and reduces the officer's night vision. This impairs their situational awareness such that they cannot see people approaching on foot or crimes in progress. Sound from the computer or a radio can be another distraction.

In addition, digital natives are used to using social networking sites like Facebook to document and to share moments in their lives, especially during "downtime"—which could mean a quiet 4 AM shift or when guarding a crime scene perimeter. In law enforcement, however, there is no such thing as "downtime." Several incidents of fatal ambushes of police officers in late 2009 prove that situational awareness to one's physical surroundings is paramount at all times.

Therefore, while digital natives are good at multitasking, they must be trained in how to prioritize tasks and remain focused. For example, on the scene of a street-corner robbery or homicide, not only does it look unprofessional for officers to have their heads down texting or tweeting, but it also carries serious consequences for both officer and public safety. Just because the incident is over doesn't mean the suspect will not return, still armed and dangerous.

On the scene of a large-scale incident, it's arguable that officers can gather important intelligence from social networking sites. However, officers should not be part of real-time information dissemination. The incident command system specifically defines roles in each part of an operation: The dispatchers are the ones who monitor intelligence, while the officers in the field must stay alert to their surroundings.

### Training for Proper Online Community Conduct

The physical safety of the officer and the public is top priority, but an officer's online conduct can also have far-reaching repercussions. Leaks of internal information, whether crime-scene photos or an agency's "dirty laundry," have been a concern of law enforcement agencies for decades. Social networking and other means of cyber communication raise the possibility that a video or tweet will go "viral." This concern applies especially with regard to use of force: Witness the proliferation of cell-phone videos in the minutes following the 2009 shooting of an unarmed civilian, Oscar Grant, by San Francisco Bay Area Rapid Transit Officer Johannes Mehserle.

Off duty, cops have always blown off steam to each other in bars and other public places, but there they were likely to be wearing civilian clothes and sitting in their own little corner. On the internet, the ultimate "public place," many law enforcement officers openly self-identify; their jobs are part of their identities, and they believe they can say anything they want on Facebook on their own time. However, when an officer uses social networks as a virtual "bar," it's not only fellow officers who are listening; so are many other people, not always known to the officer.

This problem can even extend to private data. Anecdotally, young people are reported to share their passwords so that they can update each other's Facebook statuses. In a November 2009 E-Commerce Times article, FBI Assistant Director of Cybersecurity Shawn Henry was quoted as saying, "You have digital natives ... [who] don't have the same concern for privacy, for security, as I do, as many of us here do. ... And many of the folks who are coming up the ranks in major corporations don't have the same sense that there's a threat, because they've been surrounded by the technology, the openness, that is supposed to make their lives easier and faster. Those very capabilities are the ingress for the threat" (Renay San Miguel, "An FBI Cybercrime Agent's Tales From the Trenches," bit.ly/fNN36e).

The ease of electronic sharing has created a laissez-faire attitude toward information. Digital natives tend to think more in terms of what they need or what their friends would enjoy, rather than worrying about who owns digital property such as a Wikipedia entry or an image file, or how lapses in personal security or privacy might negatively affect their professional lives.

### Molding Digital Nativism to Community Needs

The key to cyberethics and safety education, then, is not to ban social networking and other technology outright but to realize the underlying values behind sharing of inappropriate material. It isn't that digital natives don't care or are willfully ignorant. It's that they value "transparency"—a buzzword that really means "cops are human, too"—and use technology to build and further their relationships with others.

Relationship-building is a key component in community-oriented policing, and the fact that more community members are joining social networks and using digital tools every day indicates that digital natives are in the best position to take the lead in "digital community policing." But to fill this role, they need to be guided as to what constitutes both appropriate and inappropriate transparency, and the consequences of each.

This kind of guidance helps shape recruits as professional members of a professional police department, able to leverage their skills without jeopardizing the agency's credibility. Incorporated into training at the academy, field, and in-service training levels, it should both adhere to and inform an agency's policies and standard operating procedures—changing as needed along with technological advances and the recruits' skill levels.

## Field Training: Shaping Digital Knowledge to Fit the Job

Most law enforcement agencies follow the San Jose Model of field training recruits. This model incorporated goal setting and metrics, which for years have provided a structure for both recruits and field training officers (FTOs) as they work together to prepare new officers for solo patrol.

However, the old FTO maxim "Keep your eyes and ears open, and your mouth shut" is only effective when the FTO's experience outweighs the trainee's. This will still be the case when it comes to the officers' feel for the street and the people they serve. However, compared to recruits in previous generations, digital natives motivated to join the force already have considerably more knowledge about both police work and technology. Digital immigrant FTOs must take this into account.

For example, years ago it would have taken months for a new officer to acquire essential background knowledge about a street gang using a time- and labor-intensive combination of vehicle surveillance, field interviews, confidential informant development, and even undercover work. Nowadays, that officer need only run a Google search and spend a few hours reading or streaming videos to gain comparable background knowledge.

In some ways, field training a digital native is like field training a "lateral transfer"—an experienced officer from another agency—because it takes into account that officer's existing knowledge. Just as a lateral already knows how to conduct traffic stops, build searches, and so on, a digital native knows how to retrieve call records and text messages from a mobile phone or tweet information about a fleeing suspect.

Whether they should is another question. The digital immigrant FTO may find him or herself at a disadvantage when it comes to the native's natural inclination to use technology on the job. It is important for supervisors to understand the legal precedents and logistical concerns with using it. Some of this information is easily found on websites like PoliceOne.com and Officer.com and on blogs.

Other information, however, may require more advanced training. The investigation of digital devices is a prime example. Digital natives are more fully aware of rapidly advancing technological capabilities. For example, while digital immigrants may be inclined to overlook the Xbox in the entertainment center during a search, digital natives know it has enough storage space on it to function as another hard drive.

However, digital natives are also more likely to take digital devices for granted and treat them too casually. A native officer who knows that valuable information can be found on a suspect's mobile phone may be tempted to go through it looking for contact information or call detail records, the kind of search legally allowable only "incident to arrest"—depending on location (Milazzo, "Searching Cell Phones Incident to Arrest: 2009 Update," *Police Chief Magazine,* October 2009).

The digital immigrant FTO who instructs strictly from the FTO manual, without encouraging critical thinking, will likely be unprepared to educate officers on the possible consequences of their "natural" actions. In addition, budget priorities in both police departments and academies may put high-tech crimes training way down on the list.

To think ahead, department leaders may want to reassess their FTO programs. The best FTOs have always asked their recruits what they would do in any given situation; this technique makes the recruit think critically and might even teach the FTO.

Thus, the proactive agency might encourage their FTOs to guide recruits' self-education. For example, recruits may be tasked to research the best blogs about digital evidence case law, while the FTOs (and perhaps the department attorney) vet those sources for relevance and veracity.

To effectively facilitate this approach, agencies must have policies in place that address technology use specifically (as opposed to relying on codes of conduct alone). It may be tempting for leaders to want to "lock down" as much as possible, especially when they don't understand how best to leverage digital technology on the job. However, again, this is not realistic (nor optimal). A better approach would be to ask for policy input from younger recruits. As in the U.S. Army, an internal blog or wiki can be set up to post policies and request suggestions ("Army to Test Wiki-Style Changes to 7 Manuals," *Army Times,* July 2009), while internal microblogging can be used for discussions. Asking all officers to contribute and collaborate in this way makes them think about what they're doing and thus take ownership of their actions. It will also appeal to digital natives in particular, who are steeped in an open, collaborative social media culture.

This approach has the added benefit of also teaching administrators about digital (and social networking) technology and how to use it to solve problems. As a result, they may be more open to allowing their native officers to use technology to solve problems on the street. Meanwhile, however, natives must understand an administrator's need to monitor on-duty technology use to ensure it stays on track.

## First Year and Beyond: Mentoring the Digital Native

Traditional field training programs end with the newly minted officer assigned to a shift and left to his or her own devices. This is not the right approach for digital natives, whose strengths include ingrained social networking culture: collaboration, friendly competition, development of a "personal brand"—the traits by which others come to know, trust, and respect the individual—and constant connectedness, enabling faster and easier communication with both citizens and fellow officers.

This does not mean that departments should allow technology uses such that policies on professionalism are compromised. It does mean that administrators must understand digital natives, who view everyone as "friends" and potential friends, and want to feel valued. Thus disciplinary action should not be the automatic first choice in cases where native officers genuinely did not understand the nature of their misconduct.

### Guiding Digital Natives and Immigrants Together

Instead, administrators must take the time to create in-service training for all officers about digital technologies. Ideally, this will include perspectives from both digital natives and immigrants, and teach each group about the strengths and weaknesses of the other.

Digital immigrants, for instance, might learn that although they assume that "technology overuse reduces interpersonal skills," this is not the case. The Pew Internet & American Life Project found that internet social networking actually increased individuals' access to a larger, more diverse group of people ("Social Isolation and New Technology," 2009, bit.ly/dI2uxk).

This means that digital natives tend to interact across conventional boundaries such as race and gender; if technology is an equalizer, then reaching out to citizens is less of a problem for officers now than it was in previous generations. The implications for community policing should be obvious.

On the other hand, digital natives' positive attitudes toward collaborative culture may entail a certain naïveté. As internet safety expert Larry Magid wrote in November 2009 on his blog LarrysWorld.com (bit.ly/eWSEmN), current efforts to educate digital natives in schools show that they have a hard time understanding how sharing information could put them in danger or hurt their own or others' reputations, or how friending the wrong people could make them look less than professional.

Digital immigrants understand these issues all too well. Drug informants, for example, typically cooperate with police for one of three reasons: because a case is hanging over their heads, they want to make money, or they're trying to get back at a rival. None of those reasons is noble, and it's easy for police officers to believe everyone thinks that way.

The key, then, is for training to leverage both immigrants' and natives' experiences, building on the groundwork laid during field training. Immigrants help natives understand the rationale behind their cynicism that "everyone wants something." Natives help immigrants understand that sometimes, that "something" is simply "to help."

As time goes on, natives will come to learn that they can use personality rather than personal information to connect with the public, which in turn will help immigrants overcome their discomfort with online culture. This can pave the way for truly groundbreaking work, such as the use of social networking to "crowdsource" crime prevention and crime solving.

### Building Community, Internally and Externally

Traditionally, police have responded to the crime trends they saw. Sometimes public opinion matched the numbers generated from arrest reports and Uniform Crime Reports. But sometimes it didn't. Although the resurgence of interest in community-oriented policing in the 1990s helped police to listen better to public input, that decade also saw the introduction of public accountability numbers systems, such as CompStat in New York City. Policing continued to be driven by numbers rather than human-to-human feedback.

Internet social networking has changed that dynamic. Numbers are still important—there is no other way to tell whether what you are doing works—but digital natives are more inclined to build relationships to solve problems. The digital native's reliance on technology-facilitated collaboration means that over time, it's likely that "silos" of responsibility will be broken down.

As digital natives become more responsible in their technology use and digital immigrants become more comfortable with it, the police department can develop its own internal community, integrating many of the functions once "siloed" among public information, community relations, patrol, investigations, and so on.

For example, detectives who need patrol officers to collect information about a crime like identity theft could use a combination of podcasting and internal messaging to teach them. Patrol, likewise, could use the same technology to upload images, audio, or video of trends they see to dispatchers, commanders, and detectives.

The introduction of such internal crowdsourcing can lead to its application outside the department. The same technology—the social web, camera phones, podcasting, etc.—enables police to release information that can then be shared throughout the community via citizens' diverse individual networks. Indeed, some police departments have already established YouTube channels and blogs for this purpose.

Two-way communication means not only that civilians can more easily pass tips to police but also that they can better understand certain aspects of police work (such as responding to 911 calls that are not true emergencies).

All in all, technology can provide police with the opportunity to interact with civilians who genuinely want to help them and learn what law enforcement is all about. Increased awareness on both sides facilitates trust and respect, enabling police to focus more on serious crime.

### Always-Connectedness and the Native Officer's Work Flow

A final significant difference between digital natives and digital immigrants is the native's ability to go beyond "work–life balance" to work–life *integration*. In the corporate world, workers are increasingly "workshifting," working in places and at times outside of the 9-to-5 office environment.

Whether this can translate into law enforcement—with investigators wanting to work from home or elsewhere—is a question administrators should at least consider. Corporate workers are subject to many of the same information security rules that investigators would be, and their bosses have the same fears about productivity that any good leader should.

On the other hand, statistics show that workshifting in a "results only work environment" can actually increase productivity, as Kellyanne Conway wrote in her "Generation 'Y Do I Have to Work From the Office?" post on the WorkShifting blog (November 3, 2009, bit.ly/3MoY80).

In fact, digital natives' facility for information-gathering means that their always-connectedness can make them better informed than their digital immigrant colleagues. Information overload is not a concern for them because they have learned how to filter and organize all that they see. Moreover, they are able to intuit how to put it to best use, whether for their own career, others' education, their line of work, or personal use (Zaslow, "The Greatest Generation (of Networkers)," *Wall Street Journal*, November 2009).

These issues call for appropriate mentoring with regard to digital technology use. Digital immigrant colleagues, or even natives who have moved into supervisory positions, can help less experienced officers put their connectedness into a context that digital avoiders can understand. Meanwhile, native officers must adapt to the fact that not every administrator or private citizen will be willing or able to respond to their problem-solving ideas.

However, supervisors and administrators should be mindful of the fact that their own lack of understanding of digital technology and its potential applications—and lack of desire to understand—could drive digital natives away. Those who want to recruit and retain top-notch officers must be willing to move beyond their comfort level or allow free rein to others who are willing.

## Recruiting and Retaining the Digital Native

Traditionally, large police departments have always been viewed as "better." Larger budgets, more diverse communities, and more staff have (in the best of times) driven much technological innovation. These agencies gain reputations for being more progressive, and so they tend to attract both recruits and lateral transfers away from smaller agencies.

However, larger departments are also less willing to take chances with personal technology (such as video-enabled mobile phones). They have more at stake with regard to a need to "control the message," which often translates into controlling their employees—a prospect that chafes digital natives.

In this respect, smaller departments may have an advantage. They may not have the prestige of the agencies with better "toys," but in a bid for good young officers, they can afford to innovate. Thus, just as larger agencies are good at being "proactive" when it comes to protecting themselves against problems like lawsuits, smaller agencies stand to be more progressive when it comes to protecting themselves against lost personnel—and lost reputation.

An example of such an innovation: An officer who wants to join the tactical team posts a series of videos to his YouTube channel that show him excelling in a firearms competition, an active-shooter training exercise, or some other relevant experience. His proficiencies are likewise noted on his LinkedIn profile, which he can tweak to match the job he wants. He friends other tactical officers and hopefuls on social networks like Twitter or one of the many police-only groups. The agency that encourages and supports its officers' "professional branding" provides value to recruits who are digital natives.

The best mentoring doesn't just guide police officers through their first few years on the job; it also prepares them for, and leads them further into, their careers. Even if officers end up leaving the department they started from, or leaving law enforcement altogether, being given options along the way helps them make the best decisions for themselves and their agencies.

Leaders must understand that they are not only supporting individuals; they are also ultimately supporting their own department and community. Professional police officers constitute a professional police department. And a professional police department is what all citizens demand—and deserve.

Digital natives are part of the group of generations (starting with Gen X) whose members tend to be loyal to trusted individuals rather than organizations, reluctant to give up individual rights and desires to a corporate body which, they perceive, will give nothing in return. To retain them, law enforcement managers must show that they value each individual.

Law enforcement administrators who have allowed recruits some control over their field training and mentored their use of digital technology through their first few years of patrol should be prepared to shift their focus to career development. Many different specialties exist within law enforcement, and whether an officer moves from patrol to investigations, the tactical unit, training, supervising, or community/media relations, the decision will be as thoroughly researched as was the decision to become an officer.

Likewise, an officer who wants to get into investigations can "brand" his or her passion for justice by starting a blog or a podcast, where she talks about victim, investigative, and legal issues. She might choose to speak directly to community members, telling victims of domestic violence or identity theft exactly what steps they must take to contact police.

In both cases, the officers' freedom to be completely transparent—to show what can and cannot be expected of investigators, or the hard work it takes to be a tac-team member—is important. Officers who cannot transmit the full range of their passion, from joy to frustration, will lose interest. Uninterested officers are less professional, whereas those who feel valued for all their experiences on the job—and who are encouraged to channel them in appropriate ways—are more likely to value each other as well as the citizens they protect.

## Technology and the Police

Historically, technology has been a "force multiplier" for police departments. Intelligence software makes automatic connections between people and places, removing the need for detectives to spend time making phone calls and visits. Digital cameras provide immediate photographic evidence, without the need to wait for processing. And social networking sites enable a single officer to push information out to multiple sources, who can then share it among their own networks.

In other words, police work stands to go from "reactive" to "proactive," more so now than at any previous point in history. Administrators and supervisors, then, must take care to encourage digital natives even if they themselves don't fully understand the technology. They must be open to learning how it can be used, but focus primarily on the individuals using it. They can do that by:

- Allowing for the fact that digital natives learn differently because their brains work differently. They require engagement of all five senses in as many ways as possible.

- Making field training participatory, encouraging critical thinking in addition to hands-on police work.

- Building a collaborative culture. Digital natives collaborate, often electronically. Whether with private citizens, a fellow detective, or members of a regional task force, they will work better as part of a team.

- Recognizing the unique individual contributions each officer can make. Mentors who help recruits "brand" their careers can stoke their passion and turn them into professionals.

Over time, digital immigrants will learn to manage both new recruits and civilians the way they want, expect, and need to be managed, to maximize their (and the technology's) potential and abilities to the fullest. Until then, although digital immigrant law enforcement administrators may not know how to use technology nor how to train their native officers to maximize its potential in their jobs, it's better to hold on to the reins of the galloping horse rather than simply watch it run away. Digital immigrants can learn from their digital native employees and can help those employees learn from superiors' experiences on the job.

## About the Contributors

**Christa M. Miller** is a content creator and strategist specializing in public safety. She blogs about law enforcement's use of social media at Cops 2.0, drawing on her experience as a law enforcement trade magazine reporter as well as her network of law enforcement professionals. She lives in Greenville, South Carolina with her husband and two sons.

**Lieutenant David Hubbard** has been in law enforcement with the Eustis (FL) Police Department since 1989. He has worked in both patrol and investigations. Currently, Dave is the Administrative Services Commander for his agency. He has a bachelor's degree in criminology from St. Leo University and a master's degree in criminal justice from the University of Central Florida.

## Recommended Reading

### Books and Articles

Hampton, Keith, Lauren Sessions, Eun Ja Her, and Lee Rainie. "Social Isolation and New Technology." *Pew Internet & American Life Project*, November 2009. tinyurl.com/yjjyt4b (accessed October 19, 2010).

Honig, Audrey and William Lewinski. "A Survey of the Research on Human Factors Related to Lethal Force Encounters: Implications for Law Enforcement Training, Tactics, and Testimony." *Law Enforcement Executive Forum* 8, no. 4 (2008). tinyurl.com/ygqwsrx (accessed October 19, 2010).

Hubbard, David. "Officer Retention in Small Departments: Identifying Issues While Offering Solutions." Florida Department of Law Enforcement. tinyurl.com/y93flsl (accessed October 19, 2010).

Miller, Christa. "Keeping It Real: Preparing Officers for the Street." *Law Enforcement Technology* (September 2005). tinyurl.com/ykgmh4z (accessed October 19, 2010).

Prensky, Marc. "Do They Really *Think* Differently?" *On the Horizon* 9, no. 6 (December 2001). tinyurl.com/29jcr (accessed October 19, 2010).

### Websites

Cops 2.0, cops2point0.com

Personal Branding Blog, www.personalbrandingblog.com

Marc Prensky's Weblog, www.marcprensky.com/blog

# I'm With the Brand: How Generation Y Will Transform Hiring Through Personal Branding

Dan Schawbel

In August 1997, Tom Peters wrote an article for *Fast Company Magazine* (Issue 10) titled "The Brand Called You," which explored the evolution of career development and exposed a new mindset for the new millennium. Basically, he contended, instead of relying on a company for career guidance, it's up to you to take ownership of the brand called "you." The notion of *personal branding* called for everyone to become a "free agent," but not everyone bought into it back then.

Today—thanks to the rise of social media—more and more people are grabbing hold of their brand and shaping it. Before Web 2.0 changed our world, it was extremely hard for anyone to get enough press to really stand out. Before blogs, you'd have to get your local newspaper or other mainstream media and convince them to write about you. If you wanted to build your circle of contacts, you could go to a networking event and meet five to 10 people each time. Web 2.0 amplified how we network, placing increased emphasis on first impressions and personal visibility and self-promotion.

For the generation growing up publicly online, who share every facet of their lives willingly and openly with an ever-expanding network, the idea of leveraging the web to build a personal brand comes naturally. In fact, smart companies should actively seek out employees with good networks and networking skills. On the other hand, the digital natives' unprecedented openness with others online is a double-edged sword, because they may not think about how their online activities affect them when they enter the work force.

## The Demise of Job Boards and the Rise of People Searching

Generation Y and those entering the workplace after them naturally gravitate toward building brands for themselves. However, the more effective among them set themselves apart through more than massive friend lists. They succeed in creating a brand consistent with their goals, which sets them apart from the pack. This is turning job searching on its ear; it's transforming job seeking into people finding. It's time the rest of us learned from the digital natives how we can use social networks and online communication tools to secure a job (and at the same time, employers can learn how to identify the most promising candidates).

We're all familiar with the term *job board*. In fact, there are thousands of job boards in existence—some you may know about and others you may never know about. Most readers will be familiar with Monster, CareerBuilder, and Yahoo! HotJobs because they are large brands with large news distribution partners (CareerBuilder partners with CNN and Monster with the *New York Times*, for example). These sites have been around for a long time and contain millions of resumes, with thousands of job openings posted each day. Then there are vertical job search engines, such as Indeed.com, that locate and aggregate postings from the job boards. Finally, there are niche job boards for various industries and professions, such as TalentZoo.com for marketing professionals and mediabistro.com for professionals in publishing, advertising, and public relations. All function more or less like a digitized version of a newspaper's employment section, with a few added functionalities.

Right now, if you're unemployed, you are probably spending hours on job boards desperately searching for a job in your industry (or just for one that will help you pay the bills this month). As of November 2010, the Bureau of Labor Statistics reported that the U.S. unemployment rate was 9.8 percent, which is close to one in every 10 Americans being jobless. Since there are millions of job seekers, job boards are home to piles of resumes that will never even be looked at—these are long odds for success. In all probability, job boards will cease to exist in the future for two main reasons: The model is outdated, and social technologies have transformed the recruitment process forever. As the joker says in *The Dark Knight* movie, "There's no going back."

## The Research Tells All

If you work in an HR-related field, you may have deemed job boards as sacred sites that have helped you for a decade or two. Some readers may have even landed their current position through a job board. But a *Mercury News* article ("Experts Agree: Building, Tapping a Network Crucial to Finding New Job," May 5, 2009) about a woman who sent her resume to 1,700 job postings and garnered only 13 interviews and no job offers prompted me to further research my prediction about the demise of job boards. First, let's start with a quote from a very well-known author in the career field:

> For every 1,470 resumes, there's one job offer made and accepted. —Richard Bolles, bestselling author of *What Color is Your Parachute?*

Clearly, resumes are no longer the sole factor in the recruiting process as they were decades ago. A good resume is no longer enough, and a job board isn't a great place to submit even the best resume, particularly given the number of job seekers using them now. A further indication of the decline of job boards is the fact that some of the largest ones are laying off a good percentage of their staff (in February 2010, Monster Worldwide eliminated 200 positions) because companies aren't hiring, and as such, they aren't posting jobs. In 2009, only 13.2 percent of external job hires came from job boards (CareerXRoads 9th Annual Source of Hire Study, February 2010). That means that about 87 percent of jobs are filled through other means. No matter how you spin the stats, the fact is that job boards will rarely work in your favor because people hire people; they do not hire resumes.

## People Finding

*Job search* is old-school terminology—it refers to applying for jobs that are listed somewhere, such as on a job board or corporate website. The new way to look at a job search is as a *people search*. Conducting a people search means that you identify the top companies you want to work for and find people who are employed at those companies. Then, you network with them and form a positive relationship, and they perform the job search for you. Social networking sites (e.g., Facebook, LinkedIn, Twitter) put everyone on the same plane and give you access to employees who can get you jobs.

Remember that a company's employees have access to internal job boards, which can tell them who the hiring manager is and whether a job is actually available. Companies give employees access to internal job boards because they want to retain them and give them opportunities at various levels and in different departments in the company (which saves the company money, too). If you have a relationship with an employee, that person can email or call the hiring manager and connect you directly or at least forward your resume. In fact, this kind of connection means that there's no reason for you look for a job on a job board or corporate site ever again (if you're smart).

## Look for a Job Like a Native: Me 2.0

For those of you who haven't grown up online, you have two crucial steps to take: 1) Discover your brand, and 2) build up your brand presence.

While Me 1.0 was hidden behind a corporate brand, without its own voice and unable to afford excessive promotion such as PR and advertising, Me 2.0 (and I wrote a book by that title) is front and center in your company—investing your time and energy, empowered by the ability to have your voice carried across the world in a matter of seconds.

There are two main reasons why personal branding is becoming a core part of our culture. Sadly, neither is revolutionary. First, we are all being judged all the time (even when we're sleeping, our online profiles are still up). Second, we must constantly sell our ideas—to teachers, managers, venture capitalists, friends and family—to make things happen in our lives. We have to convince the relevant parties to pay attention to us, and social networks provide the means.

In 2007, a group of international brand and career experts collaborated to create a single definition for personal branding and built the Personal Branding Wiki (personalbrandingwiki.pbworks.com). After analyzing the definition and reciting it in a few presentations, I found it a bit long and hard to remember. A concise version we should all keep in mind is: "How we market ourselves to others." Personal branding is a process. And it is a process that digital natives intuitively participate in. The challenge for individuals is controlling their brand message to achieve their goals. For organizations, it means understanding how employees with a strong brand bring incredible value to the companies that employ them. There are many lessons to learn as you build your own brand in a Web 2.0 world.

## The Personal Branding Process

The personal branding process comes naturally to digital natives, who are as comfortable online as off. They have unconsciously been building their brand since they were old enough to post a profile on Myspace or Facebook, or blog about how much high school sucks. While many digital natives may already be taking these steps to build their personal brand, it is helpful to build some awareness of the process in order to fully optimize the personal brand. For those of you who are new to the game, there are steps you can take to make your first foray into personal branding.

1. **Discover.** The first thing to do is to figure out who you are and what you want to do in life (or what you want to do next in life), by focusing on your strengths, passions, and goals. You should then craft a development plan that aligns your short-term and long-term goals and, finally, create a personal marketing plan. Many digital natives can choose unconventional career paths, because they are able to combine their passions with technology savvy. They are creating their own possibilities, which is highly effective in this unsettled economy.

2. **Create.** There are traditional and nontraditional ways to create your personal brand. The traditional ways include a business card, professional portfolio, resume, cover letter, and references document. The nontraditional ways include a video resume, LinkedIn profile, blog, Twitter account, and an existence on various other social networks. As you create your brand, ensure that the content, including pictures and text, is concise, compelling, and consistent with how you want to represent yourself. Many digital natives have not yet fully grasped the importance of this last point, perhaps due to their age and maturity or due to a changing notion of what is acceptable online behavior. That said, the digital native's ability to use social networks to create a personal brand should serve as an inspiration to digital immigrants.

3. **Communicate.** After you've created your brand, it is only natural that you'll want people to see what you've done. Depending on your

audience (hiring manager, teacher, clients), you will want to tweak your materials accordingly. To properly communicate your brand through self-promotion, you need to have your story down pat and find the right channels to reach those who would be interested in what you have to say. One secret to successful communication is to remember that it is a two-way street and to promote others before you promote yourself. Communication can take the form of guest posting on blogs, writing articles for magazines, becoming your own personal PR person, attending networking events, and public speaking (personalbrandingwiki.pbworks.com).

**4. Maintain.** As you grow, the brand that people see has to grow at the same time. For every new job, award, press article, and client victory (to name a few), you will need to change everything you have created to reflect that. Digital natives know that as you become more popular, your reputation is knocked and tossed around throughout the web, from blog posts and tweets to video and more. Digital natives are also adept at keeping a close eye on where their name is. There is a variety of free tools to monitor your online reputation, including Google Alerts, blog reactions on Technorati, BackType, BoardTracker, and Twitter.

## Personal Branding Depends on Your Career Status

The majority of digital natives are still in high school and college or just entering the work force, and their use of personal branding reflects this. Soon, however, this generation will be entering the work force en masse, and it behooves the corporate world to recognize their skills. To take full advantage of them, employers will need to allow their digitally inclined employees to continue using social networks freely.

Let's consider the various stages of career status and how they affect the maintenance of personal brand.

**High school student.** In high school, personal branding applies because getting into a top college is very competitive. At this stage, the goal is to position yourself as worthy of admission to a top school.

Getting good grades and SAT scores, interviewing at schools, networking with alumni who can endorse you, and writing a compelling essay are all important—but so are all things social media.

**College student.** College students are interested in getting an internship, starting a business, or getting a job upon graduation. They have to compete on experience and network extremely hard in order to get a job. They need to position themselves as superior relative to their peers. Becoming a leader in college organizations, meeting as many people possible, and forming a personal branding toolkit starting freshman year are critical to success.

**Corporate employee.** If you work for a company, and enjoy doing so, then personal branding becomes the cornerstone for moving up the hierarchy and gaining recognition as a leader within your organization. If you are considering moving on or seeking growth opportunities elsewhere, your personal brand will likely be how other organizations discover and recruit you, or your network will be the way in which you identify the best opportunities in the marketplace.

**Entrepreneur.** An entrepreneur needs to think about company branding as well as personal branding in the process of establishing a business. The entrepreneur's personal brand must reflect the company, yet at the same time be set apart from it. The entrepreneur's brand is *very* important in securing venture capital. For instance, if Jason Calanis (who sold Weblogs, Inc. for millions) wanted seed money, he would have a better chance of getting it than someone without a track record of success.

**Consultant.** Personal branding is obviously fundamental to consultants—in fact, it's all they've got. Many consultants (at least the good ones) brand themselves as masters of a specific trade. They are able to track—and demonstrate—how their work provides value to their clients.

## Your Network Is Your Only Insurance Policy

The web has broken down hierarchies and connected everyone in disperse networks, so that you can reach individual employees directly at companies you want to work for, without applying through job boards. The best method for companies, candidates, and recruiters to connect remains networking, according to ExecuNet, which found that just 10 percent of open executive-level positions are publicly posted online (ExecuNet's *2010 Executive Job Market Intelligence Report, April 2010).* That number will probably drop to zero in five years. If you are looking for a job at any level today, it's time to follow the digital native's lead and start using those social networking sites you thought you were too old to join.

In May 2009, a Jobvite survey presented some very interesting data examining the present and future states of recruitment. Here are the major points worth noting:

- 76 percent of the HR and recruiting professionals who responded plan to invest more in *employee referrals* (68 percent in 2008).

- 72 percent of respondents plan to invest more in recruiting through *social networks.*

- 75 percent of respondents plan to invest less in more costly referral sources (job boards, third-party recruitment, and campus recruitment).

- 80 percent of companies use or are planning to use social networking to find and attract candidates this year.
  - 95 percent will use LinkedIn (80 percent in 2008).
  - 59 percent will use Facebook (36 percent in 2008).
  - 42 percent will use Twitter.

- 77 percent of respondents said they use social networks to reach passive candidates.

- 66 percent of respondents who reported hiring a candidate through social networks said they were pleased with quality of the hire.

- 15 percent of respondents tapped employees' social networks for hiring.

- HR people use social networks and other online sources to research candidates.

  - 76 percent use LinkedIn.

  - 67 percent use search engines (Google).

  - 44 percent use Facebook.

  - 21 percent use Twitter.

  - 24 percent of candidates disclose their social networking presence when applying for a job.

In reviewing Jobvite's research, it becomes obvious what's going on in the recruiting world. In the post-downturn reality, companies can't afford to pay job boards thousands of dollars to list positions, especially because many companies aren't even hiring, and it's easy and cheap to assess top talent through social networks. Unfortunately, it is also evident that few companies understand the recruiting potential of their own employees, many of whom already have established professional networks on social networks like LinkedIn (only 15 percent of companies tap employees' social networks for hiring).

Companies are beginning to understand the need to use social technologies in their business, so they realize that they need to recruit individuals who already have these new skills. One issue with this survey is that it reveals that job seekers aren't showcasing their social profiles or blogs when applying for jobs; yet recruiters are using search engines and social networks to recruit. Job seekers should make sure their presence is positive and clean, and then promote any social networking URLs on their resumes and other application materials. Of course, current practices may change as more and more digital natives enter the job market.

Remember: Your network is your only insurance policy. As companies' use of job boards declines, the need for strong professional networks increases. At some point, maybe five years or so down the road, you won't be able to get a job without knowing an employee who can refer you for a position at a target company.

There are three main areas you should focus on right now:

**1. Protecting your brand.** As the survey confirms, most hiring managers are researching social networks and using search engines to conduct background checks. Aside from using a website such as namechk.com to claim your brand name on social networks, you must ensure that you're painting a positive portrait of yourself on your profiles. You want to feel proud of those profiles, keeping in mind that they may help you get a job. Heads up, digital natives!

**2. Promoting your brand.** If you aren't visible online, you don't exist. From the research mentioned here, it's apparent that hiring managers are conducting background checks using search engines and social networks, and if your name doesn't show up, you will lose an opportunity every single time. Also, it is disappointing to see that most applicants aren't promoting their online presence to potential employers. This is a major opportunity to stand out, since only about one in four applicants are taking this step.

**3. Partnering your brand.** To survive and have a successful work life, you must have a strong network. This is a call to arms. You can't force relationships, but you need to work as hard as you can to network with other people and build relationships. If you don't, it will take you longer to get a job, you'll have a harder time landing an interview for positions, and you won't have the support system you need to rise to the top. Partner with people who work at companies you want to work for or who have skills that can help you start a business. Meet as many people as you can—treat life like a giant networking event.

## The Importance of Hiring Savvy Networkers

Digital natives live their lives online. The smartest of them strive to create a constructive personal brand that will help them achieve their career objectives. (Conversely, those who haven't invested much thought or time into developing a visible brand are at a disadvantage.)

As the most successful candidates find their way into employment via the effective use of personal branding, through social networking and other social media tools, they will also be those most adept at using these tools. Understanding how digital natives create a personal brand can do more than help others better leverage these tools for their own career objectives. It can also help hiring managers staff their organizations with employees who bring these skills with them and who can apply them toward the company's objectives.

## Three Perspectives on the Importance of a Network

Given the current economic climate and the increasing importance of social media in all aspects of business, it is imperative that companies understand how to successfully use the power of social media tools, which starts with the value of network building. Consider the importance of these tools from several different angles.

**The corporate perspective.** In a down economy, companies cut back on marketing budgets. Marketing departments are downsized, which means there are fewer people to get the message out. The problem is that organizations actually need to get their message out there, more than ever before, to foster growth and economic recovery. Social media can provide the foundation for cost-effective—and just plain effective—marketing.

**The employee perspective.** Employees, especially in the marketing department, are in desperate need of support. With a slim budget, they are still expected to see a return on each dollar they invest in their marketing programs. Employees who aren't accustomed to social media are still resorting to investing every dollar they have into interrupting random people, hoping they might decide to, at a minimum, visit the company's website. With far less money to invest, delivering ROI with this approach is going to prove incredibly challenging.

**The potential hire perspective.** More than a million people have been laid off. Most job seekers are still convinced that the old method of job seeking is the way to go and, sadly, most fail as a result. Sure, they may create a LinkedIn profile and submit their resumes to corporate websites and traditional job banks. But this will not suffice today. Attraction-based (or inbound) marketing of yourself is the best long-term strategy, so that you never have to apply for jobs and instead find job offers on your doorstep. Assuming that they otherwise fit the requirements for a job, the few potential hires who are socially connected should be (and will be) rewarded with job offers.

Essentially, building a personal brand online comes full circle: It helps people navigate along the career path they want, it helps employers find the best candidates for the job, and it brings a new wave of employees into the work force who are well-equipped to leverage social media, which will contribute to the success of the companies smart enough to hire them.

As digital natives develop their personal brands, they master a skill set that we all need in today's workplace to succeed in our careers or to build successful businesses. Everyone (regardless of their age or generation) should be developing a personal brand, and it is imperative for organizations to seek out brand-savvy employees. Once hired, an employee becomes a reflection of the corporate brand (and vice versa), and the network the employee brings to the table infuses the organization with fresh connections to spread the company's brand. What works on a personal brand level can also be leveraged to get the word out about your company, helping ensure its viability in the future. By letting your employees continue to freely live their online lives—something that is important to them on both a personal and professional level—you will harness the digital natives' natural networking abilities and also make them feel valued.

## About the Contributor

**Dan Schawbel** is the leading personal branding expert for Gen-Y. He is the bestselling author of *Me 2.0: Build a Powerful Brand to Achieve Career Success* (Kaplan, 2009) and the publisher of both the award-winning Personal Branding Blog and *Personal Branding Magazine.*

## Recommended Reading

### Books and Articles

Alba, Jason. *I'm on LinkedIn—Now What??? A Guide to Getting the Most Out of LinkedIn.* Silicon Valley: Happy About, 2007.

Brogan, Chris and Julien Smith. *Trust Agents: Using the Web to Build Influence, Improve Reputation, and Earn Trust.* Hoboken: John Wiley & Sons, 2009.

Comm, Joel. *Twitter Power: How to Dominate Your Market One Tweet at a Time.* Hoboken: John Wiley & Sons, 2009.

Fields, Jonathan. *Career Renegade: How to Make a Great Living Doing What You Love.* New York: Broadway Books, 2009.

Slim, Pamela. *Escape from Cubicle Nation: From Corporate Prisoner to Thriving Entrepreneur.* New York: Portfolio, 2009.

Vaynerchuk, Gary. *Crush It!: Why NOW Is the Time to Cash In on Your Passion.* New York: HarperCollins, 2009.

### Websites

DailyBlogTips, www.dailyblogtips.com

Mashable: The Social Media Guide, mashable.com

Pro Blogger, www.problogger.net

Seth Godin's Blog, sethgodin.typepad.com

Stepcase Lifehack, www.lifehack.org

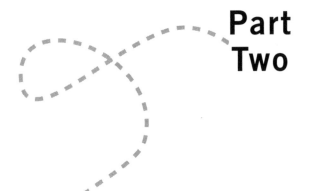

Part
Two

# Marketing and Selling to the Digital Native

CHAPTER **6**

# With, Not To: The Value of Social CRM

Marshall Lager

It is an understatement to say that the world has changed tremendously since the birth of the internet. Nowhere is this more keenly felt than in business. Entire new channels have opened up, and with them the means of communicating value and brand identity have shifted. A salesperson today who is still using tools and tactics that were popular even five years ago is probably not making very impressive numbers. We all know that the web has changed the way (successful) business gets done, and with a generation that has grown up along with the internet now entering the work force and dominating the consumer space that has grown up since the ubiquity of the internet, the pace of change is likely to increase.

"So what?" you may ask.

Digital natives are relatively young, so they probably don't make many major purchasing decisions beyond their own discretionary spending, right? And as long as they're buying something for themselves and contributing to the economy, they'll sort themselves out once they have real adult responsibilities, right?

Wrong. By the time you read this, Generation Y will outnumber the Baby Boomers (Erik Qualman, *Socialnomics: How Social Media Transforms the Way We Live and Do Business,* John Wiley & Sons, 2009) and will have outnumbered Generation X (my own generation) for some time. Generation Y, also known as Millennials, is the generation that best encompasses digital natives. This generation has more money and greater freedom in spending it at their age than any previous generation. Gen Y is already in the work force and rising through the ranks, adapting the newer technologies and attitudes to fit their work styles. They are also very entrepreneurial—if you don't see a lot of Gen Y-ers in cubicles, it's probably because they're running their own businesses. And according to Qualman, 96 percent of them participate in the digital age's version of social networking.

As I mentioned, I'm not a digital native, but I was naturalized at a fairly young age because of my nerdy youth and the degree to which the school system and my parents catered to my digital inclinations. Still, I can remember when every phone was attached to a wall or sitting on a table and when there were pay phones on the street (which people actually used). I remember when the Atari 2600 and the microwave oven were high-tech home electronics, and cable TV remote controls were switch boxes hardwired to cable boxes. If anything, my experience puts me in a great position to see how new technologies (and new applications of existing ones) are changing the way we live and interact—I am close enough to get it but still able to be awed.

Whether you choose to look at digital natives and their success stories as feel-good examples of interesting ways to run a business or as case studies for repeatable success in an industry, you can't escape the realization that the world as a whole is changing and that change will be for the better.

## The Native Business Model

Most, if not all, of the social technologies that are changing business today grew out of consumer-level applications that weren't built for business. So it's fitting that we look first for examples of how those technologies affect digital natives' daily lives as consumers. Let's examine some representative areas where the effect can be seen: fashion and music. Kids today, with their clothes and their iPods, right? Seriously, though, the following cases are all businesses that directly affect their customers' lifestyles. The band you listen to or the clothes you wear have more influence on your outlook than your favorite accounting software, so pay attention.

### Example 1: Threadless

If you spend any time on social networking sites like Facebook, you've probably seen an ad—or even received a request to rate a design—from the T-shirt company Threadless. If you've taken time to look at the designs, they've probably made you laugh, made you think, or earned your respect for the artistry involved. However, you may also have noticed that you don't see Threadless shirts in Macy's or Urban Outfitters, unless they're being worn by shoppers. That's because the company operates largely in the online social sphere, "advertised" by word of mouth. And we're talking about a lot of mouths with plenty of good words coming out of them. While the company doesn't reveal sales figures, Inc.com reports that the company made more than $17 million in sales in 2006, and the 2008 figure is around $30 million ("The Customer Is the Company," June 1, 2008, bit.ly/hDGoRW).

How can a T-shirt company do so well without the usual trappings—and advertising budget—of a traditional apparel business? According to Bob Nanna, marketing manager for Threadless, the answer is that it's run by the sort of people who are interested in original designs in the first place. "The founders, Jake Nicholl and Jacob DeHart, met on a design forum, which held a one-time design contest," Nanna says.

"They thought the idea was so cool, so why not start a company and site to do just that?"

Their idea was cool enough to attract other like-minded people, and Threadless, built on a model of community forum plus design contest, was launched with a mere $1,000 in the bank. "It was essentially operated as a hobby until 2003," Nanna says, "when they realized they needed warehouse and office space to handle the volume of shirts. They started hiring friends to fill orders and keep the site going."

Participants submit their own designs and vote on designs submitted by others in a perpetual design contest. Each periodic winner receives up to $2,500 and an additional $500 each time a run of reprints is needed. "We give the designers tools to share their designs on Twitter, Facebook, or blogs," Nanna says. "We sell the shirts for $15 to $20." The arrangement works out well for all involved. One designer, Glenn Jones, had such success through Threadless that he opened his own shop.

"People can start their own companies based on the Threadless model—there are probably a ton of carbon copies already—but they don't do as well, because Threadless wasn't an overnight success," Nanna says. "We grew virally for four or five years before viral was even a business concept. It was just two guys having fun. Threadless, at its heart, is an art community, not a T-shirt company."

### Example 2: Etsy

While Threadless shows how social media can support a nontraditional business model for T-shirts, a company like Etsy shows how it can create—or recreate—a market for handcrafted goods.

Once upon a time, there were no megastores, no brands. If you wanted something you couldn't make yourself, you had to get it made for you by a craftsperson. While that's not a very efficient structure for today's global economy, many people feel there's something lacking in the sameness of mass-produced products. Enter Etsy, a community of crafters and artisans, and of course, the people who buy their wares.

"Etsy is an example of going back to the way marketplaces and businesses used to function," says company spokesperson Adam Brown. "Consumers are bombarded with ad messages—Etsy doesn't do much advertising. Most ads come from big-box enterprises, but people want their personality to stand out. They're not buying a sweater from The Gap, they're buying one-of-a-kind, or personalizing what they find."

Etsy's creative participants hit a somewhat older demographic than Threadless—the average seller is age 35, and 95 percent are women—but the same drive to create unique items is there, and the buyers are anybody who wants to own a piece of that uniqueness. "Some of the creators are hobbyists, some are professional artisans and artists; about 85 percent are in the U.S." People come to Etsy organically and by word of mouth, so search results and personal recommendations have a large effect.

Most of the work available on Etsy is created and sold on spec, but that may be about to change. Etsy Alchemy, a place for commissioned work, recently relaunched. "Post about what you want, and sellers bid on the project," Brown says. This model hews even closer to the artisan–patron relationship of old.

"What I love about Etsy is you never know what you're going to find," Brown says. Every day, there's something new that's beautiful, weird, or different. You see the insides of people's minds, communicate with them directly, and form groups, teams, and friendships." All while money changes hands and unique clothing and crafts enter the public eye.

### Example 3: Chester French and Salesforce.com

Threadless and Etsy are both examples of businesses that look and act like businesses, with a digital twist. However, the final example in this section steps away from that form a bit—here, we'll focus on a band. When most people think of a music group, their thoughts range from high school Battle of the Bands contests to sold-out arenas. They don't necessarily think of a customer database or personalized communications, but

Interscope act Chester French (and its use of Salesforce.com) could change our notion of how music success stories are written.

I first encountered Chester French (CF) at Dreamforce '09, an annual blowout in San Francisco held by customer relationship management (CRM) software company Salesforce.com. This band of two (singer D.A. Wallach and instrumentalist Max Drummey) wasn't on stage—at least not in the traditional sense. Incredible as it seems, CF was in town to talk to media and analysts about their success using Salesforce.com for their business operations.

Wallach explained to the assembled crowd of journalists, consultants, and other CRM cognoscenti how Interscope, the band's label, had not been supporting it effectively. Realizing that a highly engaged and happy fan base was the key to being more than just another nowhere indie act, Wallach and Drummey started a major online effort with several social networking sites, with Salesforce.com providing the business processes needed to keep fans involved.

Sheila McGee-Smith, president and principal analyst of McGee-Smith Analytics, was in the crowd with me and taking better notes than I was because she was going to post something about it. I admire her opinions and insight, so I'll let her blog entry ("The Rock Band and the Cloud," No Jitter, November 25, 2009, bit.ly/g4FhVk) tell the meat of the story:

> During a press lunch, three Salesforce.com users gave interesting case studies and then answered questions. One of the speakers was D.A. Wallach, half of the band Chester French. Having played after the morning keynote, Wallach described Chester French's use of Salesforce.com. Sounding more like an MBA than a rocker, Wallach explained that 98 percent of all bands fail and that most bands starting out fill venues with their friends or friends of their friends. So to increase

the probability of success, they went about figuring out how to get more friends.

Enter social networking, including Myspace, Facebook, and Twitter. But being smart rockers, they also decided they needed a CRM system to manage their growing fan base. The use of a cloud-based application made perfect sense to the on-the-road rockers, who can now maintain personal relationships with a centralized database of fans and check sales activity from anywhere they have an Internet connection. With the release of their first album, Chester French found their VIP friends were happy to spend on average $25 for not just a music download, but T-shirts, CDs, and vinyl versions of the music.

At last count, Wallach showed 842,449 followers to his Twitter account. This kid may be one of the first to make a million dollars on Twitter.

Every email the band receives is answered personally—not with a fan club form letter. The band's website includes several package options for purchasing music and merchandise, as well as a VIP Concierge Service that includes personal invitations to backstage events and parties. The listed African Safari Package might be facetious, but who knows what will happen if a fan scrapes together $75,000 to fly the band down to Nairobi?

There are, of course, some common threads in these three examples. Foremost, there is less of a division between company and customer, thanks to social media. Social CRM practices have enabled these businesses to bring the customer inside the organization in one way or another. They don't have to advertise by traditional means because the customers (as fans, community members, or patrons) spread the word on their own, keeping interest high among the "in" crowd and bringing in new members all the time.

Chester French could have an impromptu concert on a few hours' notice and get decent attendance, because their highly motivated and digitally connected fan base would hear about it and get there, bringing their friends. Hot new designs on Threadless sell well because the company's perpetual voting process makes sure every new shirt gets face time with people who are motivated to buy. Etsy provides a venue for hobbyists and professional artists alike to interact with like-minded people who have money to spend and ideas to explore.

Also common to these ventures is the experience of starting out on a shoestring. Nowhere in any of these examples is there talk of soliciting funds from venture capitalists, hammering out a business plan that would be acceptable to a bank loan officer, or any of the things you'd expect to see with a traditional startup. (By comparison, my first entrepreneurial attempt out of college involved teaming up with friends to launch a comic book publishing company, and we even went to angel investors and the Small Business Administration for help. We didn't make it, by the way.)

Since startup budgets are slim or nonexistent, it's only natural for digital native businesses to use as many free tools as possible. Twitter, Myspace, Facebook, and pretty much every other social media venue are free, and the only cost of YouTube is what it takes to create a video, which can be done for next to nothing in many cases as well.

These are businesses that are built on passion—for design, for craft, for music—and passion drives out fear. Use of social media helps calm nerves as well, since receiving instant feedback provides honest validation of the effort, or at least shows where it's going wrong.

But most importantly, these businesses are succeeding because they don't draw a hard line between themselves and their clientele. The people who make the shirts, the crafts, and the music are indistinguishable from the ones who buy them. That's what I had in mind with the title of this chapter. By leaning on the *R* in CRM (*relationship*), these companies turn customers into friends so that they can turn those friends back into customers. This cycle makes it that much easier for the business to attract new friends, via that viral growth process mentioned in connection with Threadless, and thus continue to grow and prosper.

That's great if you're a new, alternative business. But what about a more traditional sort of venture, with employees, business plans, marketing campaigns, and all that jazz? What if you've already established yourself, but now want to secure your future? Fear not! Examples abound of major companies that have taken a page from the digital native playbook and applied social CRM to their business processes, often resulting in considerable success. The traditional model still works (good news for all the venture capital firms out there), but there's no law that says we can't add to it, enhance the customer experience, and engage the emerging generation of consumers who simply expect to engage directly with the companies they do business with. Certainly one of the best and easiest places to make a foray into the world of social media is with the customer service department.

## Keeping the Customer Satisfied

There are many examples of how digital technologies—the tools digital natives are most comfortable with—are transforming customer service. One popular illustration comes from Frank Eliason, Comcast's former senior director of national customer service, whose @comcastcares Twitter approach almost single-handedly shifted customer sentiment in a positive direction. The company went from being a goat to one that gets mentioned favorably in books about customer experience.

### Example 4: Comcast

As telecom and cable operators go, Comcast has experienced its share of highs and lows. While it's fair to say that nobody particularly likes their cable company, Comcast engendered a hate among some of its customers that bordered on mania. Those customers went so far as to create ComcastMustDie.com, a repository of customer service complaints that soon became a rallying point for thousands of angry and vocal people. It described the company as "a vast, greedy, blundering, tone-deaf corporate colossus," and the examples on the site only worsened that image. Comcast's industry ranking was horrible: It came in last on the American Customer Satisfaction Index (ACSI) for its sector in 2007.

Something changed when Eliason, then senior director of customer service, started experimenting with Twitter. He saw complaints about Comcast winging back and forth across the 140-character messaging service, many of which never made it into the traditional contact channels or were comments on how those channels had failed. Seeing this, Eliason chose one of the angry tweets and responded with some of the most important words ever sent: "How can I help?"

That simple beginning led to the creation of Comcast Customer Connect, a seven-member team of representatives who engage directly with customers to mollify their anger and solve their issues with Comcast. The @comcastcares Twitter account now has more than 49,000-plus followers (as of December 2010) and includes so many anecdotes of successfully fixing what's wrong and turning frowns upside down that it's pointless to list them here. The Comcast story has run in *BusinessWeek,* the *New York Times,* and many other major venues; it's worth your time to seek out these tales.

Comcast is still far from the top of the ACSI rankings, but it's garnering a lot of accolades for its efforts with social media. In fact, ComcastMustDie.com has changed its front page to a statement that, if far from complimentary, at least allows that a big corporation can change. Comcast is "tone deaf no more":

> As both *The New York Times* and *Washington Post* have reported, Comcast has heard our angry voices and taken concrete steps in the process of putting customers first. Meantime, it has used ComcastMustDie and now Customer-Circus.com to specifically resolve many hundreds

of customer complaints. There is a long way for Comcast to go, but there is also no question that it has been forced by us to reckon with us. Now we will employ the same formula to other serial customer-abusers.

This site, ComcastMustDie.com will remain—but we have a new and improved Consumer Vigilante Web site here—Customer-Circus.com, where other infamously arrogant corporations will be subjected to power of aggregated rage. (No worries. Comcast is still one of them.) We hope they, like Comcast, will see this not merely as a threat, but as an opportunity to connect with and regain the confidence—even loyalty—of its customers.

With Comcast, we see a case of a big corporation rebuilding its damaged image through the use of a free internet communication service. Do you really need another example? Of course you do. Luckily, this is an area in which Forrester Research offers particular insights and provides several illuminating case studies, one of which I will examine here.

Dr. Natalie Petouhoff (Dr. Nat to her friends and fans) is one of the analysts leading Forrester's study of business use of social media. Her work, and that of her colleagues, has revealed several common threads for getting social media technology to work in a professional setting. Petouhoff's focus has been on the particular impact of social media on the contact center. "As consumers rapidly adopt social media—and use it to voice their displeasure about brands and complain about products and services—customer service professionals struggle with how best to harness the power of the cloud to transform customer experiences," Petouhoff writes in the Forrester Best Practices paper, *Five Strategies for Social Media Customer Service Excellence* (2009).

It's no surprise that adoption of social media has been driven by experiences in the contact center. Customer service professionals are constantly seeking better ways to interact with customers in order to make the experience of communicating with a company better and more pleasant for all involved; social tools are first and foremost a way of communicating. The use of social tech in B2B and B2C settings is, in part, a reaction to ineffective customer service strategies of the past. When so much money is spent on technologies to deflect customers from live interaction and the job performance of customer service representatives is rated on how quickly calls are completed, is it any wonder customers would turn elsewhere?

"The resulting customer disdain, combined with a rapid rise in the adoption and use of social media by consumers have today formed a perfect storm that is driving change in the world of customer service," Petouhoff writes. "When companies blatantly ignore product or service issues, customers now can use the internet as a medium to broadcast, very publicly, their frustration to millions. This has switched the balance of power from corporations to customers. Even the press has taken up the cause, routinely reporting on companies that provide good or poor customer service experiences. The risk of corporate reputations being ruined by poor customer service interactions has greatly increased as consumers have gained the ability to share their opinions directly with each other."

Forrester has compiled a set of best practices for incorporating social media into business and offers several case studies to illustrate. They come from companies you've heard of that are using lessons learned from the digital native to achieve impressive results. Here I've analyzed one of my favorites from Forrester's research from Sage North America.

In the interest of disclosure, I will say while I was writing this chapter I was engaged in a blogging project for Sage that grew out of the company's social media efforts. Nevertheless I was aware of those efforts long before said blogging project, and before the genesis of the book you're reading now, though my experience with this company certainly lends insight into its activities.

### Example 5: Sage North America

Sage North America, a division of U.K.-based Sage Group PLC, is the company behind such small- and medium-business application brands as ACT!, SalesLogix, and Peachtree. Sage found its ACT! contact management and CRM software slipping behind in customer satisfaction at the same time the world economy was contracting. Sage directed the ACT! product group to rejuvenate itself, to update the software to regain market share and revenue growth. As part of the solution, it launched the ACT! by Sage Community in the first quarter of 2008. The community is an online resource for partners, developers, and users, with blogs and forums focused on improving customer experience.

The initiative has grown to include most if not all of Sage's product families—there are a lot of them—and these things take time. The online community is a source of new ideas for the company as well as an eager pool of beta testers. A company that had been quiet and humble has become noteworthy again, with its social CRM efforts garnering kudos from a number of industry personalities.

ACT! by Sage leveraged social technology in three main ways:

*1. It redefined the customer experience.* Sage's customer loyalty team started listening more closely to what customers had to say about ACT! products and services. Rather than the outmoded (but still widely used) approach of first making changes and then seeing how the public reacts, Sage considers the customer perspective from the get-go. This practice is a core concept of social CRM, and the ACT! team enhanced the practice by deploying social media to support it, namely the Act! by Sage community.

*2. It enabled real conversations between customers and executives.* Blogs by ACT! executives, from the general manager down, are an important part of the online community. When customers raise particular product or service issues, the execs address them in a timely manner and provide direct contact information to continue the discussion offline.

*3. It used its customer conversations as actionable data.* Surveys can be a tricky and unreliable means of collecting customer feedback and making it meaningful to decision makers. Social networks are not only a good way to make customers feel they're being heard, but they also make it clear to executives what does and doesn't work with a company's products and services. Nothing is more clear for this purpose than the actual voice of the customer. To their credit, the ACT! team used the honest, in-the-moment feedback generated by the online community to re-engineer their own product, business processes, and organization.

Those actions sparked positive results in a number of areas. During its first year of existence, the ACT! community had nearly 9 million page views and more than 260,000 searches. The company reports that emergent issues are now noticed faster and can be addressed quickly and in a number of ways, including blog posts, software patches, and new versions. This reduces both overall contact center call volume and occasional spikes in the contact center.

The company achieved a 15 percent increase in its Net Promoter Score, which was borne out in good customer word of mouth. ACT! community members passionately recommended the product to peers without being prompted, and the online customer service community has become one of ACT!'s top marketing assets.

ACT! customer data and feedback are examined every week at cross-functional department meetings, and the director of global technical support assigns action items based on the results. Every member of the ACT! team is in a position to improve the product and operation based on what customers want most. Company decisions and product development are rooted firmly in the voice of the customer.

As with the earlier examples, ACT! demonstrates clear advantages to using social media as part of a CRM initiative. While for many organizations it will not be entirely free to follow this path, once there are employees dedicated to monitoring the social media, there is very little financial barrier to getting started. While at Comcast, Eliason began by listening, and listening costs nothing. Listening enabled both

Sage and Comcast to start forging a better connection with their respective customers.

## Lessons Learned

However, the real lesson of social CRM is that customer attitudes toward companies are changing. People want to be listened to, and they also want to know who they're talking to. Social media humanizes a company in ways a traditional contact center can't. The company can take the first step when appropriate, which is the best way to show that it's listening to its customers. A May 2010 study by Aberdeen Group ("State of Customer-Centric Retailing: A Best Practices Guide for Higher Sales, Customer Retention, and Satisfaction," May 31, 2010, bit.ly/dSO2A8) noted that best-in-class companies are far more likely to listen to and act upon their customers' changing wants and needs. Top retailers were nearly twice as likely as industry laggards to incorporate customer feedback into business and product plans (30 percent versus 17 percent).

People are averse to trusting companies, but we're wired to work with people we're familiar with. By turning a corporation into a transparent group of individuals with their own voices, we create trust. Trust leads to deeper involvement. Involvement in a company's activities leads to emotional investment in how those activities turn out, and all of a sudden a big company is selling *with* its customers, not *to* them. At that point, advocacy—that most precious jewel of CRM—is the next stage.

The conclusions we can draw from the CRM success stories are clear. As long as social networks continue to have any level of popularity, consumers will use them to talk about what they like to consume. Smart companies will do whatever it takes to tap into these conversations and start some of their own. Some entrepreneurs will even use social media to launch and operate a business. Whichever way they go, these businesses will need to understand how to handle social CRM. Turning a corporate entity into a trusted source of information and assistance might not be easy, but it's necessary.

For too long, corporate decisions about being open with its customers have been governed by fear—fear of giving something away or of losing exclusivity. But by taking a page from the digital native's book, businesses are learning to be fearless and embrace transparency. They are letting customers know the company and the people in it.

## About the Contributor

**Marshall Lager** is the founder and managing principal of Third Idea Consulting LLC (www.3rd-idea.com), a firm that provides advice on the confluence of CRM, social media, and brand management. Third Idea's mission is to help businesses navigate the changing currents of customer-facing technology so that all parties can get the greatest benefit from the relationship. Prior to Third Idea, Marshall served as senior editor at CRM Media, writing news, blogs, and feature articles on the above topics for *CRM* magazine and its website, www.destinationCRM.com. During his tenure at CRM Media, Marshall was the recipient of three APEX writing awards for his feature writing and his back page column, Pint of View.

## Recommended Reading

### Books and Articles

Greenberg, Paul. *CRM at the Speed of Light: Social CRM Strategies, Tools, and Techniques for Engaging Your Customers.* New York: McGraw-Hill, 2009.

Petouhoff, Natalie L. "Five Best Practice Strategies for Customer Service Social Media Excellence." Forrester Research, August 2009.

Petouhoff, Natalie L. et al. "ACT! by Sage Uses Social Media to Transform the Customer Experience." Forrester Research, August 2009.

Qualman, Erik. *Socialnomics: How Social Media Transforms the Way We Live And Do Business.* Hoboken, NJ: John Wiley & Sons, 2009.

Safko, Lon, and David K. Brake. *The Social Media Bible: Tactics, Tools, and Strategies for Business Success*. Hoboken, NJ: John Wiley & Sons, 2009.

Shih, Clara C. *The Facebook Era*. Boston: Pearson Education, Inc., 2009.

Zabin, Jeff. "Brand Reputation Management: Using Online Monitoring to Protect a Company's Crown Jewels," Aberdeen Group, June 2009.

### Websites

1to1 Media online, www.1to1media.com

Beagle Research Group, beagleresearch.com

CRM Expert Focus Group on LinkedIn, www.linkedin.com/groups? gid=86337

CustomerThink, www.customerthink.com

Destination CRM (*CRM Magazine*), www.destinationCRM.com

Destination CRM Blog, www.destinationCRMblog.com

Forrester Research, www.forrester.com

McGee-Smith Analytics, www.mcgeesmith.com

PGreenblog, the56group.typepad.com

Social CRM: The Conversation, blogs.zdnet.com/crm

Third Idea Consulting, www.3rd-idea.com

# CHAPTER 7

# Inspired Interaction: Youth Marketing on Mobile

Peggy Anne Salz

*We are inevitably moving towards the Mobile Society, where our mobile devices become the remote control of our daily lives.*
—Alan Moore, The Glittering Allure
of the Mobile Society, November 2008

The emergence of empowered consumers—and the abundance of applications designed to give consumers more of a say in how they create, access, and enjoy content—have transformed publishing, marketing, advertising, and communications. However, mobile takes this interaction to a new level, particularly for the generation that has grown up with the internet, the so-called digital natives. With mobile, the inclination of digital natives to interact is taken to a new extreme. Mobile empowers digital natives to create, comment, and connect around content at the very moment of inspiration.

See something cool? Digital natives use the built-in camera and location capabilities provided on most mobile phones to tag real-life locations and tell the world (or at least the members of their social network) what they did there. Sensing a business opportunity, a slew of mobile companies (such as GyPSii and Rummble) have launched successful services and created entire mobile communities by simply allowing digital natives to record, rank, and rate the world around them.

Mobile enables instant self-expression and turns up the pressure on companies and brands to deliver their marketing message in the context of a two-way conversation about what matters most to digital natives: their lives, their experiences, their networks, and their worlds. Of course, delivering a message does not a conversation make; marketers also have to listen to what digital natives have to say.

## It's All About Me

Mobile is not only a communications tool that connects digital natives with everyone else; it's a technology that shapes every aspect of their daily lives. "Leaving home without my phone almost feels like leaving the house naked," noted a 17-year-old girl surveyed as part of a milestone 2008 study conducted by the wireless trade association CTIA and Harris Interactive, a market research firm.

This survey of some 2,000 teens across the U.S. revealed that respondents feel that mobile phones have become a vital part of their lives and their identities. Some 75 percent of 12- to 17-year-olds now own cell phones, up from 45 percent in 2004 ("Teens, Cell Phones, and Texting," April 20, 2010, bit.ly/hwpjrf). The vast majority of respondents said they text message as much as or more than they talk on the phone. For them texting *is* talking.

What's more, almost half of those surveyed said that having a mobile phone is "key" to their social lives. This is consistent with the findings of other reports, including a survey of 1,000 individuals commissioned by Retrevo (Retrevo Gadgetology Reports' ongoing series of studies, 2010). It found that respondents check and update their favorite social media sites at all times and in all places: when they get up in the morning, before they go to bed at night, while they are in the bathroom, even during sex. Not surprisingly, the addiction to social media skews heavily toward those under the age of 25.

Of course, it can't be verified that this data is representative of the entire population of digital natives. However, with mobile phones becoming ubiquitous and smartphone penetration on the rise, it's logical that mobile devices would accompany their owners at all times, including even the most private and intimate moments.

## Going Mobile

Connect the dots from reams of publicly available data, and one thing is clear: Digital natives are mobile, and mobile is part of who they are.

Five years ago, Mizuko Ito, a cultural anthropologist at Keio University in Japan, arrived at a similar conclusion. Her observations are captured in the book she co-authored with Daisuke Okabe and Misa Matsuda *Personal, Portable, Pedestrian* (MIT Press, 2005). Her views on how mobile and digital media are changing relationships, identities, and communities are even more pertinent now as the buying power of these digital natives increases. In her research into how mobile has shaped the way digital natives live their lives, she observed the emergence of "tele-nesting," the practice—especially among youth in Japan but now prevalent everywhere—of staying in touch through a steady stream of text messages.

Based on this, the book suggests that mobile is more than a communications device; it has become "the glue for cementing a space of shared intimacy." What's more, the writers observed an emergent social norm around frequent text messages to signal unavailability from a shared digital space, such as a forum or a chat room. "In other words, the connected state is the default, and the disconnected state is noted."

For digital natives, the connected state has indeed become their collective default. Even the disconnected state is one that they communicate, setting their status to say they are away from the desk, or sending a quick text message to say they're involved in some other activity (eating, bathing, sleeping) and will be back in the mix soon.

## The Next Mass Media

Another confirmation of the increasing importance of mobile in our lives—and particularly for the lives of hyperconnected digital natives—comes from Tomi Ahonen, independent consultant, mobile luminary, and author of the book, *Mobile as 7th of the Mass Media: Cell Phone, Cameraphone, iPhone, Smartphone* (Futuretext, 2008). In Ahonen's view, it's the addictiveness, pervasiveness, and sheer dominance of the mobile device that gives it a pivotal position in our daily lives.

Today, everything we can do on the internet with our PCs we can also do on our mobile phones. What's more, the phenomenal popularity of location-based services, made-for-mobile social networks such as the U.K.-based flirt-and-fun network Flirtomatic, Germany's itsmy.com, and the blue-collar-focused social network BuzzCity's myGamma—as well as a host of websites that encourage moblogging (mobile blogging) and content capture and creation on the fly—are paving the way for mobile to be the next, and potentially most dominant, mass media. Little wonder that Ahonen further concludes that all forms of content will "ultimately converge around the cell phone."

According to Ahonen, the power of mobile begins with its reach. There are twice as many mobile devices as TV sets, three times as many mobile subscribers as internet users, and four times as many mobile phones as PCs. Mobile is also very versatile as a media channel if we consider that it is digital, multimedia-capable, personal, and interactive. It has the ability to receive and deliver broadcast content. A growing number of mobile content companies and network operators are convinced the mobile will soon be the main device people use to enjoy radio and TV programming anytime, anywhere.

There is an opportunity here to understand digital natives' emerging mobile habits and expectations, particularly as their buying power increases. Mobile marketing opportunities will only increase in the coming years. Certain specific capabilities of the mobile phone are uniquely suited to generate massive new mobile advertising opportunities:

- Everyone has them (high volume).

- Everyone carries them around (always on, always connected).

- Everyone can use his or her user input mechanisms to interact with brands/publishers (camera phones/SMS text/voice).

- Everyone can use them to pay for content and services (a built-in payment mechanism).

Indeed, mobile can do everything that all previous mass media— print from the 1500s, recording from the 1900s, cinema from the 1910s, radio from the 1920s, TV from the 1950s, and internet from the 1990s—can do. Ahonen further concludes that all forms of content will "ultimately converge around the cell phone." This convergence is what Ahonen tells me will make mobile "at least as disruptive as the internet has been so far."

## Listen to Me

However, the real revolution here is not in the breadth and types of content we can access using our mobile phones; it's in the ability mobile gives us to communicate with the companies that created the content in the first place. Clever content companies understand the importance of user input and encourage it. What's more, the truly cutting-edge companies build user participation into all aspects of their business.

A prime example is Sony Pictures Television International (SPTI), Asia. In preparation for writing the 2009 Netsize Guide (the mobile industry almanac and analysis), I interviewed Rosemary Tan, SPTI Asia's executive director of mobile entertainment, a woman who I regard as a visionary.

During the interview, she pointed out that the mobile phone is well on its way to becoming "an entertainment center in the palm of one's hand," but she added that the bigger picture is about giving consumers choices and allowing them to access and interact with content on their terms. Considering the increasing youth-driven trend toward what Lawrence Lessig and others call "remix culture," it only makes sense to enable anytime content creation and recreation via the mobile.

## Advertising Becomes Content

In a similar vein, commerce, marketing, advertising, promotion, and customer relationship management—all communication between companies and consumers—must open up to ideas and input from their customers. And as a generation grows up with an expectation of interaction in all aspects of their lives, businesses must learn how to create and facilitate the two-way conversations that mobile enables in order to connect with consumers on their terms. Given the habits of younger consumers, companies will need to embrace tools and technologies such as social networks, microblogs, mobile devices, and video-sharing sites to create an ongoing and meaningful dialogue with their customers.

This is the view of Cone, a strategy and communications agency engaged in building brand trust. Its 2010 Cone Consumer Media Study, based on an online survey of U.S. consumers aged 18 years and older, found that consumers developed "a stronger connection with a brand" that they felt they could interact with on new media channels. Another finding that underlines the importance of conducting a two-way conversation: 60 percent of respondents said they feel better served by a company or a brand if they can have a conversation with them in a new media environment.

"If companies are going to be a mainstay in new media, they're going to have to realize consumers expect more than a passive existence," according to Mike Hollywood, Cone's director of new media. "New media are about experience, dialogue, and immediacy. There was a time when just being in new media got you the gold star for effort. But today's consumers are continually refining their expectations and more and more are looking for specific interactions."

## Tell My Story

This is where the Mobile Youth project headquartered in the U.K. comes in. The company first made its mark conducting research to find out what young people think and want (insights that can allow companies to make better products and market them more effectively). Since then, it has become a distributed youth agency helping companies all over the world understand youth in their region and draw up a marketing and execution plan that takes their views into account.

According to director and founder Graham Brown, years of researching this unpredictable but lucrative demographic have uncovered two universal constants: their need to belong and their need to be significant. While young people have exhibited these traits for many generations, the way in which they are manifested has certainly been transformed with the digital native generation. Brown reminds us that "when marketers engage young people, they have to do it from the angle of how that brand or product can fit in with youth's goal to achieve what *they* [youth] want socially."

A blueprint to follow is BEINGGIRL.com, Procter & Gamble's teen-focused website and social network. Rather than simply promoting its Tampax brand products to teenage girls, the company has turned its sales pitch into a community that listens and solves problems ranging from relationships (boyfriends and family) to health issues—and everything in between.

Brown's algorithm for success: Begin with a focus on how to solve a youth problem and then work out how technology fits into that. "It's not about the technology; it's about engagement," he explains. "It's no longer appropriate to tell the story about your brand. The story, the narrative, has to change to helping young people tell their story."

It's a lesson that Pepsi learned the hard way. Its social networks and accompanying market campaign missed the mark because they were all about Pepsi, one-way advertising that left little room for digital natives to tell their story. In contrast, beverage maker Monster Energy Drinks has harnessed similar social media tools to significantly increase market share and customer loyalty, despite a crushing recession in its markets.

"It didn't use advertising to tell its story; it focused on helping young people tell their story and provide a platform that Monster just happens to own." As a result, digital youth and 20-somethings in various countries including the U.K., Canada, and Australia have joined the Monster Army, becoming brand ambassadors and shaping the brand message to appeal to them rather than merely accepting what the company says.

Matching the right technology (mobile) and the right marketing approach (making digital youth feel they are significant) has allowed McDonald's in Japan to achieve amazing results by turning short-term conversations into long-term relationships. The company is experimenting with the use of mobile to deliver personalized greetings to customers as they enter the restaurants and works to learn individuals' habits in order to provide coupons targeted to their preferences.

The takeaway from these success stories: Marketing to digital natives isn't about selling; it's about engagement. What clinches the deal with digital natives is a company/brand that shows it is really listening to what potential customers have to say, whether it's listening to problems and offering solutions (Procter & Gamble); providing the opportunity to co-create the brand message they want (Monster); building a dialogue based on their habits, preferences, and interests (McDonald's); or enabling true interaction.

## Ask Permission

Effective marketing empowers the digital native to participate in the narrative. But it also respects individuals and puts them in control of the advertising they receive in the first place. This is all the more important when advertising is displayed on a device as personal as the mobile phone.

Understanding the requirement for permission-based marketing and advertising has allowed Blyk, the world's first ad-funded mobile virtual network operator now turned global mobile media company, to successfully target the difficult youth demographic (16- to 24-year-olds). It kicked off its service in 2007 in the U.K., offering users free text messages and call minutes in return for accepting up to six advertising messages per day. To make sure users actually want to listen to the messages, Blyk required users to choose the categories of ads (fashion, sports, music, etc.) they would want to receive.

Armed with this customer data, Blyk was able to offer advertisers the segmentation that would allow them to effectively target their message and, more importantly, collect worthwhile feedback from their target demographic.

Before it shifted its business model in 2009 to partner with mobile operators (such as Orange in the U.K. and Vodafone in The Netherlands) rather than operating a network itself, Blyk counted well over 1,000 campaigns with 100-plus advertisers, including major brands such as Coca-Cola, L'Oreal, and Sky. What's more, Blyk recorded an average response rate of 25 percent, remarkable when compared to the single-digit response rates achieved by the vast majority of online and one-to-many mobile marketing campaigns.

Alcatel-Lucent conducted grassroots research that highlights the central importance of permission (putting the consumer in control of the advertising) and preference (matching the right ad to the right person) in mobile advertising.

These requirements came through loud and clear in a comprehensive survey of 2,200 digital natives (aged 13–25) across 11 countries conducted by award-winning Alcatel-Lucent Global Youth Lab. The research, designed to assess the receptivity of respondents to SMS (text) and MMS (still image) advertising, provides valuable insights into what digital natives expect in their advertising as well as the rewards and incentives that will keep them coming back for more.

Among the key findings:

- Permission and preference are key to securing end-user adoption of SMS/MMS advertising. In total, 81 percent said it was important for a company to ask their permission before sending an ad, and 76 percent said it was important for the ad to be based on their interests and preferences.

- Sharing interests, hobbies, and personal information is acceptable if it results in the delivery of more relevant advertising. Eighty percent find it acceptable to update their preference at least once a month, and the vast majority of respondents are highly motivated to share information about their hobbies and interests.

- Privacy is a concern, but control is the solution. For the vast majority of respondents who indicated concerns about privacy (79 percent), the ability to start and stop the advertising (thus accepting advertising entirely on their terms) effectively mitigates these concerns for 73 percent of respondents.

Against this backdrop, Connie Torres, Alcatel-Lucent director of market advantage research, advises its mobile operator customers to build and maintain a database of "opt-ins" (customers who specifically agree to accept advertising messages on their mobile phones) to ensure consumers get the advertising they want. Fortunately, her research shows the vast majority of the 2,200-plus respondents surveyed would agree to answer at least four questions during the opt-in process in order to tailor ads to the topics and brands they care about most.

Based on this research and work with mobile operator customers, Alcatel-Lucent has identified the following five basic rules for effective (translate: engaging) mobile advertising:

1. An opt-in audience is a must, and operators must get customer permission before delivering any advertising.

2. Advertising messages must be relevant—period. The best advertising matches the consumer's stated preferences and interests.

3. Consumers must be in control of the advertising they receive.

4. Everything needs to be simple.

5. Incentives are key. Free texts and mobile service can be a draw, but other rewards—including offers or exclusive content, virtual goods, and one-on-one brand interaction—also motivate consumers and increase loyalty.

## Valuable Advertising

The money is in advertising that (literally) speaks to the interests and passions of the consumers, engaging them in a dialogue about what matters most to them. This conversation can be direct, connecting consumers with brands that they consider important to their daily lives. However, it can also be more subtle, involving so-called branded utilities (for example, weather information sponsored by makers of cold medicine) that deliver value to consumers by providing something they truly appreciate.

A welcome confirmation of the latter comes from the Global Web Index, a September 2009 report from market research firm Lightspeed Research that offers some important insights on the U.S. market. It found that Americans want brands that provide utility. Among the responses: Helping consumers keep up-to-date with relevant news and analysis was considered important. In addition, brands should be entertaining and become part of a daily routine. If you consider the always-connected nature of mobile-wielding youth, providing utility—useful services or information associated with your brand—may well be the best way to develop relationships with younger customers.

This research dovetails with a fireside chat with Rory Sutherland, Ogilvy Group U.K. vice chairman, that I moderated during a 2009 U.K. mobile advertising event. He pointed out that the most successful brands may be those that combine their message with branded utilities and life-simplifying services. During the interview, Sutherland advised marketers to make more use of the direct feedback channel mobile provides in their campaigns and efforts to engage customers and build brand loyalty. "Advertising is talking *and* listening. Mobile is brilliant [because] you can do it in real-time."

The takeaway: Marketers focused on the digital native demographic would be well-advised to move away from promotion (talking) to focus on increasing the ongoing value and convenience they deliver to customers. Listening—that is, harnessing the built-in feedback channel mobile offers—yields a number of business benefits. It allows marketers to connect with natives on their terms, tap their wisdom to improve products and services, and diffuse potentially explosive situations before dissatisfied consumers voice their frustrations to the world via social networks or Twitter.

## Open for Business

Sensing a business opportunity, U.K.-based Rapide Communication Ltd., launched a service focused sharply on wringing business value out of customer feedback via mobile. Its service, aptly called Rant & Rave, allows companies and brands to listen seriously to complaints before their customers voice their frustrations to the world online.

According to internal search data compiled by Rapide Communication, based on customer case studies and feedback, only 4 percent of unhappy customers will take their gripes directly to a company. This means a whopping 96 percent of dissatisfied customers are taking their thoughts elsewhere. "Digital natives want to express their ideas and feelings using the technologies that have become embedded in their daily routine and mobile is the one they always have with them," says Nigel Shanahan, Rapide's managing director. "The aim is to harness this behavior and provide customers the opportunity to express what they think about a brand or company in their own way."

To achieve this, the company has developed text analysis technology with Birmingham University in the U.K. that automatically extracts topics and then scores the sentiment from 1–5. Warwick Business School created a test research project called the Man Machine Challenge that compared human analysis of comments to the Rant & Rave "Sentiment Engine." It concluded that for an organization receiving at least 3,000 comments per month, Rant & Rave's automated analysis could result in savings of as much as £65,000 per year. Company clients including Audi, Honda, and Scherring Plough have made significant savings because they use mobile to listen to their customers.

However, listening to customers is much more than capturing feedback and sentiment at the point of service. "Where it gets really interesting is when the customers are fully engaged, and brands are able to ask thousands of people at a time, a specific question, knowing that they will get a response," Shanahan explains. With this in mind, Rapide Communication is working with U.K. retailers including Dorothy

Perkins, Miss Selfridge, Harrods, and John Lewis on trials that will enable them to consult an audience of engaged digital natives on a plan or idea. "This is real crowdsourcing, and what better way than via a device that is completely personal and 'always on' to get results quickly?"

## Next Dimension

Clearly, advertisers won't get far if they insist on using mobile to deliver a one-to-many pitch. It's about enabling a balanced exchange that respects our personal space and excites our individual passions.

So where does mobile go from here?

There are no easy answers, but the observations of Mark Curtis, CEO of Flirtomatic, a pioneer mobile flirting service and one of the most popular social mobile services worldwide, provide a fresh perspective.

During an interview, Curtis developed a thought-provoking analogy between the role of mobile in the everyday lives of digital natives and the relationship between "daemons" and human characters in the fantasy trilogy *His Dark Materials* by English novelist Philip Pullman.

The first book in the series, *The Golden Compass*, takes place in a parallel world where all human souls take the form of animal companions called daemons. These small, often-changing animals are lifelong companions. Every person in this fantasy world has a daemon. What's more, daemons can change form to reflect the moods or inner feelings of their owners. The bold and adventurous Lord Asriel, for example, has a snow leopard for a daemon. The bond between the characters and their daemons is a close relationship that can never be broken. Severing a character from his or her daemon is like separating the person from his or her soul.

In many ways, Curtis says, this relationship corresponds to *phase one* in the evolution of personal mobility. In the past decade, mobile devices, like daemons, became extensions of our "selves." Digital natives personalized them with ringtones, images, and wallpapers. And a raft of reports detailed the feelings of isolation and even depression this demographic felt when they were separated from their mobile devices, unable to receive text messages or connect with their social networks. Based on a series of surveys, interviews, and focus groups, market research firm Solutions Research Group concluded that 27 percent of respondents suffered increased levels of anxiety when separated from their mobile phones or the internet. A further 41 percent suffered occasional anxiety due to a communications blackout.

Clearly, mobile devices have become inextricably intertwined with daily lifestyles. According to Curtis, *The Subtle Knife*, the second book of Pullman's trilogy, provides a glimpse into the next phase in the behavior of digital natives, insights that directly impact how companies and brands will need to interact with this demographic moving forward. In this novel, the "subtle" knife has two sides: One can cut through any known matter, and the other can cut into different worlds. Put another way, this knife can cut through the fabric of space-time and open windows between worlds.

In *phase two* of the evolution of personal mobility, a phase that began in 2010, mobile has become the digital native's multifunctional subtle knife. Digital natives use it to create and enter parallel places and to link between the physical and virtual worlds. With their mobile phones, they can step away from the stress of their daily existence and enter personalized social networks, spaces where their representations (images and avatars) connect with friends, family, and the brands that matter most to them.

And it doesn't stop there. The advent of smartphones—equipped with GPS, compass, video, and accelerometers that allow devices to detect and respond to motion—paves the way for an avalanche of augmented reality applications. These applications harness the features and functionalities of advancements in mobile phone technology to merge the physical world around them with information compiled about people and places on the internet.

Mobile—essential to most, and akin to an appendage to the digital native—represents more than a marketing opportunity today. It is a marketing imperative. As the digital world becomes evermore entwined in every aspect of life, companies that do not develop fluency in this form of communication cannot meet customers where they are or provide endless opportunities for interaction and intelligent innovation.

## About the Contributor

**Peggy Anne Salz** is the chief analyst and founder of MSearchGroove, an online network specializing in analysis and commentary on mobile search, mobile advertising, and social media. Her drive to spark debate about issues impacting the industry at all levels has won her international recognition as a brave new voice in the mobile content market. Her report, "Mobile Search & Content Discovery," was regarded as the first in-depth study of its kind, establishing Peggy as an authority on mobile search and content discovery technologies. Her most recent series of practical how-to white papers covers the basics of mobile advertising and mobile analytics, earning her a reputation as a leading mobile advertising expert. Peggy has established a successful writing career based on vision, insight, versatility, and more than 15 years of industry experience. Her work, which includes more than 300 articles on mobile content and applications, has appeared in magazines and online destinations such as the *International Herald Tribune, Wall Street Journal, Mobile Entertainment, Mobile Media, New Media Age,* and in the Agile Minds column in *EContent* magazine, among many more.

## Recommended Reading

### Books and Articles

Ahonen, Tomi. *Mobile as 7th of the Mass Media: Cell Phone, Cameraphone, iPhone, Smartphone.* London: Futuretext, 2008.

Ito, Mizuko, Daisuke Okabe, and Misa Matsuda. *Personal, Portable, Pedestrian.* Cambridge: MIT Press, 2005.

Jaokar, Ajit, Brian Jacobs, Alan Moore, and Jouko Ahvenainen. *Social Media Marketing: How Data Analytics Helps to Monetize the User Base in Telecoms, Social Networks, Media and Advertising in a Converged Ecosystem.* London: Futuretext, 2009.

### Websites

Alcatel-Lucent, www.alcatel-lucent.com

Millennial Marketing, millennialmarketing.com

Mobile Youth, www.mobileyouth.org

SMLXL—From Interruption to Engagement, smlxtralarge.com

# CHAPTER 8

# Adapting Old-Fashioned Marketing Values to the Needs of the Digital Native

Michael P. Russell

There seems to be a great deal of uncertainty about how to tap into the digital native (the Millennial generation) market. Take a breath—the task is not as difficult or as different as some would have you think. Digital natives may be a new crop of potential customers, but many of their core drivers of demand are similar to what motivated previous generations. It's important to remember that when establishing a marketing strategy, the first step remains the same: Start by understanding what it is that the market is looking for. As David Gautschi and Darius Sabavala write in their paper "The World That Changed the Machines," published in *Technology in Society* (1995), "The engine of change is the people who populate the market—the world—rather than the technologies and products—machines." So, while a great deal of focus has been placed on the technology this group has grown up with, marketing fundamentals still hold sway. This is not to say that differences don't exist. They do, but we're in dire need of some perspective. If companies are to develop successful marketing strategies, they need to have an accurate picture of the market.

## What's the Difference?

The Cooperative Institute for Research Program (CIRP), which has been studying incoming college freshmen since 1966, has made some findings that contradict the blanket statements about the Millennial generation. CIRP shows that the top five life goals for college-bound students have not changed much over the years. For a group that is supposed to be wired so differently, their synapses are firing in a way that leads to similar outcomes.

CIRP tracks a variety of activities (socializing with friends, exercising or sports, watching TV, student clubs/groups, reading for pleasure, and housework/childcare), and since 1994, there has been virtually no change among college-going students in the time they spend on these activities. This would contradict the notion that digital natives are over-scheduled and are more focused on school and social activities than previous generations. With regard to the hypothesis that digital natives are less individualistic, according to Richard Hesel and John Pryor in their 2007 presentation at the American Marketing Association, "Marketing to the Millennial Generation: Beyond Howe and Strauss," there has been no change in first-year college students' self-ratings of cooperativeness or competitiveness from 1990 to 2001.

Let's debunk another myth: Digital natives are considered to be the savviest of all tech users. However, the 2009 Accenture "Consumer Electronics Products and Services Usage Report" found that although current thought has digital natives utilizing the technology they were born into at a high level, Baby Boomers actually embrace consumer technology applications nearly 20 times faster. The number of Boomers reading blogs and listening to podcasts increased 67 percent from the previous year, 80 percent faster than Millennials. There was also a 59 percent increase in Boomers' use of social networks, a growth rate that was 30 times faster than that of Millennials.

Nielsen's 2009 report, "How Teens Use Media," disproved the notion that teens' TV viewing is declining. The reality is that teens have shown a 6 percent increase in their TV viewing over the past five years. Ball State University's 2007 "Center for Media Design Study" explored the common belief that teens use media multiple screens at a time. The work revealed that teens viewed two or more screens at once only 23 percent of the time. The other 77 percent of the time found them viewing media one screen at a time. These partially founded beliefs are no doubt adding to the confusion of many executives as they attempt to develop a strategy to address and win the business of this sizable market. Yes, there are additional channels to establish and navigate, but meeting the wants and needs of the market is still paramount to earning their business.

## Mass Media With a Twist

It is helpful to keep in mind a simple adage coined by Ray Krok, the founder of McDonald's: "Look after the customer and the business will take care of itself." This is true for any generation (or population for that matter). Understand your customers, what motivates their demand, and meet those needs. The fact that Millennials now use multiple means to obtain and share information creates both a challenge and an opportunity. For a long time, marketers took a broad approach, as the channels available to them were geared toward a mass market strategy. The message could be targeted, but the medium reached the masses. Contrary to some current beliefs, those avenues are still available.

As far as what is creating media buzz among digital natives, television shows beat the web as the most frequent media conversation topics. In its 2009 report "How Teens Use Media," the Nielsen Company found that once an ad connected with teen viewers, their recall of an advertised brand was 44 percent *higher* than among older viewers. The research also showed that teens tend to like TV ads more than adults, making them an audience that is winnable through this old-school medium.

While an increasing percentage of TV show-viewing takes place via PC, this is not the case where cell phones are concerned. My current research on this market finds that males 18–24 are the most interested in this possibility, but little actual activity is occurring due to price, network speed, and device size. The highest number of viewing minutes per day that I have found is 15 in South Korea, where there are more established players and customers are more accustomed to the service. Even there, though, service providers are not earning significant revenue. The mobile TV/video market is only about 1 percent of the total market of potential users and has not generated the forecasted revenue.

More than half of Millennials indicate that print magazines help them determine what's "in." When digital natives go online, their internet use looks a lot like their parents'. According to Nielsen's "How Teens Use Media" report, both groups access many of the same categories and sites. Even billboards continue to catch young consumers' attention. John Erik Metcalf, a Millennial-aged blogger, posted a piece on his blog Think27 about a billboard campaign that he had seen. He was quite put off by the approach. The message on the billboard read, "Represent yourself like you present yourself. Pull them up," a reference to those in the younger population who wear their pants purposely sagging low. Metcalf viewed this as an attempt to push conformity, which he felt would not work as a way to influence his generation. Instead, he wanted to see a positive, uplifting, simple message/story, which, from his perspective, would be a much better way to convey the objective.

In effect, however, he demonstrated how an old-school means of advertising and communicating had not only gained his attention but motivated him to discuss and distribute the sponsor's message to a much wider audience. His reaction was to use the means and the channel that he had available to him—his blog—to convey his opinion to others. He broadcast his thoughts to all who had an interest, which could very well have included the sponsor of the billboard as well as the message's intended audience. By placing an old-style stationary and static message in his blog, he circulated it to a far wider audience.

There's no telling how effective the campaign was in decreasing the appearance of sagging pants in the area, but it apparently worked in getting people in the target demographic to talk about it and voice their dislike of sagging pants. While I agree with some of what Metcalf wrote about preferring a "pull" approach instead of a "push," his dismissiveness misses a key point: The billboard got his attention. It made him think. It also motivated him to talk about the issue, and he spread the word to others about it, as he showed the billboard in his blog. Digital natives may know how to use technology and expect companies to deliver messages via these technologies, but they're not immune to effective traditional advertising.

In addition to television and billboard marketing, there are other tried-and-true marketing outlets that continue to resonate with the native. Event sponsorship to introduce or promote products has a long history as an effective marketing tool. Digital natives want to see that companies are aware of their interests, of who the popular artists are, and of what the latest hot activity is. Visibility in these venues may provide an effective introduction to a product, which the digital native can then immediately find out more about through a personal mobile device, for example. It also offers the opportunity for potential customers to opt in for mobile advertising, a program that digital natives are more open to than any other demographic.

Although they have grown up in a much more technologically oriented environment, digital natives are actually not so different from you or me in terms of their life goals or the means by which they want to be introduced to messages and products. Using positive stories in marketing products is not a new concept. (Let's see, cave paintings may have started this trend.) And despite the recent hyperbolic overload on the topic, viral marketing is not a new phenomenon: In the '70s, Faberge Shampoo hoped that you would tell two friends, who would tell two friends, and so on, and so on.

## Know Your Market to Stay on Target

A number of companies have taken the "we know our market" approach by using a simple demographic definition of the market, as opposed to defining the market based on an understanding of the drivers of demand. Knowing these drivers offers far more insight when establishing a market strategy.

Helio, a managed virtual wireless network operator launched as an Earthlink and SK Telecom partnership, targeted the "youth market" (i.e., a demographic definition). During its approximately two years of operation, the company burned through its initial investment of $440 million plus additional funding. Helio's idea was to offer "cutting edge" technology devices to the tech-savvy younger generation. Since it had no in-depth understanding of what made this youth market tick, Helio ultimately attracted very few customers (170,000) before it was acquired by Virgin Mobile U.S., for $50 million, which also targeted the same market. Virgin Mobile U.S. was losing customers at the time and acquiring Helio seems to have been an attempt to maintain its customer base in this demographically defined target market. Basically, Virgin Mobile U.S. bought 170,000 customers.

Helio mistakenly believed that a "youth" message and position, along with a few different devices, would draw younger consumers to it. The company did not fully understand this market's drivers of demand. Its failure is evidence that a company needs to offer products to the target market that deliver more effectively than the relative alternatives available to them in the marketplace. The larger, better-established telecom carriers offer access to similar, if not the same, content and services as Helio and Virgin Mobile U.S., and have a broader array of the latest devices, which are subsidized to make them more affordable. The large telecoms offer unglamorous "Friends and Family" plans at an acceptable price point that include a much larger "in-calling" network. Like every generation, digital natives are not immune to a good deal. While AT&T, Verizon, Sprint, and T-Mobile are not direct mobile virtual network operator competitors, they are direct competitors for the wireless services that digital natives are looking for.

Helio would have been better off examining the market and breaking it down in a granular manner, so it could develop products that appealed to specific demand components. Helio should have examined consumers' specific desires and offered products tailored to these demands. Producing offerings that address what the market segments are seeking or repositioning current offerings to respond to specific demands provide a better opportunity to resonate with the targeted market. Listen to the market, find out where consumers are spending time, and present them with products that will provide them with the benefit bundles they are looking for.

## Market Strategy 101

A global study conducted in May and June 2008 by the Economist Intelligence Unit (EIU), titled "Maturing with the Millenials," claimed that more than half of the executives polled had not yet developed a way to target, attract, or retain Millennials as customers. This is a significant insight, since this generation is and will continue to be a formidable purchasing body. They are just beginning to graduate from college, enter the work force, and establish lives of their own. With those life steps comes the need to make purchases, including the most basic ones such as a car, furniture, and food. Digital natives didn't just appear on the horizon, and it is surprising to see that companies are, to a great extent, still up in the air about how to go after this audience.

Further research by the EIU in October 2008, sponsored by Genesys, illustrates this pervasive malaise, as none of the techniques cited by executives in this report mentions offering products that the market wants or needs. The closest reference is "Delivering great products at a great price," which ranks third (35 percent) in its list of most effective techniques for targeting Millennials. Ah, but who is defining "great"? That tag is usually decided on prior to market feedback. It falls into the trap of "we have developed something that everyone will want." The EIU found that, according to executives worldwide, the four best techniques for tapping into the digital native market were: 1) participating in viral marketing and peer-to-peer recommendation sites (41 percent); 2) sponsoring or advertising in areas populated by Millennials, such as extreme sports, music venues, and social network sites (36 percent); 3) delivering great products at a great price (35 percent); and 4) focusing not only on Millennials but also on their key influencers (e.g., parents, peers) (30 percent).

Many "great" products have fallen by the wayside because demand never materialized, and executives were left scratching their heads unable to determine what went wrong. The Segway is a great example of this. It generated enormous buzz prior to and immediately after its launch. Jeff Bezos made the claim that Segway would reach $1 billion faster than any previous company. Cities would be architected around the Segway. None of this has come to pass. All the funding, great engineering, and fanfare could not make up for the fact that the Segway did not fill a need or a want for that matter. It missed the mark in price, application, and access to use.

Since digital natives were born into a technology-abundant world, it's not the technology that is changing them. They explore their desires, wants, and needs via technology as those are the tools that have always been available to them. And businesses certainly need to take advantage of these additional channels of access that digital natives rely on. These new channels provide an opportunity for immediate contact and feedback.

*Speed* in obtaining information and responding to it is the most significant difference between this generation and those that preceded it. Digital natives want things now and/or want them improved immediately, and this expectation compresses the time companies have for engagement and potential sale.

Because this generation is still young, they have not yet fully developed their interests and needs, unlike older consumers in the market. Therefore, a well-crafted marketing strategy that targets digital natives must go beyond convincing them to buy a product. At the heart of the challenge is trying to better understand why they are buying and what is motivating their demand. Gautschi and Sabavala appropriately point out in "The World That Changed the Machines" that strong demand in the market comes as a surprise and thus results in lost sales due to insufficient capacity. Companies that lack the ability to quickly react or respond will see the market pass them by. Effectively defining its market can help a company better gauge what the potential demand will be. Seth Godin, author of a number of wildly popular marketing books, put it very well (as quoted on the mobileyouth.org site): "We're moving from an era of finding customers for our products to an era of finding products for our customers."

## Brand Recognition

With the emergence of digital natives, companies are questioning how best to gain brand awareness with this sizable new group. As Celia Goodnow of the *Seattle PI* noted in her article "Millennials Thrive on Choice, Instant Results" (March 12, 2007, bit.ly/fgEhxm), Millennials are the second-largest generation in U.S. history after the Baby Boomers. They are coming into their own and companies want to determine how best to market to them and generate sales from them.

In our hyperconnected society, companies are no longer in complete control of the time and place by which they communicate to the market. They need to make adjustments to their strategies if they hope to reach the digital native market. In 2006, Teen Research Unlimited (TRU) found that U.S. teens spent $179 billion on everything from clothing to music (bit.ly/dNq6iG). A 2009 AOL study, "Three Screen Nation: Marketing to Gen Y," states that members of Gen Y spend an average of $2,200 per year, with cell phones and fashion topping their list of expenditures (bit.ly/hnReZx). They also influenced purchases of food and other items for the household. Clearly, going forward, this generation will have a significant impact on the bottom line of many companies.

Digital natives were born into a world where they have always had multiple means to access content and communicate—sometimes simultaneously—and it can be a daunting task to figure out the appropriate mix of message and channel strategy to reach them. The challenge facing companies out to woo this market is to break through the abundant white noise and capture their attention, to build awareness and an enduring customer base.

Scion, a car manufacturer launched in the U.S. in 2003, worked off Microsoft's *New Marketing Playbook*, which outlines the so-called important strategies for winning over and establishing brand loyalty with the digital natives. "Scion's target buyer is information rich, time poor and highly technology savvy," said Jim Farley, vice president of Scion. "Scion will cater to this influential generation with unique products, a distinctive dealership environment and a revolutionized sales process, all complemented by an astonishing sticker price."

Armed with an interactive website for product information, a lifestyle/automotive magazine, and participation in lifestyle events, Scion was poised to take over this new consumer group. Initial response to products was good. Sales grew through 2006 and then saw a dramatic decline with the introduction of updated models. In addition, the demographic Scion had been targeting was overtaken by older buyers: The median age of buyers was 30, but 42 percent of Scion sales were to those 36–55 and only 38 percent to the 16–35 age group. Scion set up its showrooms along the lines suggested by Microsoft's automotive study: available products, self-serve internet kiosks, big screen TVs highlighting the vehicles features, and the opportunity for customers to discover the product at their own pace. Customers were presented with basic models to keep the decision process very simple and straightforward. They were then offered the ability to customize and personalize the vehicle with an assortment of 40-odd accessories.

Scion was left wondering why the 36–55 age segment snapped up cars in even larger numbers than its target market. First, even though digital natives grew up immersed in technology, they are not the only ones using it. The sort of sales tactics used in Scion showrooms actually appeals to individuals across many market segments. However, what Scion failed to identify and leverage were any benefits of Scion ownership that would appeal specifically to Millennials. Scion is now focused more on the potentially negative effect of the car's popularity among older customers, and the effect this will have on its perceived "coolness" among younger buyers. Scion should instead invest energy into discovering why, even when digital natives did purchase the car, these "trendsetters" didn't share positive reports with their peers. The company should be trying to determine whether the car failed to deliver in the eyes of these potential consumers.

## Time Is of Essence

Digital natives do have a heightened expectation of immediacy in their desire to gain information and be able to react to it *now*. A key element in gaining and keeping the attention of this generation is to regularly modify and update your product and message. Don't be stagnant. Keep the message simple and to the point. Accustomed to the rapid evolution of the tools that they use, digital natives want something fresh from companies trying to market to them.

The technology that digital natives have grown up with and are adept at using—these new channels marketers speak so much about—also offers quick and easy access to them. Online social networks, blogs, and mobile phones offer instant two-way communication and one-to-many communication. These channels are much more personal in nature, and in the case of the mobile phone, always with them. Leverage this access to make quick adjustments or improvements in a shorter time cycle. But beware: While social networks are now a regular aspect of digital natives' daily activity—they check and update their profiles several times a day—they visit with a purpose and are not interested in being interrupted by advertising that will draw their focus from the task at hand. They filter out extraneous information that does not relate directly to their interests. That said, these new bi-directional communication channels do let companies get a sense of whether their marketing is having the desired effect much sooner.

Although Millennials appear to be brand focused, they do not seem to be all that brand loyal. A poor experience can sink a product in the blink of an eye. The fundamental rules of marketing apply. The language may be different; the places to interact may have changed; the channels to reach potential customers may have increased as well. However, creating awareness, eliciting trial, fostering adoption, and earning customer loyalty are still fundamental objectives.

Moving beyond one's ability to send a letter, email, or place a call to a company in regards to a product, social networking and blogs have expanded the range, reach, and lifespan of an opinion a consumer may put forth about a product. Viral marketing can be a double-edged sword. Social networks are not just a way to connect and stay up to date with what is going on with everyone; in large part, these are platforms for self-promotion and self-branding. Thus, enabling these customers to develop status with relation to your product can be beneficial to both you and them.

## Engage and Interact With the Market

Engage this generation with marketing that calls them to action. Interaction provides natives with a sense of contributing, which feeds into their propensity for teamwork. YouTube provides myriad examples of how digital natives in particular like to create their own version of a music video or commercial. Encourage this behavior with a marketing effort that requests customer feedback and guidance. It will be a precarious tightrope to walk. The technology enables users to siphon off some of the company's control over message, as their input is immediate and broad, and their responses are not filtered by the corporate brand first.

To effectively reach the digital native market, use all of the tools and channels at your disposal. Don't fall into the assumption that you can only connect with them via their mobile devices or PCs. As we saw at the beginning of this chapter, old media still have the power to capture this generation's attention, and ignoring traditional channels will result in missed opportunities. It is increasingly important for companies to have an integrated, multifaceted approach. Have one piece or channel build upon the others, and link them so that customers can seek out the next piece and assist you in spreading the word by posting various elements on blogs and social networks. Adopting the Millennial's language, imagery, and practices will help as well. However, I must reiterate that a company that expects to gain these customers by just using the new technology to market a product that was not developed for their needs will not see the impact that it was hoping for.

Companies need to be extra careful about how they view the customers—trying to see the product through their eyes, and not being blinded by their own preconceptions about how it should be used. For example, while doing research in the mobile space, a big growth spot for Millennials, I encountered a company website that referenced developing regions of the world. It indicated that in these regions, where PCs are less ubiquitous, mobile phones are becoming the primary means of accessing internet content. Yet, barely a paragraph later, the company makes the blanket statement that "consumers want—and expect—a PC-like experience on the mobile phone." This makes no sense. People living in developing regions who have little to no exposure to the internet via PCs are clearly not expecting "a PC-like experience" on their mobile phones. Here is an example of a company projecting its preferences onto the market regarding what mobile should be on a global level. It seems to be openly disregarding the differences in various people's habits and needs.

It is important to recognize that digital native consumers do not want to stand idly by and just accept what companies want to sell to them. They are not only looking to engage in immediate feedback to improve products available to them, but they are voicing those impressions through blogs, social networks, and corporate sites. Potential consumers can easily access these views by means of a search on the products they are interested in. While a letter to a company, or an email for that matter, is limited to the two parties involved, comments posted on the web have a much broader and longer-lasting impact. Microsoft's "Automotive Industry Survey—Millenials' Technology Preferences," conducted by Wakefield Research in April 2010, highlights this generation's desire to also interact with companies and brands through multiple technology channels. Ford, for example, is launching an effort to introduce the new Ford Fiesta by tapping into newer technology. The company believes that this generation has not yet established a preference for car brands, and Ford wants to win the group over by using "young trendsetters" to create excitement around the Fiesta by driving the vehicle and spreading the word via social networks.

There are some good and some not so good aspects to Ford's approach. It has tapped into the social networking, word of mouth, and peer references, but it is brushing past some other elements that Millennials are known for. There is an assumption that younger buyers will want to break away from Honda, Toyota, and Nissan, as these are the brands that their parents drive. However, a 2006 TRU study states that this is a generation that respects and looks for input from their parents on major decisions. Therefore, it would make sense that they would take guidance from their parents about which make of vehicle to purchase.

Even following Ford's logic, it is unclear why Millennials would gravitate to a brand that has been in the market for 30 years. "This new car embodies the very essence of Fiesta—fun, vitality and emotion," said John Fleming, president and CEO of Ford of Europe. "We know there isn't a better name for the new model, and we have over thirty years of investment in the Fiesta brand to consider." The question to ask is whether the brand currently carries any credibility with those the Millennials admire or aspire to be like. Has the vehicle been developed with their wants and needs in mind? The latest model was designed and sold in Europe and Asia and is doing quite well there, since demand for quality smaller vehicles is high on these continents. However one wonders about the claim that the instrument panel has been designed in a "futuristic" layout similar to that of a cell phone. Futuristic, really? Cell phones are old news! Apparently, the company actually believes that being similar to a cell phone will win over the Millennials because they are avid cell phone users. Simply relating the design to another popular device, which not incidentally has a completely different benefit delivery, is talking down to this desired target market.

It is important to keep in mind that Millennials are also looking for things that are genuine. Digital natives are savvy to the fact that they are being advertised to. Thus, it seems unlikely that they will be swayed by the "Ford Fiesta Agents" posting pictures, videos, and endorsements to blogs and social networks when they know that Ford has provided the agents with the vehicles so that they can be evangelizers for the product. The agents are even assigned activities to post about. Regardless of the fact that these canned testimonials may negatively affect digital natives' opinions, to have any chance of being effective, these activities need to reflect what the Millennials regularly do in their daily lives. It is possible that after the six-month "free" period, when it becomes clear how many of the agents actually spent their hard-earned cash to own a Fiesta outright, the agents' views will carry more persuasive weight. While I give credit to Ford for making an effort to add new avenues to their marketing and advertising, I get the sense that its efforts still rely more on pushing their developed product into the market, instead of listening to the market and meeting the needs of the Millennials.

## Mobilizing the Message

Millennials are a driving force for mobile services and will increasingly be so as they move into the world and take on more responsibility for their own lives. According to Nielsen's 2009 "How Teens Use Media" report, 77 percent of teens in the U.S. already have a mobile phone. Wireless communication, a constantly evolving space, presents a big opportunity for companies. Mobile marketing and its promise has been hyped for a number of years, but only recently has it shown signs of delivering on that promise. There have been a number of hurdles holding back mobile as an effective channel: privacy concerns, the expense of data plans, ease of use, speed, and consumers' not wanting spam on their mobile devices, to name but a few.

The addressable market is growing though, as Millennials adopt mobile data in larger and larger numbers. According to "How Teens Use Media," 37 percent of U.S. mobile subscribers ages 13–17 access the internet on their phone. The report also found that more than half of teen mobile media users are open to mobile advertising. Teen mobile media users were roughly three times as receptive to mobile advertising as the total subscriber population. In addition, they demonstrate a willingness to use mobile devices to spread the word about a company or product. BIGresearch's December 2007 "Simultaneous Media Survey" showed that more than half of 18- to 24-year-olds communicate with others about a service, product, or brand via cell phone, second only to face-to-face communication (66.9 percent). Digital natives are also taking advantage of location-based services that leverage mobile handset technology to determine where a customer is located at a given time. An October 2010 report by Pew Internet, "Americans and Their Gadgets," found that 96 percent of 18- to 29-year-olds own a cell phone of some kind (bit.ly/eiabFW). In its "Mobile Access 2010" report, Pew also notes that young cell phone owners are significantly more likely to use mobile data applications, such as texting, social networking, playing music and games, watching videos, and making purchases (bit.ly/gVqhjY).

For many people, digital natives in particular, mobile phones are considered as essential as an appendage. It is coming to light, however, that Millennials view their mobile phones as more of an entertainment device, while older cell phone users still see mobile devices primarily as a tool that blends work and personal communication. In any case, thanks to the ubiquity of mobile phones, companies are no longer limited to specific times and places for reaching customers. That said, however, it is crucial that mobile ads be relevant and offer benefits to the consumer if companies hope to gain a positive impact through this channel. Harris Interactive's "Mobile Advertising" research points out that mobile ads need to appeal to "real interests." Younger consumers are more susceptible to mobile ads that are geared to their areas of interest, such as sports and entertainment. They are also interested in location- and time-specific ads.

BIGresearch's December 2007 "Simultaneous Media Survey" reveals that the 18- to 24-year-old segment, more than any other age group, is swayed by video messaging on their mobile phones. This type of message influences purchases across the board, from electronics, apparel, and home improvement to medication, telecom services, and eating out.

## Something Old, Something New

In the information circulating about digital natives, there are many references to the idea that older generations always think the upcoming generation is different from previous ones, but that this generation of digital natives *really is different.* They have more communication devices at their disposal. They are much more comfortable with them and much more adept at using them. Having grown up in a tech-heavy environment, they are quick to pick up on new technology and expect improvements or new offerings to come rapidly.

Younger generations learn from previous generations and feel compelled to try to improve upon their achievements—and this holds true for marketing as well. However, while many companies are quick to abandon the old rules of marketing when dealing with this generation, some of the old rules may actually apply even more to digital natives. Yes, this is a generation that wants to "know" and "friend" companies. This actually makes it even more important for marketers to genuinely know this market and to help companies they represent deliver real, honest value to them.

In some cases, however, marketers will need to abandon old rules and techniques — particularly those that tried to convince the market that they needed something that they never wanted. Technology—in particular, real-time feedback—now allows for deep and detailed insight into customers. Companies should take advantage of this. Segment the Millennial market in a way that defines what they are doing and what benefit bundles they are seeking, and personalize your product and message just for them. Build genuine understanding into your product, into your market position, and into your message. Take advantage of the multiple channels out there. Listen and respond to the feedback you receive to improve the value of your product. Focusing on genuine benefits gives you a better chance of building a lasting brand, known for delivering on its promise. You may be surprised to find that this approach to marketing and selling to Millennials will attract Gen X and Baby Boomers as well.

## About the Contributor

**Michael P. Russell** is the founding principal of Open Water Consulting LLC, which provides strategies to bring new products to market, gain market share, and create distance from competitors (referred to as "open water" in rowing races). Michael focuses on providing companies with the contextual market information they need to make product decisions and providing insight into their customers' decisions. His work is founded on segmenting and sizing market demand. With over 20 years of experience in a variety of industries, spanning the fields of the internet, wireless communications, software, CPG, and manufacturing, Michael has developed a foundation of knowledge that can be applied to multiple business situations. He produced contributions for the publication of *Net Markets: Driving Success in the B2B Networked Economy*, co-authored by David Gautschi and Tom Dagenais. He assisted in the development of key frameworks that he now applies to assist companies in gaining a rich context of the environment in which they are operating. Michael has also been a guest lecturer on Studies in Technology Commercialization, developing an effective market strategy and identifying key target markets.

## Recommended Reading

### Books and Articles

BIGresearch. "Simultaneous Media Survey." December 2007.

The Economist Intelligence Unit. "Maturing With the Millenials." September 2008. *The Economist.* bit.ly/hnE2nN (accessed January 18, 2011).

Gautschi, David and Darius Sabavala. "The World That Changed the Machines: A Marketing Perspective on the Early Evolution of Automobiles and Telephony." *Technology in Society* 17 (1995).

"Marketing to the Millennial Generation: Beyond Howe and Strauss." American Marketing Association 18th Annual Symposium for the Marketing of Higher Education. www.artsci.com (accessed November 28, 2010).

Nielsen Company. "How Teens Use Media: A Nielsen Report on the Myths and Realities of Teen Media Trends." June 2009. bit.ly/gQCuTr (accessed January 18, 2011).

Wakefield Research. "Microsoft Automotive Industry Survey—Millenials' Technology Preferences." May 2010. bit.ly/fCBDoH (accessed January 18, 2011).

### Websites

GigaOM NewTeeVee, gigaom.com/video

Marketing Pilgrim, www.marketingpilgrim.com

MarketingVOX: The Voice of Online Marketing, www.marketingvox.com

Millennial Marketing, millennialmarketing.com

Mobile Marketer, mobilemarketer.com

MobilizedTV, mobilizedtv.com

OldSchool SEO, www.oldschoolseo.com

Youth Marketing Connection, youthmarketing.com

# The Social Media Imperative: Learning to Engage Digital Natives Where They Live

Shashi Bellamkonda

When speaking to groups on the theme "Social Media to Grow Your Business," I ask the audience to tell me by show of hands how many have purchased something in the last three months because they saw an ad in the paper. A couple of hands go up. Next I ask about how many bought a product because a friend or coworker recommended it. This time more than half the audience raises their hands. As this simple example illustrates, businesses have to realize that their traditional marketing audience is deserting them in droves. This trend will only accelerate as digital natives, who have grown up in a digitally connected world, increasingly rely upon social tools and methods to get information. Undoubtedly, their relationship with social technologies will have an impact on which companies they choose to do business with.

Rohit Bhargava, author of the book, *Personality Not Included* (McGraw-Hill, 2008), explains this phenomenon by saying: "Many marketers assume that just because the younger generation has grown up with digital technology as a part of their lives, they will be much better at ignoring your marketing messages and therefore will be tougher to reach. That's dead wrong. Actually, they can be a marketer's best friend. When you grow up with instant access to the knowledge of the world, you actually become much better at finding what you want." He goes on to say, "The implication for marketers is this … that content becomes so much more important because a 'digital native' can find it and share it with her entire network—including people older, like their parents. Not only are they more likely to be reachable online, but if you're not offering your content to them in that way, you're missing a huge opportunity."

In the *Wall Street Journal* article "The Greatest Generation (of Networkers)" (November 5, 2009, on.wsj.com/1SMuPi), Steve Gallagher, the vice principal of Millwood High School in Halifax, Nova Scotia, is quoted as saying, "Young people today are connected socially from the moment they open their eyes in the morning until they close their eyes at night. It's compulsive." He points to an example: Once, when he was reprimanding a student for texting during class, he noticed the student's fingers moving on his lap. The student was texting while being reprimanded for texting.

Gallagher's experience is not unique. The article goes on to say that almost a quarter of today's teens check Facebook more than 10 times a day, according to a 2009 survey by Common Sense Media, a nonprofit group that monitors media's impact on families. August 2010 research from Common Sense found that 22 percent check social networking sites more than 10 times a day and 51 percent of teens check social networking sites more than once a day.

If you have a business, understanding the role of social media is essential for survival. It is clear that a generation of customers is growing up today with a level of immersion in, and reliance on, social media that must influence the ways businesses communicate with their customers. Given the rise of the digital native as the dominant consumer base, social media savvy may well become the factor that separates the successes from the failures.

## Recommendation Nation

Today, when people consider purchasing a product, many turn to social media first: 61 percent rely on user reviews for product information or research before a buying decision is made (Razorfish, "FEED, the Razorfish Consumer Experience Report," 2008, bit.ly/80TOTI). Recommendations can take the form of reviews on sites, in blogs, or within individual pages in social networks. On Facebook or Yelp, for example, friends and acquaintances trade recommendations.

This trend will be even more pronounced with younger buyers. According to Pew Internet & American Life Project's "Generation 2010" report, 73 percent of teens and 83 percent of Millennials use social network sites, significantly more than older generations, especially adults over 55. While half of younger Boomers use social network sites, only 16 percent of adults 74 and older have (bit.ly/ikk19Y).

At a GrowSmartBiz business summit I attended, customer relationship management guru Brent Leary pointed out that customers today *expect* companies to engage with them via social media. He said that if a business is not monitoring the conversations, it will not know what is already being said about it online. Thus, if businesses are hesitant to engage with customers using Web 2.0 tools because they are afraid that bad things will be said about them, chances are that such negative conversations are already taking place online (of which they are probably woefully unaware).

Engagement in social media is imperative for business today. It also levels the playing field to some extent: If you master digital technologies, your company will have the same chance as the major players in your industry to be heard, quoted, cited, and interviewed about your expertise and your business. Remember that not so long ago, the only way a reader could communicate with the newspaper was by writing a "Letter to the Editor." Today, only seconds after an article is published, readers can comment and have their comments responded to by writers, editors, or fellow readers.

And the news media is only one example of how times have changed. In an August 2009 article "Twittering May Have Impact at Box Office" (Michael Sragow, August 20, 2009, bit.ly/7lVLxk), the *Washington Post* replied, "Although word of mouth could always make or break a movie, it usually took days to affect the box office. But the rise of social networking tools such as Twitter might be narrowing that time frame to hours. And that has Hollywood on edge."

This is very true. For example, because of the time difference, the East Coast audience could easily impact opening day viewership on the West Coast by using Web 2.0 tools. Audiences no longer wait for a mainstream movie review when they can look straight to their networks for a virtual thumbs-up or -down.

The entertainment and media industries are not alone in feeling the incredible impact of social media. Yelp began as an online network for people who eat out and write restaurant reviews. The site boasts a devoted following: In fact, according to an October 2009 user survey Yelp conducted, a whopping 94 percent of respondents turn to Yelp first to make a purchasing decision. Contrast that with the 43 percent who indicated they would consult a friend and the mere 2 percent who would turn to the Yellow Pages. It seems the community aspect of Yelp, where people share information about themselves and get to evaluate their fellow reviewers, plays an important part. Indeed, 80 percent noted that they prefer Yelp because it emphasizes reviews from trusted members of the community.

This trend is clear in the activities of digital natives in particular: In its 2010 ECAR Study of Undergraduate Students and Information Technology, EDUCAUSE found that the percentage of students 25 or older who use social networking sites increased from 33 percent in 2007 to more than 75 percent in 2010. Facebook use increased from 89 percent in 2008 to 97 percent in 2010 (bit.ly/g9SGlN). In May 2009, Youth Trends found that Facebook was the number three source among college students for learning about new products and services—after word-of-mouth and television commercials.

## Business Advantage

There are certainly some notable examples of social media being used by major organizations to engage with customers. Comcast, Dell, and Best Buy are among the leading brands using social tools to connect with their customers. For example, Comcast provides Customer support using the Twitter handle @comcastcares, which was launched by Frank Eliason, previously senior director of national customer service operations. "If anyone wants to tell me good or bad experience with myself or my team please email me frank_Eliason@cable.Comcast. com." His candor and style captured more than 43,000 followers in his first two and a half years on Twitter.

However, as previously suggested, one particular advantage of using social media tools—in addition to reaching digital natives where they live—is that they have the potential to level the marketing playing field between large and small organizations. The following are just a few of the many illustrations of businesses that are using online tools to help them lead their field.

Gary Vaynerchuk of Wine Library TV (tv.winelibrary.com) is a wonderful example of a digital native who was successful in reaching digital natives. Tara Hunt writes in her book *The Whuffie Factor* (Crown Business, 2009): "In less than a decade, [Vaynerchuk] helped turn his family's New Jersey store with 10 employees into a global business with 100 employees and annual sales in multiples of 10 million dollars." Vaynerchuk did this first by taking the business online with a website (winelibrary.com) in 1997. As social networking grew in both audience and participation, he decided to start an online TV show at tv.wine library.com.

On this homemade show (presented in a video blog), Vaynerchuk tastes two or three different wines every day and makes recommendations in a seemingly unrehearsed style. People like the frank and conversational nature of this daily webcast. His audience has grown quickly; Tara Hunt writes, "A year after [Vaynerchuk] began Wine Library TV, he had over 15,000 daily downloads and nearly 100 comments on every show."

While downloads provide a good metric for your viewership, the comments that people make on this site are even more significant as a sign of engagement and audience interaction. Vaynerchuk reinforces his use of Web 2.0 tools for marketing by speaking at conferences about his success and inspiring others to do the same, as well as creating a community of wine lovers, which in turn has helped his business. On the Wine Library TV website, he writes, "WLTV has blossomed into a full-fledged community." The viewers (self-named "Vayniacs") convene on an extremely active  forum and have organized numerous offline gatherings. Vaynerchuk and the viewers have teamed up with Crushpad in the past year to create the first ever *community wine*, "Vayniac Cabernet."

Another example of a relatively small businessman who has leveraged social media to improve its exposure is that of Chef K.N. Vinod, owner of Indique Heights and two other restaurants on the border of Washington, D.C. and Maryland. After much persuasion, this busy chef started blogging at chefvinod.typepad.com about his travels, recipes, cooking techniques, and other topical subjects related to his culinary adventures. The blog includes photo albums with themes such as "foodie friends" and "heads of state, ambassadors, and celebrities." Since he started blogging, Vinod has noticed that more food critics visit the restaurant, which in turn has triggered an increase in clientele and raised his overall profile as a chef. Thanks to the success of his blog, he decided to launch a Facebook page for Indique Heights to engage with his customers and provide information on activities and offers in the restaurant. Customers actively participate on the Facebook page: Guests discuss the food ("best desserts ever!") and even the New Year's events months in advance.

A very different culinary example is provided by two enterprising businessmen—themselves digital natives—who have a food truck called Merlindia in the Washington, D.C. area and use Twitter to tell their customers where their van is parked to serve customers. A typical tweet from these lads might be "the fojol bros. are set up and ready to serve at 14th & K." These young businessmen are taking advantage of their customers' connectivity and use of Web 2.0 tools to create a totally new business model. They have been so successful that they are going to have another brother join them in the business, and they attribute much of this success to the simple, low-cost marketing they achieve through social media.

Social media can work for businesses of all types. For example, Steven Fisher led a workshop on social media tools for car wash owners. As an impromptu demo, he discussed the Canton Car Wash in Baltimore (www.cantoncarwash.com), which actively encourages customers to join its Facebook page. It is clear this strategy is working, as demonstrated by comments about the quality of their car washes and other conversations.

As I write, I see a tweet from one of our Network Solutions customers, a well-known author, telling another friend, "I know Network Solutions is expensive, but their service is top notch." Since I monitor the social media sphere for the words *Network Solutions*, I saw the message and thanked her right away. Had I missed it, I would have been alerted when another Twitter friend, who saw the same message and knew it was valuable to me and Network Solutions, sent it to me via a Retweet, which allows Twitter users to repeat someone else's tweet to their own followers. This example demonstrates not only how important it is for companies to monitor social media but also how effective these tools can be in helping companies engage with customers to receive both positive and negative feedback.

It is a positive sign that an October 2009 online survey by Internet2Go and MerchantCircle found that 45 percent of small-business owners use Facebook to promote their businesses, and 46 percent have Twitter accounts. In total, 53 percent had created a social network profile. As these statistics, and the other examples, provide evidence that companies see the value of social media to engage with customers of all ages, the need to master these techniques will become increasingly important.

According to Pew Internet's "Twitter and Status Updating Fall 2009" report, age is a strong, independent predictor for use of Twitter and other status updating services. Internet users ages 18–44 report rapid uptake of Twitter, whereas internet users age 45 and older report slower adoption rates. In an April 22, 2010 presentation, Pew's director Lee Rainie reported that 57 percent of online adults were using social network sites as compared with 73 percent of teens.

The good news is that even if you aren't already on board, social media tools are freely available, so now is the time to experiment with them and begin to develop the essential skills you will need as the generation of digital natives become the dominant consumer force.

## Mastering the Art of Conversation

At its most effective, social media is a two-way conversation. Companies must leverage the tools as a way to connect human beings with each other, as well as with information. A great example of this is Lionel Menchaca, chief blogger for Dell Inc., who helps answer customer questions using his Twitter account @LionelatDell. With tweet responses like "Sorry for the delay in responding to you. Please [direct message] me an order number or service tag #. Happy to help if I can." and "Just getting back today from the flu. Sorry for the delay. I'm willing to bet

@LisaG_atDell can take care of you," Twitter allows Menchaca to re-inject human contact into the overly automated customer service experience we have all come to loathe. Therefore, I would advise against sending tweets to feed followers using an automated message such as, "Thanks for following me. Here is a report you can download <link to the download>." These kinds of impersonal messages will likely cause you to both lose your followers and result in digital natives blocking you from the conversation.

While many aspects of social *life* remain mysterious, there are three steps that can be taken to engage digital natives in social *media* conversations: listening, participating, and contributing. The following are some tactics, tools, and strategies for effectively engaging in social media to reach users of all ages, digital natives in particular.

### Listening

During the listening phase of engagement, you need to monitor social networks and other places where people are mentioning you, your company, and/or your brand online. Conversations often take place in online communities, which may or may not be open.

Closed communities require membership. People join these communities to discuss common interests and ideas, causes, or particular celebrities. For example, I wrote a blog post on the Network Solutions blog, Solutions Are Power, about how fans of singer Josh Groban banded together and raised money for charity. While checking my analytics, I saw several visits from board.friendsofjoshgroban.com, which is a community of Josh Groban fans. However, since I was not a member, I could not see what was being written about my blog post by the "grobanites."

Listening to open conversations is easier, particularly given the various alerts technology provided by search engines and software companies. With these tools, you can set alerts for your name, your business name, and names of your products (and even those of your competitors), and also be notified when anything appears online mentioning these terms. Perhaps you'll want to set up alerts around keywords, technologies, or trends that impact your business. The listening phase will provide you with an indication of where your audience resides and, therefore, where you should channel your time and resources.

Some alerting and other real-time awareness tools include:

- *Google Alerts* (www.google.com/alerts) lets you choose to get alerts for the terms you specify when they first appear in a Google search—either instantly or at daily or weekly frequency. (Yahoo! provides similar service at alerts.yahoo.com.)

- *BackType* (www.backtype.com) gives you results from the comments sections of blog posts and social media. You may not find these results on other search engines.

- *Technorati* (technorati.com) is a blog search and ranking site that can tell you if your search terms have been used to tag any blog or microblog post.

- *Radian6* (www.radian6.com) provides reports and alerts for any mention of your predetermined terms in the social media sphere.

- *Search.Twitter.com* (search.twitter.com) gives you real-time results on conversations about your brand or business or even your competitors.

- *Alterian* (socialmedia.alterian.com) is a tool used by PR and marketing agencies to monitor and measure social media.

- *Social Mention* (www.socialmention.com) is a real-time social media search and analysis tool that sends you alerts and lets you know the predominant sentiment about a brand.

### Participating

Keep in mind that an actual *conversation* is never one way. You must be prepared to actively contribute to the discussions that mention you or your company brand. Use the knowledge you gain from the listening phase to participate in the discussions.

To become involved, you must create profiles and join (the appropriate) social networks. Here is a description of some of the most popular social networks in use and how to approach your participation:

- *Twitter* (twitter.com) is perhaps the most widely discussed social tool today, although interestingly, it is less popular with younger users (which is not the case with most other social tools). Twitter provides a way to join the online conversation by collecting a following around 140-character messages. With Twitter, you should adopt the language of the people (i.e., Twitter followers): Send genuine tweets that share feelings, accomplishments, and interesting things happening in the company. Self-promotion, continuous marketing messages, and one-way communications are to be avoided.

- *LinkedIn* (www.linkedin.com) is a business-oriented social network designed to facilitate professional connections. It is frequently used for recruitment or finding contacts at companies you want to do business with. It can be very useful to create or join LinkedIn groups of like-minded business folks. LinkedIn is particularly useful in that it allows you to leverage your connections (and those of your first- and second-degree connections) to build interest in your group and extend the reach of your network.

- *Facebook* (www.facebook.com) provides a place where users create personal profiles to connect with former and/or current classmates, colleagues, family members, and other contacts. Facebook "friends" share news and recommendations about information, products, pictures, and events. Your organization can have a public profile to share information about your business and products with Facebook users, and Facebook's newsfeed makes it easy to spread ideas virally.

- *Myspace* (www.myspace.com) is useful for building a following for a music group or other arts-related endeavor, although it has declined in popularity since it moved to an ad-supported model. On Myspace, you must build a network of "friends." Myspace bulletins can be used by businesses to promote products or events to all of their Myspace friends. The more friends they have, the larger the audience they reach. Myspace offers many ways to reach specific audiences through its blogs, forums, and video site. As with other social media sites, providing your "friends" with genuine news, information, and other benefits will encourage them to spread the word, thus increasing your network.

- In some cases, during the listening phase, you will identify *niche social communities* (listservs, wikis, etc.) where lively conversations about your brand, product, or product segment are already taking place. If you do encounter these opportunities, find a way to become a genuine community member who contributes useful information.

Digital natives have an overload of messages coming at them from all directions, so they seek refuge in social networks and do not expect (or want) to receive sales pitches there. They will follow and cultivate networks with people who are genuine and who provide useful information and unstinting advice when asked. If you develop a relationship with this audience, they will return the favor.

In addition to social networks, you should also contribute to forums and community boards related to your business or the interests of your potential customers. These are communities of users or experts with the common goal of helping each other. On forums and community boards, experts answer questions and, by doing so, establish their leadership and expertise. Users get their questions answered and can rank the answers, which can be a useful lead generating tool.

Some examples of ways in which you can contribute to forums and community boards are:

- On *LinkedIn Answers* (www.linkedin.com/answers), LinkedIn members post questions and other members give their answers. The questions are often about specific products and companies. In addition to making connections by sharing your expertise, you also have the opportunity to have your answer be voted "best," which will elevate your standing in the community and lead people to click to your profile, thus potentially connecting with you and your business.

- In addition to actively commenting on key blogs in your digital space, you should volunteer to write *guest posts* for blogs related to your industry. Often, all you need to do is send an email to the blogger with your idea for a guest post. It is essential to offer an idea that is valuable to the community. (Darren Rowse, a well-known blogger from Australia, gives good guest blogging tips at www.problogger.net.)

- The spirit of collaboration and communication on the internet includes the sharing of favorite links and articles through *social tagging* and *bookmarking*. The easiest method is to join social bookmarking sites like Delicious (www.delicious.com) and Digg (digg.com), although tagging content on Flickr (www.flickr.com) and other sites that provide this option can also demonstrate your commitment to being part of the conversation. When you bookmark a link, everyone who connects with you on the social bookmarking site can see your "favorites" (if you choose to make them public). Links that are bookmarked by several people usually rise to the top of the page. If this happens to any content you create, increased traffic back to your website or blog will be generated. In order to establish credibility, it is important to use social bookmarking to provide value to your network, and your network will reciprocate by recommending you and the links that you bookmark.

### Contributing

Once you know where your target market is and you have established a presence, you can then begin to develop your own personal contribution tool. A blog is fundamental to establish your thought leadership. It also provides a place for your customers and connections to converse with you by commenting on your posts. In addition to text posts, you can also use audio (podcasts), photos (Flickr), or video (YouTube, Livestream). For example, you can make videos of yourself or your business demonstrating new product features. Videos can also contribute useful how-to instruction or standards information for your industry as a whole. You can share exciting stories about your business or about your employees' activities and interests. Just remember that even when you are discussing your products, the information you provide must be of genuine interest and value to the community. Obvious sales messages will alienate your audience.

You have to set the right tone on your blog. A blog has to be conversational yet cannot be taken lightly. Successful blogs have a definite theme to engage and hold readers who are looking for specific content. A blog should be updated regularly; establishing a constant flow of blog posts will help elevate the search engine results for that topic, which will help you get more visitors.

Starting a blog is easy with free services like Blogger or WordPress. The fact is that a blog does not need to originate from your own domain to be considered "valid" within the blogosphere, so free tools will often suffice. However, many blog hosting sites offer premium levels with relatively easy mapping and configuration.

However, technology shouldn't be your primary concern. Before you start, you need to identify the type of blog you want to write: a CEO blog with high-level musings, a group blog written by your development team, a customer support blog in which your help team provides near real time feedback, or a thought leadership blog written by an executive or other leader in your organization.

Once you have carefully conceived of your blog's focus and approach and have launched it with some initial posts, connect with other bloggers in your space to link content and promote each other's stories. Again, to be part of the larger community, you need to read and comment on other people's blogs.

Keep in mind that building an audience for your blog takes time. Some general ways to build readership include making it easy for readers to subscribe to your blog, including your blog's URL in your email signature and whatever other social media sites you belong to, and specifically inviting comments in some of your posts.

Providing links to others' blogs and feedback on their posts will help build traffic. It is important to recognize the link economy online and make it easy to share your posts. You should also enable comments in your blog settings and engage with readers who do comment. This is particularly important when trying to attract digital natives, as they expect to be able to interact with information.

This aspect of the digital native's information consumption behavior is documented in Capgemini's TME Strategy Lab analysis from April 2007, which reports that "youth are also constantly engaged in community interactions, sharing opinions on what content is worth seeing or experiencing ... Conversations between peers then arise around that content in the form of blog comments, links sent by email, [instant messaging] discussions, merging communication and content into what one could call 'conversational content.'" The report goes on to conclude that "for an increasing number of young users, content gets added value from the ability to consume and discuss it collectively." These online community dynamics alter traditional patterns of trust: Consumers, especially the younger generation, have more confidence in peer-generated or "crowdsourced" content.

The term *crowdsourcing* was coined by Jeff Howe in a 2006 *Wired* article to describe a situation in which a problem is broadcast to an unknown audience and the crowd/audience submits the solutions ("The Rise of Crowdsourcing," June 2006, bit.ly/BHpY). We see it at work on Twitter when someone tweets a question, perhaps asking where to eat or what to buy, and dozens of followers respond or in similar real-time conversations on Facebook.

Perhaps the most remarkable example of crowdsourcing comes from Shel Israel, whose pivotal book on social media called *Twitterville* (Portfolio, 2009) is based on stories that he "crowdsourced" from among his 22,500 followers (as of this writing). Israel described how he conceived of *Twitterville*: "In April 2008, I was stunned by the story of James Buck, a UC Berkley student who was in Egypt doing a photo journalism project as a grad school project. When Egyptian police arrested him for taking photos of food strikes in the Nile Delta area, he posted a one-word tweet: 'arrested.' This set off a series of events that got him released within 24 hours. As he was being driven to the airport, he posted a second one-word tweet: 'freed.'"

Israel continues: "That incident gave me some sense of Twitter's amazing potential on several levels. I posted a tweet, saying someone should write a book about this incident. I received a reply—I don't recall who sent it—but it went something like: 'How about you, Shel? You haven't done much lately.'"

It was a good point. And that turned out to be the start of *Twitterville*. In writing the book, Israel collaborated with his followers using Twitter. He explained each chapter before he started writing and then asked followers to send him ideas for the book. He received more than 200 story suggestions, about 75 of which ended up in the book. He also started a "Twitterville Notebook" section on his blog and received more ideas there, as well as receiving fact-checking tips and other insights from readers.

While Israel's *Twitterville* experiment was extensive, it demonstrates how readers increasingly expect to participate in the process of content creation. Contributing to the conversation is important, but with social media, the interactive and participatory nature is an essential aspect to keep in mind.

There are many ways to appeal to the digital native's remix and mashup nature, for example, by sharing content and information that others can freely use. This not only demonstrates your knowledge but also promotes your openness. Here are some places where you can upload documents like PowerPoint presentations, white papers, and ebooks that you want to share:

- SlideShare (www.slideshare.net): Share PowerPoint presentations, documents, and videos

- Docstoc (www.docstoc.com): Share public documents

- Scribd (www.scribd.com): Share books, documents, presentations, and spreadsheets

Beyond text-based information, there are other dimensions and channels to create and share content, including multimedia tools for photos, audio and video. A few popular ones are:

- Flickr (www.flickr.com): Share photos

- Photobucket (photobucket.com): Share photos

- YouTube (www.youtube.com): Share video

- blip.tv (blip.tv): Share video

- Viddler (www.viddler.com): Share video

- TubeMogul (tubemogul.com): Share video

- Seesmic (seesmic.com): Share video

To ensure that you gain maximum value from your social media experiments, you should use tools like FeedBurner and Google Analytics to track where your traffic is coming from. This will provide insights into the places your would-be audience is congregating. It will also provide you with insights into which sites you could collaborate and build partnerships with.

## Social Media: More Than Tools

While I've focused on leveraging technology, the underlying theme of a company's use of social media must be contributing valuable insights and information to the community in ways that encourage participation and develop genuine relationships based on an exchange of ideas.

There will always be technology haves and have-nots, yet increasingly technology plays a part in everyone's life: Grandparents are joining Facebook to connect with their kids and grandkids. My own parents in India now keep in touch with me thanks to my Facebook status updates that my brother reads to them. I once even found a barber online; perhaps this doesn't sound all that surprising until you learn that the barber doesn't have a website and has never used a computer. In fact, he hadn't even realized his customers were reviewing him online. Luckily, he does a good job and is excellent at customer service so the reviews are positive.

Not every company will be so lucky, however. If conversations about your business are occurring online and you fail to be a part of them, you risk not being aware of your reputation. With the emergence of the digital native—who relies on social networks, peer reviews, and online communities to influence her decision making—as the preeminent consumer, you risk being left behind. As we move forward, social media is no longer an option; it is an imperative for business success.

## About the Contributor

**Shashi Bellamkonda** is a digital immigrant who serves as the director of social media at Network Solutions, with the unique title Social Media

Swami. In this leadership role, he has helped Network Solutions aggressively move into online space so as to actively listen to and interact with its customers. He was included in *Washingtonian Magazine*'s list of Tech Titans in 2009. Shashi has presented to several audiences on "Social Media Tools for Small Business," "How to Sell Social Media to Your Boss," and "Online Reputation Management: Best Practices and Lessons Learned" at national and regional conferences. He blogs at blog.networksolutions.com and www.shashi.name, and participates in a number of community sites such as GrowSmartBusiness.com and UnintentionalEntrepreneur.com. A resident of Maryland, Shashi speaks seven languages and ardently works to spin his favorite hobbies into his profession.

## Recommended Reading

### Books and Articles

Bhargava, Rohit. *Personality Not Included: Why Companies Lose Their Authenticity and How Great Brands Get It Back*. New York: McGraw-Hill, 2008.

Hunt, Tara. *The Whuffie Factor: Using the Power of Social Networks to Build Your Business*. New York: Crown Business, 2009.

Israel, Shel. *Twitterville: How Businesses Can Thrive in the New Global Neighborhoods*. New York: Portfolio, 2009.

Scott, David Meerman. *The New Rules of Marketing and PR: How to Use News Releases, Blogs, Podcasting, Viral Marketing and Online Media to Reach Buyers Directly*. Hoboken, NJ: John Wiley & Sons, 2007.

Weinberg, Tamar. *The New Community Rules: Marketing on the Social Web*. Sebastopol, CA: O'Reilly Media, Inc., 2009.

### Websites

ChrisBrogan.com, www.chrisbrogan.com

Small Business Trends, smallbiztrends.com

Social Media Explorer, www.socialmediaexplorer.com

Mashable: The Social Media Guide, mashable.com

CHAPTER **10**

# Social Capitalism and the Reputation Economy

Michelle Manafy

People are social beings. Starting with our first awareness of our place in the familial structure, through middle school when the influence of our peers comes to the fore, then on to adult life where we seek the approval of coworkers, employers, and other members of our extended community, we are socially motivated. From brownie points to peer review and recognition, the opinions of others matter.

Online, this tendency has been altered and amplified. Social networks reach far beyond our ability to connect in a brick-and-mortar context. Of course, it is not only the scope that has changed. The opinions of others—be they strangers or friends, celebrities or confidants—have an increasing influence on every aspect of our decision making.

We do business with firms our friends recommend; we avoid companies with bad user ratings; we buy products bearing the most rating stars or with user reviews that specifically remark on features we desire; we shape future iterations of products through user feedback and forum comments.

The opinions held by others about us (and about our opinions) have an increasing influence on the decisions made about us. We are recruited for a job because of our Twitter or blog following; LinkedIn connections lead an employer to us and recommendations seal the deal; a potential business partner looks us up on Facebook but doesn't think our style meshes with his and moves on to another candidate; we collaborate, innovate, or launch a startup based on a round of comments about a video or slideshow presentation we shared online.

Along with more prominent iterations such as blogging and other user-generated content, this spectrum of activities falls under the broad heading "social media"—which describes online technologies and activities that people use to share information, including opinions, insights, observations, news, and experiences with each other.

While the term itself is relatively new, social media traces its origins to the first iterations of online connectivity, which focused on facilitating information sharing and collaboration. True to its online roots, the most popular web-based application is (and probably will remain so for some time) email, because it makes it easy to correspond and collaborate with anyone online, regardless of geographic location. Massively multiplayer online role-playing games (MMORPG)—which are often characterized by robust community interactions and connections—rose to popularity online in the late 1980s and early '90s. Then came the first widespread social applications in which file sharers began to build up reputations based on their illicit content exchanges, which took the form of first generation P2P file sharing, such as Napster, starting around 1999.

While the social networking aspect of social media as we currently think of it came to the fore as part of Web 2.0, starting in 2002 with the launch of Friendster, then Myspace, and then Facebook soon after, the underlying tenets have been around for decades. As the names of these social media sites suggest—though a lot of information and ideas are exchanged under the auspices of social media—it ultimately centers around people and connections.

Most consumers are becoming accustomed to increasing interaction online. However, given the way their expectations have been shaped by the steadily increasing impact of digitally augmented social influences, the generation of digital natives has grown up to expect conversation, community, and interaction in every aspect of their lives.

As Marc Prensky put it in "Digital Natives, Digital Immigrants, Part II: Do They Really *Think* Differently?" (*On the Horizon,* MCB University Press, vol. 9, no. 6, December 2001), "Our children today are being socialized in a way that is vastly different from their parents. The numbers are overwhelming: over 10,000 hours playing videogames, over 200,000 emails and instant messages sent and received; over 10,000 hours talking on digital cell phones … all before the kids leave college."

As Prensky recognized almost a decade ago, when he coined the term *digital native,* this generation has developed a distinctly different mind-set (in fact, he argues their brains are actually wired differently) about how to interact with the world, from friendships to shopping and business decisions. According to Prensky, "As important as it may be to the digital natives, their online life is a whole lot bigger than just the Internet. This online life has become *an entire strategy for how to live, survive and thrive in the 21st century,* where cyberspace is a part of everyday life."

This distinct world view will shape the way this generation decides with which companies to do business. Smart organizations will begin to conceive of their customers as part of an extended social network with whom they communicate, connect, and collaborate. While there's been a great deal of hype about user-generated content and viral marketing, there are myriad ways that social media will impact business, particularly with regard to properly valuing (and evaluating) online reputation.

## Social Workers

In the Gartner report "2018: Digital Natives Grow Up and Rule the World," author Monica Basso explored how digital natives were already challenging many aspects of information technology in 2008 and then predicted what this implies for "our approach to technology, business processes and organizational structure." In 2008, she observed, "A process of democratization and commoditization in communication products and services has empowered individuals to reach a universe of information, opportunities and people, despite the geographical distance, time zone differences and cultural diversity." Her prediction for 2018 is that "Thousands of people and parties will have the power to influence their direction, the services/products they offer and their reputation almost randomly—across global markets, outside official channels and through a potentially infinite web, at a head-spinning pace."

There is no disputing the way in which the web has transformed our notion of "community" and has expanded the opportunity for connection and commerce well beyond our local sphere. The stunning growth and popularity of social networks and community sites has the business world scrambling to mine them for profit: "There's gold in them thar networks!" So it is not a surprise that, when we look at innovation online today, much of it centers around social media.

At first glance, it seems that social media success will be defined by the way in which social networks themselves find a way to become profitable through advertising or subscriptions. There is also a perception that organizations should focus on social advertising—be it in-your-face interruption-style, in-context personalized placements, or by influencing the influencers to chat up your products and services casual-style.

However, the impact and influence of social networks on business will go far beyond inventing a way to post targeted commercials on Facebook walls. When we consider the digital native—who lives a social life profoundly impacted by extended web-based communities and the immediacy and persistence of who-said-what online—the potential impact and opportunities presented for business that understand the value of online reputation are as infinitely vast as these networks themselves and as infinitely complex as any relationship between two people.

## Transactions vs. Interactions

Social media and social networking are giving rise to more than just improved relevance and better advertising and sales targeting; they are providing ways to get to know each other and to leverage that knowledge to do better business. As consumers become increasingly resistant to sales and marketing (and many other propositions) that appear to be transactional rather than interactional, understanding the distinction will be significant for success. As we seek to expand our markets to embrace younger consumers, we need to understand their distinct demands.

U.K. consultancy Capgemini identified four key themes to summarize digital natives' expectations with regard to new media and communication:

> This younger generation desires *Control*, with the ability to access content and communicate whenever they choose, regardless of location. *Impatience* is also characteristic of this age group, as it seeks to make the most efficient use of its time through multitasking and 'media snacking.' The youth are also constantly engaged in *Community Interactions*, sharing opinions on what content is worth seeing or experiencing. Additionally, they are looking for avenues of self expression that enable them to showcase their creativity and portray their *Originality*. ("Digital Natives: How Is the Younger Generation Reshaping the Telecom and Media Landscape?" October 16, 2007, bit.ly/hsIPIW)

While the influence of peers is nothing new, the digital native has a uniquely digitally impacted social nature that differs from that of earlier generations. In 1985, the entire student body—a few hundred, or maybe a thousand other teens—might have been superficially familiar with the activities and opinions of a popular girl. However, while some of her fashion choices might have filtered down, it isn't likely that those outside her immediate clique would have been privy to her innermost thoughts on fiction or films, much less intimate details about her dating life. A popular girl on Facebook might not be "known" to any more people than her '80s ancestor; however, her 100 or so friends (the average Facebook user has 130, according to the company's statistics page) *all* hear about her latest shopping experience, the fit of her favorite jeans, and just about anything else that pops into her head.

And unlike her '80s counterpart, the modern girl's friends aren't limited to her vicinity; they can reside anywhere. The facility of sharing her opinions might still appear relatively small—to her buddy list of 100 or so. However, when we consider how likely it is for some of her friends to rebroadcast these opinions to their hundred friends and so on, the scale and reach of any given social networker is potentially immense. The ease with which social networkers can share information with each other and about each other, and the simplicity of including a link directly to a site or product or to include a video or image—these carry with them powerful viral sway as marketing gurus the world over have proclaimed.

One significant impact of these recommendations and community feedback loops that gets less attention, however, is how these "popular people," these "influencers," gain reputation based on the quality of their recommendations, and, to take it further, how these reputations become currency in their own right. While most organizations focus on how to tap into social networks as a new way to sell products, they fail to recognize that this emerging reputation-based culture will become an economic force as digital natives become business decision makers.

## Bad Rep, Good Rep

Reputation—like that of high school girls—is not a new concept for corporations. Companies with bad public images arising from the exposure of financial scandal, environmental misconduct, worker exploitation, and the like are the frequent focus of magazine pages, documentaries, and the news. However, scandal writ large may well be easier for spin masters to manage than the day-to-day business of monitoring and monetizing reputation in the age of millions of opinion-shaping microcosms.

Gone are the days when corporate dirt could be concealed under floor coverings or when high-price advertising and marketing firms could rehabilitate your image by using traditional media channels to broadcast your newfound impetus to do good. Every interaction with a customer today can be reported on firsthand and passed around via network circles so that it reaches numbers far exceeding a Super Bowl ad.

The same can be said of our personal reputations: While once only a chosen few could build global reputations through a major book deal, public speaking, or by rising through the ranks of business, academia, or politics, today you can build a following of tens of thousands on Twitter simply through the power of good recommendations. This relevance-based clout-building exposes the ideas of anyone and everyone to a potentially global audience. Certainly, as with all previous roads to prominence, having thoughts and opinions that others deem worthy carries great sway. In this case, though, the barriers between a person and a capital reputation do not include the likes of rarified Ivy League pedigrees or birthright. Today, social capital can be amassed purely through the value of opinions, openness, and interaction. This is knowledge that the native comes by naturally and on which future reputations will be staked.

Prensky points out that, while some digital immigrants may dismiss online rating systems and recommendations as "intrusions, or wastes of time, natives know their online compass depends upon them and are often more eager to comply … Of course at the same time one is evaluating others' behavior and content, one is building up one's own reputation" ("The Emerging Online Life of the Digital Native," 2004, bit.ly/2tOezT).

This process of reputation building is maturing along with the native. According to Capgemini, "Members of online communities do not just discuss their favorite bands or films, but are also keen to share their own knowledge and experiences with others. This is evident from the growth in user contribution to sites such as Trip Advisor, Wikipedia, and Yahoo! Answers."

The transition from casual ranking to a willingness to share hard-won knowledge is not one that most digital immigrants will easily make. For most holding positions of power in academia or business today, their store of knowledge is what sets them apart from their peers. It represents a lifetime of hard work, education, and unique experiences. While all people learn from others and benefit from connections, the road to the top usually feels like a long and lonely one. This reinforces a mindset of privacy and knowledge hording.

Not so for the native.

## Knowledge Capital

As Prensky wrote, "In contrast with their parents, who used to love to keep any information they had secret ('Knowledge is power' was their motto) digital natives love to share and report information as soon as they receive it (perhaps 'Sharing knowledge is power' is their new, unvoiced, motto)" ("The Emerging Online Life of the Digital Native," 2004). Significantly, sharing valuable opinions and other information becomes part of a feedback loop, in which contributors are evaluated by the quality of their contributions and they build reputation as they go.

Increasingly, this community-based reputation has tangible value. It influences everything from online commerce to hiring decisions. And there are those who believe that beyond being a relatively intangible asset—like knowledge—reputation will form the basis of a new online currency, known in some circles as "Whuffie."

The term *Whuffie* is defined by Wikipedia as "the ephemeral, reputation-based currency of Cory Doctorow's science fiction novel, *Down and Out in the Magic Kingdom* (en.wikipedia.org/wiki/Whuffie, 2003). This book describes a post-scarcity economy: All the necessities (and most of the luxuries) of life are free for the taking. The term has since seen some adoption as a synonym for social capital."

From a business perspective, this concept is explored in Tara Hunt's book, *The Whuffie Factor* (Crown Business, 2009), which examines the ways companies can develop their Whuffie for marketing value, better customer engagement, and relationship management. Hunt also applies this pragmatic view to business professionals, contending that an individual's opinions, insights, responses, comments, feedback, and interactions with their network all add up to "currency," which they can "spend" to obtain things they desire, such as introductions to others, answers to questions, participation in projects, etc.

Understanding online reputation and how—like other aspects of social media—it must be viewed as an interactive relationship, in which everyone feels they give and receive, provides businesses with a distinct advantage. While Hunt focuses on the personal and organizational marketing aspects of Whuffie, there are other ways to leverage this native tendency for business advantage.

One way in which this may manifest itself is in extended enterprise communities—those that encompass not only employees but also include business partners and consumers. This idea is discussed in the *Social Computing Journal* article, "How Social Computing Will Improve the Enterprise Value Chain: 8 Predictions" (December 22, 2009). People management firm Saba predicts that in the "new post-Great Recession landscape'" we will see an era in which "learning connections will matter more than learning transactions."

The article proposes that, "When enterprise real-time collaboration becomes associated with learning and knowledge sharing, it can be self-reinforcing, enabling people to discover others who can help them in a grass-roots way, which in itself fosters information sharing." The authors encourage businesses to "share everything they can—smart and motivated people who can both contribute and gain access to lots of pertinent information will make better decisions."

Saba also predicts that employee performance within organizations could take a cue from the natural order of social networks online. They suggest that performance could "be judged by how much individuals contribute to their connected communities and that emergent thought leaders could be identified not only by monitoring how much they contribute, but more importantly, by evaluating how well their ideas and suggestions are received." Taking this further still, Saba envisions a future in which the traditional organization chart "will be replaced by social influence maps ... traditional hard-lined hierarchical organization structures will give way to the connections between employees, customers and partners across the extended value chain." While it might be difficult to conceive of how this would play out in the enterprise, it would essentially mean that those with the ideas and influence would lead a given endeavor, rather than an existing manager leading by default.

## Old Money, New Money

However, while there is incredible value to organizations and individuals that master web-based reputation to effectively build and monetize their businesses and careers, the notion of reputation-based currency has been taken up by others online. Beyond practical applications of "social capital" and "reputation branding," there are more extreme experiments afoot that provide insight into what the future of social capitalism may hold.

One ambitious foray into converting reputation into viable currency is that of the Ingenesist Project (www.ingenesist.com). This open source economic development program has been put forward "to challenge America's financial meltdown" by creating an innovation economy in which users trade rallods (*dollar* spelled backwards) backed by innovation. The Ingenesist Project claims to have identified three web applications which, when applied to social networks, "will allow human intellect, social capital, and creativity to become tangible outside the construct of Wall Street and Corporations."

Participants in the Ingenesist Project Development Forum will award rallods to each other on a reputation scale for their work in design, development, and improvement. While an actual currency with which one might buy bread may not emerge from the project, its founder has developed an "Innovation Bank," which he describes as "a knowledge inventory that contains knowledge assets that exists in the format of a financial instrument between people's ears and can be deployed for the purposes of increasing productivity."

Founder Dan Robles, though not a digital native himself, has tapped into some ideas that may well resonate with digital natives. According to Robles, "When things are really good, people need a currency that reflects productivity, not debt—i.e., social capitalism priorities, not necessarily Wall Street capitalism priorities." Robles's project promotes an open peer-based evaluation of productivity, something natives do daily in their evaluation of each other online. Essentially, Robles proposes a "meta-currency" that would tap into communal, knowledge-sharing behaviors to drive innovation (and as such, prosperity) forward.

Without a doubt, openness, collaboration, and sharing are high among the native's values. This is exemplified by RentAThing, which Dave Chiu and Didier Hillhorst undertook while they participated in the Applied Dreams project at Milan's Interaction Design Institute. RentAThing clearly illustrates the native's perspective on how reputation should factor into commercial transactions.

RentAThing is a tool for negotiation that provides additional information about the reputation of the parties involved in order to enable smoother transactions. Instead of silos of reputation, with various services, companies, and individuals developing isolated reputations,

RentAThing provides a centralized means of managing and developing a single reputation: *yours*.

As people go through life, they develop a reputation for things like paying bills on time, whether they return borrowed objects or money, how they treat the things they borrow, and so on. Given social networks, the notion of "credit rating" may well be transformed. These students suggest that, "In the future, with ... smart objects as actors in a world of ubiquitous information, objects could be rented to anyone at any time. Gaining access to those objects could be as simple as having a great reputation." Just as credit ratings affect one's ability to borrow money, RentAThing puts forward the notion that social reputation could be factored into negotiations by addressing risk, or that service providers, such as those in Amazon's marketplace, could improve their own reputations by choosing to do business with customers and businesses with high reputations.

While working on RentAThing, it was likely Chiu and Hillhorst had not yet entered the world of Better Business Bureaus and credit ratings. However, they instinctively believed that social reputation—something that is perpetually tracked online and that can be quantified and applied—will affect our ability to do business in the future.

The clearest example of social reputation as currency is the Whuffie Bank (www.thewhuffiebank.org). Founded in April 2009 by a group of digital natives inspired by Doctorow's vision, the Whuffie Bank is a nonprofit organization dedicated to building a new currency based on reputation that could be redeemed for real and virtual products and services. The higher your reputation, the wealthier you are. The founders suggest that, "In a world where reputation is wealth, only those who do good and well unto others are the richest ... That's the social change we want to achieve through the use of a new kind of currency as the Whuffie."

In a presentation at TechCrunch50, one of the Whuffie Bank's founders, Santiago Siri, somewhat simplistically correlated the evolution of modern currency to technological developments, pointing out that paper currency has its root in the printing press and credit cards in computers. He believes that today we have a new currency coming to the fore: social network reputations.

Whuffie bankers earn a monthly "Reputation Salary" calculated by how often the information they share is shared with others—for example, something they tweet via Twitter is then "retweeted" by others or a Facebook post is "liked." A Whuffie score is essentially based on how relevant your messages are to the people you're connected with. Those enrolled in the Whuffie Bank can offer Whuffies to others as payment, for example, they could ask for design services in exchange for 100 Whuffies. These social economic transactions can take place on the Whuffie Bank site or within the social networks it supports. The bank has also developed an API to allow third-party developers to incorporate these transactions on other sites.

While going out and doing a day's labor for a day's pay is a relatively clear proposition, reputation capital markets can be dauntingly uncertain. As the Whuffie Bank's FAQ page puts it, "Unlike capital, reputation is never under the control of a single individual, it always depends on your peers." Siri believes that the rising power of reputation as tracked through social networks and online information exchanges "changes the relationship you have with money … not as an accumulation of work or capital … to be wealthy on the Whuffie Bank, you have to be a person that is respected by other persons that are respected."

Despite the apparently altruistic intentions of these early experiments in social currency, crowdsourcing one's reputation has potential downsides as well. When we look at star ratings on Yelp or Amazon, for example, a disgruntled former employee or a malcontent might appear to have the power to bring down the average rating. However, it turns out that with consumer sites, this has not been the case as a rule. Having collected nearly 5 million customer reviews from more than 350 retailers,

PowerReviews InSite has a pretty clear picture of the distribution of product ratings, and it has found that "92 percent of all reviews are positive."

Additionally, while there may be a concern that an evil ex-roommate, boyfriend, or even a stranger could hold the power to damage one's Whuffie with ill will, many reputation-based systems only provide the opportunity for positive feedback such as re-tweeting, liking, and recommendations. This way, one has the option to act either in a positive way or not at all. However, as we see with the constructive influence of negative feedback on consumer products, when it is well intentioned, a bad review can have a good outcome in terms of improvement and engagement. It will be interesting to see how reputation-based monetization and social capitalism will factor the bad and ugly into their good work.

## Capital Ideas

These examples of experiments in social currency demonstrate how highly online reputation is valued and how it continues inevitably to increase in importance. As digital natives become business leaders, their lifelong experiences with web-enabled reputation building and reputation-based shopping and interaction will shape the way they expect to do business, as well as how they lead businesses of their own.

In his paper "Reputation as Property in Virtual Economies," Duke Law Professor Joseph Blocher writes:

> Reputation itself—social status and the respect of others— can usefully be understood as a form of property ... reputation can be property-like even without demonstrating economic value. Virtual reputational economies show that reputation can be gained, lost, traded, protected, and shared, all in property-like fashion, without regard to whether it has independent economic value ... This is the *reputational economy* exemplified by Myspace, Facebook, and gossip blogs. Status fortunes can be made in this economy, but they can

also be easily and quite dramatically lost." (Yale L.J. Pocket Part 120, 2009)

Reputation systems abound, such as star and thumbs-up or -down ratings, seller ratings on eBay, elaborate user reviews on sites like Yelp or TripAdvisor, and rating others' opinions on Yahoo! Answers. Through these avenues—as well as those emerging daily through social networking apps, social search algorithms, and more—reputation online is increasing in value at an exponential rate. Participating in the reputation economy will be a fundamental personal and professional activity going forward. There are fortunes to be made (and lost) by understanding how to invest wisely in the future of social capitalism.

## About the Contributor

**Michelle Manafy** is the director of content of FreePint, Ltd., a publisher of sites and resources for the business information industry. Michelle previously served as the editorial director of the Enterprise Group for Information Today, Inc. In this role, Michelle was editor-in-chief of *EContent* magazine and the *Intranets* newsletter. She was also the chair of Information Today's Enterprise Search Summits and the Buying & Selling eContent Conference. Michelle's focus is on the emerging trends in digital content and how they shape successful business practices. She has written on a variety of technology topics including digital publishing; social media; content development and distribution; streaming media; and audio, video, and storage technologies. Michelle speaks at a variety of industry events and serves as a judge for many content and technology competitions. She has worked in book and magazine publishing for more than 20 years in areas ranging from pop culture to academic nonfiction and holds a BA in Journalism from San Francisco State University.

## Recommended Reading

### Books and Articles

Crumlish, Christian. *The Power Of Many: How The Living Web Is Transforming Politics, Business, And Everyday Life*. Hoboken, NJ: Sybex, 2004.

Lessig, Lawrence. *Remix: Making Art and Commerce Thrive in the Hybrid Economy*. New York: Penguin, 2008.

Li, Charlene. *Groundswell: Winning in a World Transformed by Social Technologies*. Cambridge: Harvard Business School Press, 2008.

Shirky, Clay. *Here Comes Everybody: The Power of Organizing Without Organizations*. New York: Penguin, 2008.

Tapscott, Don and Williams, Anthony. *Wikinomics: How Mass Collaboration Changes Everything*. New York: Portfolio, 2006.

### Websites

Altimeter Group Blog, www.altimetergroup.com/blog

Conversation Agent, www.conversationagent.com

Groundswell Blog, blogs.forrester.com/groundswell

Mashable: The Social Media Guide, mashable.com

Web Ink Now, www.webinknow.com

# Part Three

# Entertaining the Digital Native

# CHAPTER 11

# The Digital Natives *Are* the Entertainment!

Richard Hull

I called my favorite neighborhood chicken wrap restaurant recently and was impressed to find that it had added a perky recording detailing its new items while I waited on hold. I was clearly motivated and hungry at that point, and as a result of this enticing menu recitation, I actually tried the suggested Chicken Caesar Wrap. But then the recording said, "Be sure to follow us on Twitter!" and I laughed loud enough to earn a disapproving glare from the new guy in my office. Let's face it, unless it saves me money (and even in spite of a borderline-obsessive love of chicken wraps), why would I care in the slightest what sort of minute-by-minute nuggets Frank's Chicken Wrap Café serves up on Twitter?

Frank's is certainly not alone in missing the point of mechanisms like Twitter. When companies perceive these new entertainment avenues as little more than pipelines for the same old marketing messages, it degrades their relationship with consumers. Unfortunately, this happens all too often.

As we examine the emerging entertainment marketing culture, let's discover why disobeying the rules within digital natives' indigenous entertainment zones can have particularly catastrophic consequences and learn how to navigate this largely uncharted territory.

## Fragmented Consumption

Fragmentation is the new reality. Gone are the days when a campaign of television spots would get the message across. However, the same can now be said in relying solely on a Facebook campaign. Digital natives are rewriting the rule book in that they consume entertainment through multiple avenues, often concurrently. They have an on-demand lifestyle that combines watching TiVo'd shows while trolling Facebook, peeking at YouTube, and texting friends. As underscored in an August 2010 Nielsen report, "Consumption of video across multiple platforms is now a global phenomenon …While technological and cultural variations put some markets ahead of others, online consumers in all corners of the globe have demonstrated their appetite for anytime, anywhere video consumption" ("How People Watch—The Global State of Video Consumption," bit.ly/g1QvXa).

Marketers must understand that this fragmentation has not only created a landscape with ever more pipes through which digital natives consume entertainment but also a new paradigm for accessing and creating the entertainment itself. Whereas traditional television networks could be compared to the one-stop shopping of Walmart, this fragmented reality is akin to a massive mall filled with limitless niche boutiques.

For instance, in the case of traditional entertainment distribution methods, a filmmaker might create a documentary film about purple tarantulas but could never expect any theater, DVD store, or major television network to offer it, as they all survive only if they serve the general masses. These days, however, there is likely a Facebook community where purple tarantula fans congregate. And thus, entertainment makers can now locate and leverage existing communities, or even go so far as to aggregate the correct niche audiences themselves for such highly targeted content.

As much as this new consumption pattern is driven by innovation and rebelliousness from outside the traditional media establishment, some entertainment companies are actually beginning to figure out how to funnel media to these fragmented pipes. While the model is still in flux, studios are working to deliver films in a way that can be described as "platform agnostic," meaning that they don't care where you get their films, just as long as you get them. Although these studios have been somewhat slow to adapt to emerging technologies, the lessons of the music business have forced them to admit that a movie must now be made available throughout a patchwork of theaters, retail outlets, Redbox kiosks, Netflix mailers, television screens, mobile devices, iTunes downloads, Xbox game consoles, video on demand channels, and more—and increasingly, all at the same time. Yet they cannot rest there, because new entertainment avenues and destinations pop up every day, so it is no surprise that, according to a July 2009 Pew Internet & American Life Project report, online video viewing through these sorts of emerging avenues nearly doubled over the prior three years.

This reality mandates a new standard of marketing in bits and pieces—call it *piecemeal marketing*. It changes the way successful entertainment companies market to digital natives and, additionally, how nonentertainment companies market to them using entertainment.

The problem is that a traditional "big brand" marketing machine is a behemoth propelled by its own momentum on a path that, today, only goes halfway to where it needs to go. Think of it as an Indy car that works best when it is racing at 200 miles per hour, hurtling toward the finish line. Using that powerful Indy car to market to digital natives in their fragmented entertainment universe, however, is akin to running the Indy car over a track made of Post It Notes. Native marketing is a difficult task—one that demands nuances and soft touches as much as massive media blitzes. And that has been a tough lesson for traditional marketers to learn.

## Consumers as Entertainment

As digital natives immerse themselves in these emerging entertainment channels—and concurrently force old ones to change in order to meet their expectations—they are reshaping the way people are entertained, as well as how they entertain. In the natives' world, the tools of content creation available through these emerging platforms are free (or cheap) and readily accessible. And they have been that way since a native first thumbed his name into a smartphone.

Natives find it exhilarating (or perhaps just a basic expectation born of their lifelong experiences with social media) that they, themselves, are the editors, directors, and actors in their own entertainment. This participation could be as routine as self-editing an online mashup containing clips from their favorite movie, it could be as voyeuristic as directing their own 24/7 life-casts, or it could be as wish-fulfilling as the role-playing involved in creating a Facebook profile that reflects the way that you want people to see you instead of the way you really are.

The big reveal then, is that digital natives in fact, *are* the entertainment. With this perspective, we realize that this is a generation that will not think twice about letting your cameras follow them through even the private intimacy and rejection of the search for true love. Each time a television network creates a new twist on the find-someone-to-marry reality show, they have to beat off 20-something potential contestants with a stick. This phenomenon is not difficult to understand when you realize that digital natives have never been without this all-access television genre. It makes them natural entertainers. And it puts a premium on their ability (or need) to have a voice in the simplest of ways: from posting hourly status updates on Facebook to engineering emotional webcam conversations with strangers on the other side of the world to creating videos that rally around a cool brand. And yet, as any Hollywood producer will tell you, dealing with entertainers can be a very delicate dance.

## Sneaking Into Their Watering Holes

With every *Wall Street Journal* article using the "social networking" vernacular, reactionary companies originally surmised that they should create their own social networks. However, when no one showed up at these standalone sites, companies had to face their harsh—and often expensive—miscalculations. Now, smart marketers are shifting their focus toward interacting with digital natives in their "natural habitat," particularly in social entertainment hubs Facebook and Myspace.

However, when entering the native realm, companies must play by the rules or risk being ousted by the community they seek to woo. In order to get noticed, brands are forced to feel around in the dark for the nuanced (and ever evolving) differences of each habitat—nuances that natives instinctively understand. Facebook, for instance, is about dialoguing with friends; Myspace is where one keeps up with musicians and celebrities; Twitter gives a personal, minute-by-minute connection with the idols and class clowns who revel in the spotlight; Hulu is where you go to watch a television show if your TiVo gets hit by lightning; and all of these specific sets of rules are subject to change tomorrow (or sooner).

An August 2009 Nielsen report found that, beyond simply being considered gathering spots, 18 percent of all online users also view these social media entertainment platforms as core navigation and information discovery tools. This is particularly significant when you consider that the same Nielsen report marks year-over-year growth of unique visitors to Twitter, from 2008 to 2009, at a whopping 959 percent, and in July, Nielsen reported that 22 percent of all time spent online was on social networks and blogs. Users are essentially looking to their *friends* to point them toward the information they desire. A shift is occurring from an information economy to a social economy; people are moving away from a sole reliance on using Google to get information and instead are looking to discover it also via social platforms like Facebook and Twitter. Digital natives are leading the shift, which offers exciting opportunities for marketers seeking fresh opportunities to forge closer connections with them.

"Moviegoers 2010," a report on movie-going habits by Stradella Road and Nielsen NRG, reinforces the reality that, as part of their interest in customizing their entertainment, movie-going crowds of teens and 20-somethings are particularly anxious to quickly share their opinions digitally. The report estimates that 94 percent of all moviegoers are now online, so the natives themselves become key in spreading word-of-mouth about movies, with a powerful 73 percent maintaining profiles on social networks and 58 percent acknowledging that they regularly socialize online with friends. Hollywood is realizing that digital natives are inclined to spend a good amount of time opining about movies via social networks, even though, in our fragmented world, 73 percent still say that they initially hear about a movie by seeing a 30-second TV commercial.

Yet we must remember that the guiding principle is that digital natives congregate at these locales to share entertainment and to have entertaining, digitally enabled conversations. Maybe they do talk about chicken, but don't mistake that for an invitation to pull up a chair and tell them how yummy your new wrap is. Rather, these are *entertainment* mediums, so you, as a company, have to entertain or get out. Considering that digital natives have themselves become the entertainment, the Holy Grail then becomes your ability to entertain so well in these environments (or, likewise, provide the tools to entertain) that natives actually become your ambassadors and start using their natural propensity to entertain to create their own entertainment around your brand for you.

The band Fatty Spins, for instance, wrote a down-and-dirty online hit song, "I Fell in Love at the Apple Store" (bit.ly/EeSuA), only to find the video (shot guerilla style at the Mac Store on New York's Fifth Avenue) receiving almost a million views on YouTube in its first three weeks and generating immeasurable online buzz. Let's face it, the song combines two of the digital natives' favorite pastimes—toying with technology and meeting girls—and it does so in a catchy and entertaining way that has Steve Jobs dancing right along.

Of course, viral video is a lot less fun when digital natives turn on you (dare we say they "go native"?) and create video rants, short films, or songs about how your product sucks. Consider the singer Dave Carroll, who fought with United Airlines for almost a year about reimbursement for his damaged Taylor guitar that had been checked as luggage. When United repeatedly refused to pony up, he and his band Sons of Maxwell recorded multiple songs trashing the airline, songs that—much to the dismay of big wigs of the friendly skies—found massive online viral audiences with almost 6 million views of the first song in its initial three months on YouTube (bit.ly/9vZ3uD). And its impact did not stop there, as the songs have taken on virtual lives of their own through video responses by Taylor Guitars, countless media reports, user comments, and hilarious parodies.

While each medium has its own subtle rules, the basic tenets of entertainment do not change just because you are watching something online. Key to the viral success of online entertainment is that it must actually be good. And it holds true too that advertising masquerading as entertainment must actually entertain. If it does, natives will embrace it. The July 2009 report by Nielsen Online found that audiences age 30 and younger are more inclined than older viewers to find relevant, online video advertising funny, emotionally touching, and informative—all qualities that become essential for native marketing in our new era. You can love or hate the Apple and United songs, but you cannot deny their engaging appeal, which will surely have you humming along.

While progressive marketers are making strides in placing their messages in the appropriate online spots, the strategy of their messaging, unfortunately, has hardly evolved. It is true that brands must seek to understand these new mediums on a philosophical level in order to properly craft messages without being offensive or irrelevant. But they also must explore them on more practical levels in order to identify the new opportunities associated with this entertainment. And there's no better way to learn about these new mediums than to be brave enough to just get out and do it.

## Go Forth and Experiment

It is no secret that digital natives do not watch traditional commercials. A 2009 Magna Global report confirmed that television's fastest growing network is, in fact, the DVR. As recently as November 2010, 37.2 percent of American households are equipped with DVR technology. Given this, brands are forced to try a variety of alternative techniques to reach these fast-forwarding time shifters. Many have tried online display ads, pre-rolls, and banners, which may have a place in a large campaign. Ultimately, though, these oversaturated devices have little impact on most digital natives, because the natives simply want be entertained and to entertain each other. By choosing to dive into these often uncharted entertainment waters, a marketer's challenge becomes one of having the cajones to *experiment* with ways that both cleverly entertain and channel the natives' culture of entertainment into actual purchasing. This experimentation clearly dictates that marketers must push to break some of the traditional rules of advertising, while still understanding—as noted by a July 2009 MTV Networks/InsightExpress study—that anything that feels intrusive, out-of-the-blue, or disruptive to the natives' entertainment experience immediately becomes offensive.

Take, for instance, the British company Cadbury, which created a one-minute viral video known as "The Eyebrow Dance." In it, a young boy and girl sit in chairs while "dancing" their raised then furrowed eyebrows to the beat of a techno song. The clip generated an impressive number of views—more than 4 million in the first month, according to Cadbury. And yet, while mildly entertaining, the video never delivers a message that would sell Cadbury chocolate. Instead, most of the comments on YouTube center on whether the eyebrow movements were real or digitally enhanced, with a few smart ones actually wondering how the clip sells candy. While a video of this sort may represent a moderate success for the PR department, it is not enough to simply plant random, quirky entertainment clips into social networks.

Luckily for Cadbury, this experiment likely did no harm beyond simply denting the company's checkbook. And in some respects, the audience applauded its willingness to take a swing. The good news is that if a message adheres to the correct philosophical ground rules—namely, that it does not feel like an ad and is, in fact, entertaining—digital natives have a high tolerance, and even respect, for experimentation. Still, respect probably won't sell chocolate (or anything else).

Where these one-off viral experiments may have actually succeeded is in punctuating specific lifestyles that are consistent with a brand—truly, *branded entertainment*. For instance, clothing magnate Marc Ecko reportedly generated well over 100 million views of his two-minute guerilla-style video clip, "Tagging Air Force One." In it, he jumps fences in shadows and sneaks close enough to Air Force One to tag its engine with graffiti saying "Still Free." The clip caused quite a stir until it was revealed as an elaborate—and wildly expensive—hoax that involved actually repainting a rented 747 airplane as Air Force One. But the video worked because it both wowed people quickly and promoted an irreverent, politically savvy, throw-caution-to-the-wind lifestyle associated with the Ecko brand and its audience. And as a one-off effort, it had the luxury of never having to consistently repeat, or even one-up, its own entertainment factor.

Though experimentation of this sort inherently involves conquering a fear of losing control, some mega-brands have taken the leap as well, and natives are taking notice. A 2009 study by Scott Galloway, associate professor of marketing at New York University's Stern School of Business, pointed out that Apple and Sony have been at the forefront of creating successful digital presences that incorporate video and (somewhat fear-inducing) user-generated content. The report notes that Ralph Lauren has also made notable, if cautious, strides with the launch of an iPhone app, as has Estée Lauder, which created a game-style makeover application that allows users to upload a photo and virtually test various products on their faces.

Hollywood has also made some meaningful efforts in its movie marketing to conquer its fear and let digital natives take the wheel. While it is difficult to break old habits, interesting experiments do break through and become significant cogs in a movie's marketing plan. For Walt Disney Pictures' 2010 release *When in Rome*, audiences saw a marketing campaign weighted in television and relatively well-established online locales. However, they also noticed a valiant effort to tap into Twitter, which many attribute to a well-coordinated behind-the-scenes push from strong insider executives on the corporate side and outside producers on the movie's side. In a lesson with far-reaching implications, Hollywood is starting to suspect that successes in this regard will elevate audiences' affinity not only for the movie itself but also for the corporate brand in general.

## Branding Together

Creating one-off online videos is surely a natural evolution of the tried-and-true model whereby a brand spends a lot of money on a video spot in the hopes of grabbing your attention quickly. However, common sense tells us that the most valuable audiences are those who consistently come back for more—something that is much harder than it looks. And so the boldest experimentation with branded entertainment is being done in a serialized, or episodic, fashion. These efforts attempt to generate advertiser-created entertainment that is at once engaging and highly targeted, and that somehow integrates itself with a product relevant to the native—and does so in a way that keeps the audience repeatedly coming back for more. Because episodic-branded entertainment does not fit the rules of old-school TV timelines, control structures, or business models, most efforts in this area have focused on exploiting online and occasionally mobile mediums.

The professional entertainment creators of Hollywood have been slow to come to the party, and so the early batches (and even many of the more recent offerings) of branded entertainment have not been very good. Second-tier advertising agencies, up-and-comers just out of film school, and amazingly copious numbers of ad salespersons slick enough to get a brand to buy in have been the players creating this content. And it shows. Quite simply, it feels fake. Given a savvy audience with whom truth and relevancy always prevail, fake is the kiss of death.

However, we are now entering the golden age of episodic-branded entertainment and things are getting incredibly exciting. If online episodic video content feels truthful and relevant, digital natives will not only tolerate it, they will seek it out. The live-action, scripted online video series, *The Guild*, for instance, began as multiple grassroots episodes exploring the relationships among a fictional team of players for the World of Warcraft online role-playing game. The roughly five-minute episodes were distributed through almost every online destination where digital natives watched videos—from YouTube to *The Guild*'s own website to dozens of destinations in between. And the bootstrapping paid off. Soon, a major Hollywood talent agency took notice, and brands like Microsoft's Xbox Live and Sprint came knocking.

More experienced Hollywood players are now following in the footsteps of these homegrown successes with their own, more evolved offerings. *Buffy the Vampire Slayer* creator Joss Whedon, for example, scored massive points with his aggressively loyal digital native fan base through his self-funded, three-part online series starring Neil Patrick Harris, *Dr. Horrible's Sing-Along Blog*. Established entertainment brands such as MTV are dipping their toes in as well, with short-form episodic series like *Valemont*, a video series that begins with clips aired on television and involves the search for a missing person. Verizon mobile phones play a major role in the series, and the entire mystery resolves online, thereby tying the television, online, and mobile platforms together.

While positive anecdotes of this sort abound, advertiser-created episodic-branded entertainment is still waiting for its first major break-out success story—and there will be huge dividends for the brand that accomplishes it. Perhaps the biggest obstacle is that many marketers continue to resist the concept that the natives actually want a voice in what the final product looks like. The age-old process of creating episodic entertainment and then hoping audiences will show up does not fit the playbook here. Creators of branded entertainment should take their cues from those emerging mediums that are showing the most robust signs of life—social games, virtual worlds, Twitter, and the like—which all exhibit an unconscious understanding that the digital natives *are* the entertainment. They are proving that when you treat your audiences with respect and indulge their need to have a voice, the entertainment you create for them—and even the entertainment they create on their own about your brand—will naturally adhere to your message. When you demonstrate an interest in playing on these sorts of leading edges in these entertainment mediums, you signal to digital natives that you might be worthy of their attention.

## Playing Their Games

Other emerging native entertainment forms remain underutilized by both entertainment and nonentertainment brands, and are surely worthy of increased experimentation. The games world in particular offers a considerable amount of available entertainment real estate that smart brands can tap into. Really, in some respects, games themselves are one of the early entertainment and monetization success stories of social media and social networking in general. In this regard, "social gaming" companies (such as

Zynga and Playfish) are emerging as powerful entities, with games that exist solely as applications on people's Facebook pages. Surprisingly, their consumers appear not to be the classic teen boy demographic but instead are the highly sought after "non-gamers" who nevertheless play games like Pet Society and Farmville, which appeal to all ages.

Moreover, virtual world games, like their cousins the social networks, are constantly evolving environments—from the early buzz-getters like Second Life to role-playing platforms like World of Warcraft to younger-skewing sites like Neopets (purchased in 2005 by Viacom for $160 million) and Club Penguin (purchased in 2008 by Disney for $700 million). In general, its seems to be the pattern that brands have learned that it is easier to associate with existing virtual worlds where natives already congregate than to try to create new ones entirely from scratch. While it is relatively easy to launch a virtual world, it has become obvious that the hard part is keeping it fresh every day with new content that brings people back and supports genuine engagement.

Engagement is the lifeblood of a virtual world (as it is in all native entertainment mediums). In May 2008, Nickelodeon announced that, thanks to the Neopets virtual world, its conglomerate of family- and child-oriented sites achieved an eye-popping 80 minutes of time spent per visitor per month. This announcement received considerable attention from other media companies and has inspired other brands such as Skittles to be particularly progressive in creating in-world virtual destinations where users can play games, create content, and watch video.

The 2008 report by interFuel, "Virtual Worlds for Kids, Tweens & Teens: 7 Must-Have Features," laid out guidelines for increasing engagement with virtual world marketing. Its tips included mantras such as it must be fun, fun, fun; it must provide fresh content so that it becomes part of a user's regular routine; it must provide ways to socialize with others; it must provide the user a feeling of control; and it must encourage creative self-expression. These rules drive the virtual worlds' conversion of engagement to purchasing and have led to an emerging and quite successful model known as *freemium*. With this strategy, sign-up and avatar creation are free, but pimping out that avatar will cost you. The sales potential of this sort of virtual goods can be limitless, and the model has spurred the creation of related sales mechanisms such as pre-paid cards. Put plainly, virtual goods are proving to be a way for virtual worlds, as well as the brands associating with them, to make copious amounts of money.

## All A-Twitter

It is important to remember that Twitter only works if you are listening as much as talking. Used in this way, it allows for real-time communication with your audience, and it may very well be one of the most under-utilized (and poorly utilized) native entertainment avenues today. Simply consider its power to pacify irritated natives: Motrin and Pepsi each launched ad campaigns that some people found offensive. Online chatter about both campaigns started in social networks and quickly spread to Twitter. Motrin had no mechanism to monitor mentions of its brand on the platform, but Pepsi's director of social media was paying attention, saw the controversy, responded publicly and in a personal manner, and quickly defused the negative situation created by the Pepsi ad.

In December 2010, the Pew Internet & American Life Project found that 14 percent of internet users ages 18–29 use Twitter—about double the number of those ages 30–49 or 50–64 ("Who Tweets," bit.ly/gBjtrD). While few brands have figured out how to sell products through Twitter, research seems to indicate that the type of user on Twitter is more likely to engage with a brand, even if they do not necessarily do it on Twitter per se. A 2009 report from tech and media research firm Interpret indicates that Twitter users are twice as likely to engage with brands—in multiple ways—than other social network users. Interpret found that roughly 24 percent of the respondents who use Twitter review or rate products online, compared with only 12 percent of people who use social networks but not Twitter. Twitter users are also almost twice as likely as non-Twitter users to visit company profiles and to click on ads or sponsored links. Clearly, these are people who crave the ability to influence and dialogue.

## All About the Conversation

In all of these emerging entertainment mediums, tailoring a brand message to the digital natives as entertainers must be built around a genuine back-and-forth conversation. Think of it more like telemarketing, which works because it is a conversation. While telemarketing scripts are expertly written in ways that push toward a specific goal—a *close*, if you will—they are inherently dialogues between people. So as a brand, it is your ability to provide and enable entertaining content that keeps the conversation going—a strategy we might call *content-as-a-conversation*. Conversely, having a Frank's Chicken Wrap Café junior marketing executive blindly send out chicken tweets on Twitter is a one-way push that is unlikely to spark any conversation.

While it is hard to be too open with the natives in a conversation, it is easy to be too aggressive, because digital natives visit their entertainment watering holes to be entertained, not to buy things. When you blatantly push them to buy your product, you lose their trust. Here, we might look to Hollywood for a lesson in relationship building: This is an art form that reality television producers demonstrate handily in their day-to-day relationships with show contestants. (Here, the producers' role is analogous to a brand's efforts to build trust with digital natives.) Over the course of filming, a reality TV producer builds up an authentic, if fleeting, friendship with the star. During the first week of shooting, the producer only asks the star to do simple, non-threatening tasks, such as picking the woman he most obviously would not marry and dismissing her from the show.

However, by the fourth week of shooting, their relationship has developed to an extent that the producer can increasingly push the star toward dastardly deeds like kissing multiple suitors and pitting friends against each other. While the star would have been reluctant to do these things initially, he is more than happy to indulge his new friend, the producer, by week four. It is a function of trust. The producer's goal is to make a great show, overflowing with tension, drama, and intrigue—a show that will hook the audience. In turn, a successful show leads to the fame and adulation that the reality star ultimately wants but would not have achieved if left to his own mild-mannered devices.

The same holds true for brands that find inroads into entertainment locales where natives congregate. Start the conversation simply. Engage with the native and build trust. Inch toward the close by saving the hard stuff until after you have established that trust. Then, convince the native that your product helped him get what he always wanted in the first place. Since digital natives are all at once consumers, commenters, and entertainers, it is an approach built on truly engaging them in the conversation. With this in mind, Frank's Chicken Wrap Café might consider starting a conversation with digital natives via in-store signage that encourages them to "help us choose new items by joining in real-time brainstorming on Twitter." Such an effort imparts that customer feedback is key to the outcome and that maybe the most vocal participants might be rewarded with free food, gear, or acclaim for their efforts.

## Who Am I Talking To?

Within these entertainment venue conversations, marketers must adjust their expectations regarding the sort of information they expect to gather and really, the sort of information they use in making their own marketing decisions. They need to focus more on the emotional and activity-related components of the people they are marketing to, rather than simply the traditional demographic hard numbers—in other words, on *psychographics* instead of *demographics*. Ultimately, such a shift actually allows marketers to gather much more highly personalized information, the kind that really tells you what makes a particular native tick—likes, dislikes, emotional needs.

Evolving beyond hard-and-fast demographics is an understanding that, in this new world, you never quite know who you are talking to. A Facebook profile may say age 99, 26, or 17, and none of these ages may be accurate. This phenomenon can be traced back to the digital natives' need to entertain. Their online identities are built upon a series of self-reported profiles at various sites where it is OK to represent yourself the way you want people to see you. This could mean building an avatar that sports the hippest fashions when you, yourself, are quite style-challenged, or reporting your age as 25 instead of 18 because you aspire to appear more mature. With Neopets, for example, you are allowed to create up to five profiles, which means you get to be anyone you want ... five times over. Hollywood calls this phenomenon wish *fulfillment*. In these virtual worlds, digital natives do not see these as lies but rather as free passes to craft personas that they (and their peers) find inherently more entertaining.

Moving beyond pure demographics means also being brave enough to not make decisions based upon guaranteed eyeballs alone. Embarking upon new paths of this sort can be nerve-wracking trips dominated instead by gut instinct decisions, particularly because, while the major measurement services have adequately conducted generic usage surveys, they have been largely ineffective at measuring the impact of specific content spread across the multiple nodes of the digital domain. This keeps many old-school media types away for fear of losing their jobs when they cannot point to specific demographic and quantitative measurements. It is still an unfortunate reality in most of the media world that if you cannot count eyeballs (or at least point to someone else's faulty measurements and thus shift the blame), you get fired. But in this new world, guaranteed impressions take a backseat to entertaining the right audience in the right way. If digital natives themselves are the entertainment, then logic dictates that advertisers who wish to create these truthful, on-going, two-way conversations would do well to adopt the same intense focus on emotional, lifestyle-oriented connections that Hollywood films and television programs perfected long ago ... and to do it across a plethora of mediums.

## Where Are the Lines?

As we move forward over the coming years, we will see that, once you have hooked the natives into the conversation in one entertainment medium, you will have the opportunity to segue to other mediums. Consider Aaron Karo, who started emailing a few friends his ruminations on college life from a University of Pennsylvania dorm room. Those email exchanges led to Karo's book *Ruminations on College Life* (now in its ninth printing) and the *Ruminations on Twentysomething Life* sequel, both published by Simon & Schuster. A third book, *I'm Having More Fun Than You*, which explores Karo's thoughts on being the only single 30-year-old male among his friends, was published by HarperCollins and became a number one humor seller on Amazon. The writer continues to exploit his online success for recognition in the offline world of books, movies, television, and stand-up comedy, all while continuing the conversation with his fans through his email newsletters and Ruminations.com website. Savvy brands will soon be able to do the same as they learn to seamlessly move the digital native from Facebook to television to mobile apps to even some of the newer entertainment mediums like the mobile internet and the networks of flat-screen televisions popping up in retail locations.

In the digital native universe, the lines between marketing, entertainment mediums, and entertainment itself are no longer merely blurred; they are vanishing altogether. In fact, you might argue that the success stories are coming from those who attempt to perforate the lines in numerous places. In a world where passive television viewing has only a limited place, because you cannot fast forward through the broadcast, you have to ask yourself: If your brand was a human, would I be friends with it? And today, the answer lies in how much that brand entertains and how that brand enables *me* to do the entertaining. In a word (or maybe up to 140 characters), marketers should have fun. Experiment. Chill out. Be creative. And rejoice when your customers are creative around you. When digital natives love a brand, they naturally want to engage with it. With that engagement as the new currency of marketing to the natives, may you go forth and experiment, and build brands and revenue streams while you do it.

## About the Contributor

**Richard Hull** occupies a rare position at the heart of traditional entertainment, digital media, and finance: He is an expert on using entertainment to market content to teen and young adult audiences. Richard was most recently recruited to salvage and rebuild the asset value of Blowtorch Media & Entertainment, a company backed by Ignition Partners, a venture capital firm comprised of early Microsoft employees with almost $2 billion under management. Previously, as an early pioneer in Hollywood's charge toward online and mobile content, Richard created and led digital entertainment and finance strategies for major media companies such as Warner Bros., Walt Disney Company, Universal Studios, and MTV Networks, as well as major private equity and venture capital groups. A former film and television producer/financier constantly on the leading edge of market trends, he quickly proved himself as one the most sought-after experts in the business, with collaborations that include virtually every major studio and network. His 20-plus projects, primarily geared toward teen and young-adult audiences, have grossed hundreds of millions of dollars worldwide and include films like *She's All That*, one of the most successful teen movies in history.

## Recommended Reading

Advertising Age, adage.com

Digital Hollywood Conference, www.digitalhollywood.com

EContent, www.econtentmag.com

paidContent.org, paidcontent.org

TechCrunch, techcrunch.com

Variety, www.variety.com

# CHAPTER 12

# Ethics, Technology, and the Net Generation: Rethinking IP Law

Albert M. Erisman

Ethics is something we contemplate on a daily basis, though we are often unaware that we are doing it. It is simply identifying right and wrong. Yet in our highly digitized society, understanding how the introduction of new technology changes the ethics agenda requires our increasing awareness. Digital natives, who are very comfortable with technology and don't relate well to the pre-digital world where many of today's laws and practices were established, are faced with ethical dilemmas they may not even have considered. The intersection of technology and ethics will continue to be a messy place for some time to come, and digital natives will be embroiled in the midst of it. We can expect future technological developments to take us to places even digital natives may not find comfortable.

While there are copious advantages to the global digital connections of our newfound era, there are downsides as well. More connectivity means more and more people can use technology for nefarious ends. We can readily move from place to place with a smart card, and then find that our movements can be tracked, violating our privacy. Numerous publications have explored the way technology changes people and society. My favorites include Neil Postman's *Technopoly: The Surrender of Culture to Technology* (1992), Robert Reich's *The Future of Success: Working and Living in the New Economy* (2002), and Don Tapscott's *Grown Up Digital: How the Net Generation is Changing Your World* (2009). This societal transformation raises important ethical questions. At the moment, we are experiencing a cross-generational, cross-cultural divide over understandings of right and wrong. Digital natives have inherited a technology-laden world replete with pressing ethical questions that must be resolved.

I have organized this chapter into three sections. I begin by defining what I mean by ethics. I then introduce the relationship between digital technology and ethics. Finally, I explore the intersection of these topics as they relate to digital natives and their digital world, specifically in regard to Intellectual Property Law.

## Ethics Primer

People often associate ethics with simply staying out of trouble. For some this means simply knowing the law and not violating it. This area is called compliance, and it is an important part of the ethics agenda. Ethics, however, is much more than obeying the law. I argue that ethics is about three things:

1. Knowing the law and not violating it (but recognizing where the law is inappropriate and working to change it)

2. Acting appropriately where there is no applicable law

3. Doing the right thing

Where there is clear law, we need to follow it (or change it). There are penalties associated with violating the law. Society can even break down when legal violations are commonplace. Unfortunately, most of us tend to approach the law from a self-centered point of view. For example, in the rules of the road, "red light stop, green light go" is well accepted because our lives would be in peril if it weren't. But "speed limit 60 miles/hr" is often less readily accepted because the interpretation of a safe driving speed varies widely. And intellectual property laws are often much murkier.

Add to this the fact that the subject of the law becomes vastly more complex in an increasingly globalized world, in which laws and enforcement practices differ from one country to another (see *Asia's New Crisis*, 2004, edited by Richter and Mar). Compliance issues can be very challenging for 21st-century global citizens, particularly those working in a global business.

The law cannot be the only restraint on behavior because it cannot ever be detailed enough to cover everything. Further, it tends to look backwards to address problems where egregious behavior took place in business or society but the actions in question were perfectly legal. For example, in the U.S., the Sarbanes-Oxley Act of 2002 added numerous controls to the way financial issues needed to be disclosed and also placed limits on the way a company's auditors could do consulting as well as auditing for the same company. These rules were put in place because of the abuses of Enron.

On the other hand, we have laws on the books created in a pre-digital era that may no longer be appropriate. In *Remix* (Penguin, 2008), Lawrence Lessig points out that our intellectual property laws make criminal the popular activity of creating new cultural artifacts (remixed songs and videos, for example) by our younger generation. He advocates re-examining these laws in light of what technology now makes possible and current practices by digital natives.

However, outside the law, there is the large gray area where it is not good enough simply to ask, "What does the law say?" It would be impossible to create laws for everything, and no one would want to live in a society that tried to do so. Additionally, emerging technology opens doors to things that were not previously possible, and hence to areas where no laws exist. In these cases, we must rely on ethics.

When considering whether something is "right," the ethical person might ask, "What if my actions were to appear in the newspaper?" or "What would my mother say?" For the digital native, this ethical litmus test might be, "What if my actions were the subject of a popular blog?" In these situations, ethical behavior is not about avoiding arrest but rather focused on what might others think of what the person did.

This may seem like a very personal, subjective approach, and one might think that it would be difficult to gain agreement on what this would look like in our pluralistic world. But in fact, ethics is usually based on foundational virtues and practices that have widespread acceptance in the world. Aristotle suggested that there is a set of virtues that are broadly held and that are at the foundation of a just and vibrant society. Examples include collaboration, excellence, courage, humility, and many others that continue to be broadly accepted across the globe. We may also consider a set of universal practices (for example, value life, value property, and tell the truth) that are part of a just society. These virtues and practices serve as a basis for evaluating appropriate action. Though for many people, such virtues and practices are rooted in their religious faith or code of personal conduct, there is remarkable agreement across the world and across the ages at this level. Some ethicists also consider the outcomes of a particular decision, evaluating it on the basis of what happens and who gets harmed when the decision is made.

However, there are two other fundamental points we need to make about ethical practice. For some, the question is: How do I draw the line between right and wrong and then make sure to be on the "right" side of that line? In other words, the goal is to avoid doing wrong, whether breaking the law or making a decision when there is no law. I refer to this as "damage control" ethics since the focus is on avoiding damage to my reputation or to others. A second approach is to think carefully about the kind of person you want to be and what you have committed to do, and make a decision on the basis of doing what is right, what best aligns with your personal mission. I call this "mission control" ethics. The distinction is between trying to get by with minimal criticism and staying focused on what is right.

The second point about ethical practice is to recognize the difference between knowing what to do and doing it. Many people draw on their religious faith or personal moral commitment for support in this area, but it is an area none of us will solve completely. I have talked with many digital natives (my students in particular) who acknowledge that it is wrong to illegally download music, but (like many older people) they do it anyway.

## Solving an Ethics Problem

There is a tendency for many of us to approach ethic problems in a very personal way. But ethics is a matter not simply of opinion but of reasoned opinion. There are many models for considering an ethics challenge, and I will offer one here as well, in five steps:

1. Ethical awareness and sensitivity: Identifies the ethical decisions in the case, gathers facts, and identifies what decision needs to be made

2. Stakeholder considerations: Identifies who is impacted by the issues, including those who are secondarily involved; understands their viewpoints and legitimate interests and considers possible tradeoffs

3. Ethical values and theories: Identifies the set of values and principles for the individual or organization involved in the decision

4. Consideration of alternative actions and potential consequences: Plays out the consequences of the decision both short term and long term; engages others in understanding the potential outcomes

5. Takes action: Identifies needed communication; looks for potential secondary decisions that may need to be made

Skill and experience are required at each step of the process. The third step in particular draws on the virtue and practice discussion earlier. This step suggests that each person should think through in advance what they stand for and what kind of person they want to be. The fourth step requires thinking through what might happen when a particular decision is made. It is here where we might need another perspective, because in a tough call, we may not have the objectivity we need for the decision.

Consider the application of this model to intellectual property law. It might be tempting to say that reusing digital content must be acceptable since it is so easy to do and so many are doing it. Step 1 would cause us to think about the law. Step 2 might bring the rights of the artists and publishers into consideration, in addition to our own rights. This would call for making tradeoffs as the model suggests. Step 3 might cause us to think about the value of fairness. Finally, Step 4 would force us to consider alternatives beyond what everybody is doing.

Before addressing other examples of ethical decisions, I will look briefly at the significant impact of technology on the ethics agenda.

## Technology and Ethics

Technology has a strong impact on all three areas of the ethical agenda. (Is it legal? Is it appropriate? Is it good?) At the heart of this observation is the fact that technology often allows us to do things we have never done before. We have little shared wisdom or experience in this new place, and it takes time and judgment to determine the right thing to do.

There are two ways technology affects the *role of law* in ethics. First, in many cases there are no applicable laws because the situation is new. For example, digital natives are used to always being connected to people and information. What happens when they get behind the wheel of an automobile? In this case, the law varies. In some places, there is no law against texting or talking on the phone while driving, while in other places, it is legal to talk while driving only if you are using a hands-free device.

On the other hand, laws persist on the books that made sense before technology but make little sense in light of the new capabilities. Lessig (2008) provides an interesting parallel with an earlier technology: the airplane. Early land ownership included property rights that extended below the surface of the land owned and above it indefinitely. This worked fine until 20th-century flying machines appeared, and then the law desperately needed to be changed. It is more than unreasonable to require airlines to pay fees to every property owner they passed over. In this case, after a period of uncertainty, the law was ultimately changed to meet the realities of the new technology of that day.

Another example involves the definition of stealing. In an earlier era, stealing was understood as my taking something belonging to you so that in the end, I have the object in question and you do not. However, in the digital era, I can have the object and so can you. This modifies the concept of stealing. The same goes for trespassing. If there are no physical borders, it is difficult to determine whether someone who pokes around in your computer, but doesn't take anything, has broken the law.

Technology also affects the second question in the ethical agenda: Is it appropriate? Returning to the example of talking on the phone while driving, in some places there is no law against it, particularly if a hands-free device is used. In determining whether this is appropriate, however, we should consider our model again. Who might be impacted by our decision? Research shows that talking on the phone while driving results in the reaction-time equivalent of drunk driving. How does this fact affect our decision?

Take another example: Digital natives post things on social network sites they would not want to share with prospective employers, not thinking through the fact that a prospective employer can find all sorts of things about them on the internet. Take, for example, a young person who posts a "party picture" on a social network. Such a picture can live in cyberspace indefinitely, and the person who posts the picture may not even be able to remove it later when applying for a job. Tapscott (*Grown Up Digital*, 2009) warns, "Some day that party picture is going to bite them when they seek a corporate job or public office." Things people do every day turn out to be inappropriate in other contexts.

In all of these examples, digital natives focused on "damage control" ask whether they can get by with it. The "mission control" natives ask if their decision fits with their values and does good for society. The second requires more careful thinking than the first.

The digital world we now live in has a strong impact on the ethics agenda and raises new questions about the law, appropriate behavior, and even what it means to do the right thing, to guide the mission, either personal or organizational. Digital technology is constantly introducing new products, services, or ideas that demand new inquiry regarding ethical behavior. Digital natives are therefore faced with ethical questions they may not even be aware of. The media is one area where these questions abound.

## Innocent Entertainment or Unethical Behavior?

Reducing text, pictures, music, and video to a series of 1s and 0s raises a whole array of new ethical questions. Applying the ethics model outlined here serves to illustrate the difficulties digital natives are confronted with as they consider what the right choice might be.

With inexpensive, easy-to-use tools, digital natives with little training or money can modify a picture, thus blurring the line between photographic record and fiction, something that was relegated to professionals only a few years ago. This behavior presents no legal problem as long as the rights of the photographer and/or the subject are not violated. It is easy to come up with innocent, creative, and fun applications for these tools. Yet, potentially less innocent uses also exist: A photograph that could mislead jurors in the courtroom; a touched-up photo designed to deceive; photos modified to sell products. In these less obvious cases, it is helpful to think through what should be done using the model for solving ethical problems:

1. Start by identifying the issues in the situation. What are the facts? What is the intent?

2. Next figure out who is impacted. Is it an unsuspecting buyer? Is it a guilty person who might get away with a crime? Is it my own reputation?

3. Then consider your own set of values and commitments: How would actions affect who I am and desire to be? What might happen in our community if everyone did the kind of thing I am considering doing?

4. With several possible paths to take, it is helpful to identify how each path might play out. Who might get hurt? How might an objective third party help me see the issues more clearly? One thing I might think about here is what might happen if the action I take is destructive to others and many other people do something similar. In addition to people getting hurt, new laws are likely to be created, adding another legal burden.

5. Finally, you need to take action. Ethics is not about simply thinking about something. It also involves making a decision and taking action.

## Digital Piracy vs. Sharing the Goods

Illegal content-copying is nothing new. In the 1970s, I visited a friend's home in Budapest and noticed he had a two-volume mathematics text by an author I knew. I expressed surprise to see it in two volumes, because I had always seen the book in one volume. Then he showed me that it was in fact a one-sided copy, nicely bound (although the title was misspelled on the second volume) and available for purchase in Budapest. As I thought about that book, I realized the copy had been expensive to make and bind. Perhaps as expensive as buying a new copy at a book store. The reason the book was available in this bulky format was because original copies were simply not available in Hungary at that time.

Today we see the same scenario played out but with some important differences. In the digital world, copying and shipping a book, music, or video in digital form is both instantaneous and free. In the case of the book in Budapest, there was no monetary motivation to make such a copy, only a motivation based on (lack of) availability. In the digital world that natives inhabit, there is a huge monetary difference.

Chris Anderson makes the following point in his book *Free* (Hyperion, 2009): When digital technology makes it possible to make and distribute copies instantly at effectively no cost, the world becomes a very different place. In spite of the clear illegality of this behavior, piracy is rampant in all parts of our world, particularly among digital natives. There are many reports indicating that file sharing of music and games is commonplace and that many do not see the activity as being wrong. Statements like, "Everybody does it," "I can't afford to buy it," or "I am only testing it and will perhaps purchase the music if I like it" are commonplace and used to validate the behavior. Yet the artists don't get paid and publishers who invested in the projects don't get paid either.

Regardless of whether it is easy, it seems right, or everybody is doing it, it is hard to make the case that such file sharing is ethical. We can't get past the first question in our ethical test: Is it legal?

## I Mix, You Mix, We All Remix

In 2005, YouTube was founded by three former employees of PayPal to enable anyone to share videos with the world. We have now moved from sharing protected content to creating content. However, it is the way this content is created that causes it to run up against the law again. With a $1,500 computer and free or inexpensive software, anyone—not just professionals—can combine video and music into new art forms called remixes or mashes.

The basic idea is to combine music from one or more artists into a new mix, often including video content from films and news sources, to make a statement that none of the pieces was originally intended to make. My favorite example of such a remix is the video of George W. Bush and Tony Blair singing "Endless Love" to each other. You can find it by Googling *Bush, Blair, Endless Love*. It is the work of an amazing editor who managed to match the lip movements of the protagonists (Bush and Blair) in clips lifted from the news and combine the video with the song. It is an incredible demonstration of what can be done relatively simply today, though it could have only been done by professionals with very expensive equipment less than a decade ago. It is also illegal, because the individual pieces from which this video is made are private property.

## Problems With the Law

Now here is the challenging issue: We would say it is unethical to create such remixes because we can't get past the first ethical question, "Is it legal?" In some of these areas at least, the digital native's behavior may well pass the appropriateness test, "Is it appropriate?" For many, the "mom" test for this question would be no problem: Mom either doesn't care or thinks it's as funny as we do. The question to ask is whether we are in a situation where the law protecting digital content is outdated because of digital technology currently available.

Lessig (*Remix*, 2008) and Anderson (*Free*, 2009*)* argue "yes." Lessig says that we have reached the point where there is a growing divide in our societies. On one side are those who would vigorously defend the laws already in effect. To support these laws, products are being developed to find and track down anyone who posts a video to YouTube containing any copyrighted material. There are products for identifying file sharers as well. There is a growing effort in both America and Europe to prosecute violators, many of them digital natives. On the other side is a generation that is increasingly thumbing its nose at the law. Digital natives may or may not be consciously choosing to live their lives beyond the law, but the fact is that more and more of them are doing so.

Anderson makes the point that digital content "wants to be free." We need a new model, he says, where digital recordings are used for promotion, not for sale. Digital files (music videos, for example) would be a form of advertising for the artists, who would make their money from concerts and other sales rather than from the digital content.

Not everyone agrees with these proposals. One author holding out for the existing law is Jaron Lanier, one of the founders of the artificial intelligence movement in computer science. In his book, *You Are Not a Gadget: A Manifesto* (Knopf, 2010), he calls for greater protection of digital rights on the basis that the loss of these rights will stifle the creative work of many artists.

## New Laws for a New World

Lessig supports the right of artists to protect their work but not in the restrictive way it is done today. He proposes two directions for changes in the law. First, he suggests extending the "fair use" concept to digital content beyond text. In the text world, at least in America, "fair use" is associated with quoting text from a copyrighted article. As long as the source is credited and the amount of text is small (a subjective measure left purposely vague), no prior permission from the owner of the material is required. To date, however, no "fair use" exclusion exists for video or music, likely because when the laws were established, no one thought of these media types as candidates for "quoting." Thus to create a remix (now quick, easy, and widespread) legally, you would need advance approval from the corporations owning the rights, and there is little incentive for them to offer such approval. Most digital native remixes are made for sharing rather than for commercial use. Adding fair use rights for video and audio "texts" would clear up the ethical issues remixers are currently faced with.

Lessig also has offered a variation on the open source software concept, Creative Commons (creativecommons.org), for managing rights to digital content. Using Creative Commons, individual artists decide to share their digital content, and various forms of creative commons licenses allow them to offer much more flexible terms for the reuse of their content. If the choice to share comes from the artist, some of the more restrictive laws would be irrelevant. Until this approach becomes the way all artists choose to work or corporate content makers get on board, the issues of legality remain.

Another idea that does not involve changing the law, but simply changing practice, might be for publishers to offer various levels of pricing for music and video, the way today's software is offered—with a steep discount for students. At Seattle Pacific University, a student can buy Microsoft products for a fraction of what they cost on the market. Microsoft apparently views this as a marketing opportunity. Perhaps this could be done with music and video as well (e.g., download a song for 10 cents rather than for 99 cents. It is difficult to know whether students would still copy files if they could get them legally for such a small amount, but it certainly seems worth trying. (Of course, the act of paying for the content needs to be as easy as, if not easier than, stealing it.)

Of primary concern to Lessig is the untenable position we are in at the present. It is more than an issue over a law that is broken, he argues. Rather, when a large group of people begins to live its life against the law, as is the case with the significant percent of digital natives who copy and share protected digital content, it is "extraordinarily corrosive and corrupting" for society as a whole.

## The Digital Native's Dilemma

The advances in technology have created the opportunity to easily do things that used to be difficult and expensive. Whether sharing music and video or creating new art through photo editing and remixing, digital natives have grown up doing these things with little regard for content rights. Some of them do not know it is illegal, some simply don't care, while others believe it is OK to disregard the law since it doesn't make sense in a digital era. I have identified some areas where proposed changes in the law are being considered. Changing the law, however, is a long and difficult process. Some alternative practices that publishers could offer would perhaps help the situation, but these have not yet been tried. There are some alternatives for artists who would choose to share their content more freely, though most have not gone in this direction.

At this point, digital natives are confronted with a choice. To act ethically, a person must pass through the first question. There is the option to work for change in the law, and I would challenge many digital natives to get engaged in thinking about this and to participate in making such changes real. The changes must consider all of those involved, not just the one who wants access to the content. To act ethically, we need to act legally as well.

In discussing this with many natives, I have heard the response, "Isn't civil disobedience a way to change the law? Isn't that what was done to eliminate laws supporting segregation, for example?" Indeed, in situations where a deep moral principle is involved, disregarding the law may be the best approach. However, is it possible to suggest that not wanting to pay for music or video content is a deep moral issue?

For example, people who are poor simply can't afford the digital content, and since there is no cost to copy and ship it, isn't it only reasonable for them to copy it? Perhaps this would be a good argument for basic necessities of life: food, clothing, shelter, adequate healthcare. I would be hard pressed to agree that digital content sharing could be justified today on this basis, but it may not be outside the realm of digital natives' thinking. When you can move the conversation from "I didn't know it is illegal," "I don't care," or "Everybody is doing it" to building a case for a moral imperative, then we are making progress. In the meantime, we all need to work toward rethinking laws that no longer fit the digital era.

## Conclusion

Ethics is more than a matter of opinion. It involves careful thinking and action according to a set of principles and virtues that enable a just society and support its missions. Technology has played a strong role in creating change at every level of our lives, from work to play to personal life. It has also created many new situations where we have little wisdom and experience to guide us. Technology challenges ethical traditions. When these changes and challenges come together in digital media, it is no wonder we have a great deal of uncertainty and confusion.

We have arrived at a version of the "tragedy of the commons." When people walk past a vacant lot filled with litter, it is all too easy for them to add their own trash to the pile. If the same people walk past a well-manicured lawn, they would not think of tossing their trash there. So it is with ethics applied to digital media in our digital world. As Lessig said, when a society lives against the law, it has a corrosive and corrupting affect. This needs to be fixed. While it is being fixed, each of us individually (digital native or not) needs to think carefully about making right choices. We need to remember that as technology continues to develop over time, we will keep walking into the land of the unknown and need to start processing all of this again.

## About the Contributor

**Albert M. Erisman** is executive in residence at Seattle Pacific University and executive editor and co-founder of *Ethix* magazine (www.ethix.org). He spent 32 years at the Boeing Company, the last 11 as director of technology, managing a staff of 300 computer scientists and mathematicians pursuing new technology ideas for products and processes of Boeing. Since 2001, he has been in his present position examining issues at the intersection of business, technology, and ethics.

## Recommended Reading

### Books and Articles

Anderson, Chris. *Free: The Future of a Radical Price.* New York: Hyperion, 2009.

Brown, John Seely and Paul Duguid. *The Social Life of Information.* Boston: Harvard Business School Press, 2000.

Downes, Larry. *The Laws of Disruption: Harnessing the New Forces that Govern Life and Business in the Digital Age.* New York: Basic Books, 2009.

Lanier, Jaron. *You Are Not a Gadget.* New York: Knopf, 2010.

Lessig, Lawrence. *Remix: Making Art and Commerce Thrive in the Hybrid Economy.* New York: Penguin, 2008.

Negroponte, Nicholas. *Being Digital.* New York: Vintage Books, 1995.

Postman, Neil. *Technopoly: The Surrender of Culture to Technology.* New York: Knopf, 1992.

Reich, Robert. *The Future of Success: Working and Living in the New Economy.* New York: Vintage, 2000.

Richter, Frank-Jürgen and Pamela C. M. Mar. *Asia's New Crisis: Renewal Through Total Ethical Management.* Hoboken: John Wiley & Sons, 2004.

Seidensticker, Robert B. *Future Hype: The Myths of Technology Change.* San Francisco: Berrett-Koehler Publishers, 2006.

Tapscott, Donald. *Grown Up Digital: How the Net Generation Is Changing Your World.* New York: McGraw-Hill, 2009.

### Websites

Center for Social Media, www.centerforsocialmedia.org

Ethix, ethix.org

Fast Company, www.fastcompany.com

Wired, www.wired.com

# The Old News and the Good News: Engaging Emerging Readers Through Social Interaction

Michelle Manafy

It's not news that magazines are anorexic, newspapers are dropping in droves, and industry leaders are calling for solutions that range from forbidding the use of headlines for linking to building mile-high pay walls around anything and everything. It feels frantic, even desperate.

Though tempting, it would be a mistake to write off the dire state of the news business as simply a reflection of the general decline in print readership since the rise of the internet or as just another casualty of the recession. The problems run deeper: Print media came late to the internet party, viewing online distribution as "cannibalizing print readership." And, in large part, once media brands came online, they often viewed their sites as little more than an additional outlet for their print content, reproduced word for word. Then, for better or worse, they offered this content for free on websites, though the same content in print products may have garnered subscription fees.

While print may never go away, the days of newspaper's print preeminence are passing us by. Beset upon by myriad free alternatives and nimble web-native news outlets, venerable brands have been forced to slash staff, go digital only, and reduce the frequency of print delivery. In 2009, the Tribune Co. filed for Chapter 11. The *Seattle Post-Intelligencer* and *Rocky Mountain News* are among the numerous newspapers that have closed altogether, and the Pew Project for Excellence in Journalism reported that, by the end of 2010, roughly one-third of journalistic jobs that existed in 2001 will be gone. To make things worse, the newspaper industry finds itself in this sorry state just as a new generation enters the work force, one with less connection to traditional news media than ever before—the digital native.

## Meet the Next Generation of Consumers

Digital natives are voracious content consumers. However, they have grown up surrounded by so much media that it has lost its value, at least in the sense of price point. Awash in a sea of information, this generation not surprisingly has little connection with any one source. They are notoriously lacking in brand loyalty, instead congregating at social hubs, reading the "news" written on Facebook "walls." Without a doubt, this generation will transform the way news is produced and consumed. To stay in the game, the traditional news media will need to join the native and read the writing on the wall.

While most newspapers today have an online presence, they continue to rely in large part on print revenue to support their infrastructure. It is not all that surprising that about half as many adults ages 18–34 read a daily newspaper as those in the 45–54 age group, according to Pew's 2009 State of the News Media report (bit.ly/ifluSp). However, while newspaper readership has traditionally increased with age, the Newspaper Association of America (NAA) found that this is no longer the case. Its 2005 report, "Lifelong Readers: The Role of Teen Content," points out that historically, young people who were not avid newspaper readers in their teens and early 20s usually changed their habits as they aged; yet it was found that this was not the case with Generation X and Generation Y.

There is hope, however. In 2008, the NAA found that as many as 75 percent of young people surveyed had some interest in news, from modest to strong ("Youth Media DNA"). It seems that "kids today" are interested in news, just—apparently—not in reading newspapers or visiting newspapers' websites. The simple fact that the NAA is now devoting itself to research specifically targeted at engaging this demographic is indicative of how important it is for news media to engage young readers.

Not surprisingly, the NAA reports that television and the internet are the forms of media used most frequently by young people. This is reinforced by the 2010 L2 "Gen Y Affluents: Media Survey," which found that on a daily basis, Gen Y affluents are as likely to read newspaper content as they are to watch TV, four of five readers in this demographic access newspapers digitally, and one in eight do so using a mobile device. However, this report points out that, "If Baby Boomers are the TV generation, then Gen Y is the blog generation." Nearly half of Gen Y affluents read at least one blog daily, making blogs as popular as newspapers with this cohort (bit.ly/gxRvyU).

It is significant to note that while one chart in the "Youth Media DNA" report indicated that of the websites that respondents accessed during a week, 20 percent were online newspapers, 35 percent were information sites, and 52 percent were social networking sites, the NAA fails to recommend engaging young readers through their social networks.

The importance of this oversight becomes apparent when we look closely at how digital natives are using social networks. EDUCAUSE, which has tracked social network usage on campus for the past several years, found that the percentage of students visiting sites such as Facebook or Myspace on a daily basis has risen from 48.7 percent in

2007 to 59.3 percent in 2009 (ECAR study of Undergraduate Students and Information Technology, 2010, bit.ly/g9SGIN). In December 2009, Anderson Analytics' "American College Survey" reported that social networking sites are the number three source for learning about products and services, after regularly visited websites and friends and family (bit.ly/fggHmE).

Without a doubt, in the larger information landscape we are seeing a marked shift from one in which the media as a whole (or even select premium information brands) are the sources readers turn to for information to one in which the filter of one's personal network carries vastly more weight. This tendency to rely on one's trusted network for information will only increase as digital natives become the predominant content consumers. As we examine the decline of media brands and the rise of social networks, the path to news media survival will require "friending" this new breed of content consumer.

## Passive Consumption

In his 1985 book, *Amusing Ourselves to Death*, Neil Postman postulated that the rise of television as the primary news delivery mechanism would lead to the decline of news as a substantive medium for discourse. Postman recognized that television was an optimal medium for the delivery of passive entertainment and, as messages are molded to fit their medium, news was deformed during the process of its TV makeover.

As Postman wrote, "The single most important fact about television is that people watch it, which is why it is called 'television.'" He emphasizes that in a one-way medium, discourse becomes impossible. TV news is delivered by soap-star attractive talking heads, who read scripted sound bites, transitioning between catastrophe and film critique with little more than a "now … this." Information exists in shiny little bursts that, devoid of context and discussion, do little to actually inform.

When we consider the effectiveness of television as an entertainment medium, it is easy to see how efforts to transform news into entertainment (in an attempt to make the function fit the form) contributed to the declining value of news. And, for better or worse, much of the print news media followed television's lead in an effort to make print newspapers more like television. This can be seen everywhere, from *USA TODAY*'s Technicolor TV-screen front page to the expanding waistlines of even the most "serious" newspapers' lifestyle sections.

However, it is very important to note that Postman's interpretation of the impact of television on news media is predicated in large part on the historic print news medium—neither the one contemporary to his writing, nor that of today. His work reflects the notion that, as printing presses were released from the restrictive grasp of church and government, the common man became part of news creation and dissemination, rather than a passive recipient of what the powers that be wanted him to know.

Yes, TV news is a one-way street, dead-ending discourse not only in its narrow coverage, but in the very nature of broadcasting information. Yet even in print—as professional journalism and media monopolies arose—news delivered as an exchange of ideas and public debate had faded well before the advent of television.

## Interactive Consumption

Postman's brilliant analysis of the effect of the primacy of television as a communication mechanism has had on discourse among average Joes stops short of predicting the impact of the internet. This is certainly no reflection on Postman's prognosticating prowess: In 1985, when the book was originally published, computers had just started their march to desktop domination.

Where the evolution of media takes a significant turn away from Postman's predictions for news as discourse is in the fact that the web is not a passive one-way medium. Yes, it is dominated by searchers and lurkers, but the generation of content consumers maturing today grew up steeped in a web-based communal culture—one in which any idea is ripe for comments, linking, co-opting and incorporating, mashing up, and remixing.

Not only are today's information consumers not content to wait for news to be delivered—instead opting to search it out or have it piped into inboxes, personalized portals, or directly into their workflow—they expect to be part of its dissemination and creation. While the phrase "join the conversation" may seem dated, there is no denying that the rise of social media has transformed the expectation of the content consumer.

The news media has an opportunity to meet the demands of this emerging reader by opening communication mechanisms via sharing, linking, commenting, contributing, and more. It also has a powerful opportunity to reshape the value of news by listening and responding.

Building upon Marshall McLuhan's work, Postman says, "Each medium, like language itself makes possible a unique mode of discourse by providing a new orientation for thought, for expression, for sensibility." This notion is reinforced by Lee Rainie, director of the Pew Internet & American Life Project's February 2009 report, "The New News Media-Scape" (bit.ly/dVYFOE), in which he cites the differences between the "information ecosystem" of the Industrial Age and that of the Information Age: Information today is abundant, cheap, personally oriented, and designed for participation.

Twentieth-century media, however, was not participatory by nature. Over time, media took on the role of information gatekeeper, in which it governs the flow of news, acting as wise intermediary who will deliver necessary information to the masses. While print media does provide feedback mechanisms, such as Op-Ed or letters to the editor pages, until recently, there has been little opportunity for readers to quickly and easily comment on—much less create—the news.

Clearly, this is not the case today. Since the first listservs rose up around shared interests back in 1986, content community tools have steadily grown easier to find and use, with the prices dropping to (or near) zero. Blogs have been around for a decade now, Myspace since 2003, and Facebook and YouTube since 2005. These simple, accessible, free, social media poster-children illustrate the ease of use and ubiquity of content creation, sharing, and proliferation among the masses. Whether media moguls like it or not, publishing is easy and everyone is doing it.

However, simply providing feedback mechanisms (such as links to Comment or Rate This Article) isn't enough. The emerging content consumers want to interact with is information whenever and however they choose. This starts off with allowing content to be readily shared and linked to—but this is only the beginning.

For the news business to succeed, it must evolve to fit the new shape of discourse: by rebuilding the lines of communication, and upon these lines rewriting the rules of content creation, so that news will regain its rightful place as a creation by the people to inform the people.

## Creators as Consumers

The NAA "Youth Media DNA" report states that, "Respondents were more likely to recall reading school newspapers prepared by their peers ... rather than newspaper youth content prepared for them." For the digital native, content written by their peers is good, and content that they can become actively involved with is even better.

A 2006 Economist New Media Survey elegantly bracketed the age of mass media between the advent of movable type and the creation of the popular blogging software, Moveable Type, with the latter marking what the article calls "the age of personal or participatory media."

Early examinations of blogging often focused on the personal, diary-style blogs that initially dominated the medium. Since that time, we have seen a boom in independent blogging sites that are giving mainstream media a genuine run for its money—not only in terms of audience, but in breaking news and ferreting out the story behind major events. In some instances, these sites have been acquired by traditional media for large sums, as in the case of Guardian News & Media's $30 million acquisition of ContentNext Media, known best for its paidContent.org blog, which was founded by an unemployed journalist only six years prior to the buyout. Another notable example was MSNBC.com's estimated $75 million purchase of Newsvine less than a year after the launch of the citizen journalism-based site.

These, however, are still relatively rare occurrences. In the early days of blogging, mainstream media dismissed blogs as unprofessional, unreliable, and often inaccurate. Yet as more and more professional journalists launched independent blogs using many of the same research, reporting, and ethical tenants practiced in print, blogging began to be viewed as a reputable form for delivering journalistic content. Today, independent bloggers are given press passes to everything from national political conventions to the hottest entertainment and sporting events. Mainstream media have also joined the blogging fray, with trusted writers and emerging voices contributing blog-style commentary on venerable media sites. While not all blogging is journalism, today we see that some blogging certainly is.

Blogging was the first of many tools that comprise what has become known as social media, which also includes wikis, podcasts, social bookmarking, microblogging, crowdsourcing, and more. New means of content creation, participation, and dissemination are emerging every day, and their integration with the deeply social activities of digital natives have allowed them to spawn increasing numbers of do-it-yourself news outlets.

Pew Research Center's Project for Excellence in Journalism 2009 State of the Media Report demonstrates how social media has become a genuine force: "What began as a few podcasts, RSS feeds and email alerts a year or two ago has mushroomed into a more serious emphasis on developing multiple forms of distribution. One form involves helping citizens grab and share information with one another ... Most news websites now have links attached to stories so readers can more easily share that content, and many have gone further, creating their own Twitter or Facebook accounts to put more content into consumers' hands and allow them to pass it along." Social networks are becoming media powers in their own right, with Facebook breaking out of its social networking niche in 2010 to surpass Google News in referral traffic to news and media sites. The same year, Facebook launched its "Facebook + Media" page, engaging media companies directly to identify ways to drive more traffic to their sites ("Gen Y Affluents Media Survey," bit.ly/gxRvyU). Pew also points out that this "movement represents a dawning realization that the nature of the Web is something the news industry cannot fight and might even begin to employ."

In addition to its role in content sharing and delivery, social media tools have given readers an unprecedented ability to report on news themselves, and in some cases these tools have given rise to so-called citizen journalism. As was the case in the early days of blogging, it is easy (and a mistake) for established media to dismiss the citizen journalist as untrained, unprofessional, and unreliable.

While there is a case to be made that the vast array of information options has diluted the demand for professionally produced content, there is no way to stuff this genie back in the bottle. The public has the tools and increasingly—given that the next generation of content consumers will have never known a world without access to these tools—they will expect to be part of the process. It is important for established media outlets to recognize that the citizen journalist is not necessarily the enemy. And—whether traditional media views citizen journalists as friend or foe—there is something to be said for keeping your friends close and your enemies closer.

## We Are the News

Today's information consumers have the tools and the desire to participate, and increasingly, they are demonstrating their ability to contribute
valuable newsworthy content. Consider the coverage of the U.S.
Airways crash in January 2009, in which Janis Krums of Sarasota,
Florida, posted the first photo of flight 1549 on Twitter from his
iPhone. About 30 minutes later, MSNBC interviewed him as a witness
live on TV. Similar cooperative coverage of terrorist acts in Mumbai in
2008 and the 2009 Iranian elections, and even MTV's deployment of a
"street team" of 51 amateur journalists (one in each state and the District
of Columbia), demonstrate the way in which traditional media can
leverage community contributions to enhance professional content
offerings.

Facilitating this sort of open content exchange goes well beyond the
content itself, however. For a generation that expects to read about
itself, reported on and written by itself, enabling this generation to easily contribute content to a site in the form of photos, video, and commentary will go a long way toward developing a relationship with them
as readers.

News Media Mogul Rupert Murdoch was quoted in 2005 at the
American Society of Newspaper Editors as saying that young readers
"don't want to rely on a god-like figure from above to tell them what's
important ... the digital native doesn't send a letter to the editor ... she
goes online and starts a blog." Murdoch bought one of the most popular online communities, Myspace, that same year. In December 2010,
Myspace continued to rank in the top 10 social networks in the U.S.
(bit.ly/gFFrom).

Pew's director, Rainie, suggests that media outlets focus on assisting
younger readers in acting on information by offering opportunities for
feedback, remixing, and community building, and by being "open to
the wisdom of crowds." Specifically, Rainie points out that to get the
digital native's attention, you should "find pathways through his/her

social network, offer 'link love' for selfish reasons, and participate in the conversation about your work."

Thus, this interaction with the content consumer cum creator means media companies must give readers (more aptly, content users) control. Content must be linkable, bloggable, and shareable, so that it becomes integrated into the fabric of readers' online activities. This also requires delivering content into the places where emergent readers "live," such as Twitter, YouTube, Myspace, Facebook … and whatever the latest tool or informational or social hub might be.

However, it also means inviting readers to participate in the creation process, not only by seeking out their potential contributions on sharing sites (when you need them), but by making it easy for them to help shape ideas as you develop them, to submit video and photos for consideration, and to contribute raw content.

## Rethinking the Path to the Bottom Line

More recently, Murdoch's comments about the business of news have centered around the need to make consumers pay for the content they've taken for granted (and for free). There are many media pundits who indicate consumers are unlikely to pay for news. In fact, only 5 percent of readers would choose to pay to continue reading a news site if it shifted to a paid model, according to September 2009 research from paidContent:UK and Harris Interactive. More recent research does provide a bit more hope, though, as a November 2010 Pew tracking survey found that 18 percent of internet users age 18 and older have purchased news online (bit.ly/hVoFSF). Yet the latest entrant onto the content delivery scene, Apple's iPad, brings with it mixed messages about the future of paid news consumption. According to a December 2010 study by the Reynold's Journalism Institute, reading breaking news is the most popular use for the device, though 81.5 percent of those surveyed read books, newspapers, and magazines on it. However, more than half (58.1

percent) of the respondents who subscribe to printed newspapers and use their iPad at least an hour a day for news said they are very likely to cancel their print subscriptions within the next six months. While there was a rush by early adopters to purchase magazines for the iPad (notably *Wired* magazine), pundits generally agree that no device can "save" the industry.

The challenge for newspapers is understanding that subscription revenues and advertising are not the only ways to fund news production. On his blog The Equity Kicker, Nic Brisbourne (a software and media venture capitalist) wrote an extensive analysis of the trend in news media to convert from a largely free, ad-supported model to a fee-based one (bit.ly/gy5Mud). He writes that, "The web is more than just a new medium. Rather than thinking about how they can sell the same old news via a new channel, media bosses should be taking this opportunity to re-examine old assumptions, to rebuild their product for the 21st century."

It is clear that today media consumers have an abundance of news options—in terms of a multitude of outlets as well as delivery and consumption mechanisms. With abundance comes devaluation, certainly. Yet Brisbourne points out "the good news is that every abundance creates new scarcities and this is where the news industry must go to make money in the 21st century. The scarcities created (and enabled) by abundant news are interesting stories, thought provoking analysis, conversation and community, and trust/verification … Conversation and community will both make the experience richer for the active participant and improve the quality of the content on the site for more casual reader."

However, Brisbourne does not suggest that finding a way to re-engage readers through quality and community will suddenly make them willing to pay for news. He points out that niche and new media brands are finding alternative ways to leverage their brand to make money—

beyond buying and selling content or selling advertising space to support content creation.

The Nieman Journalism Lab Blog highlights some interesting ways that news media is leveraging brand to diversify revenue (bit.ly/gxjTri). For example, the New York Times Knowledge Network offers weeklong courses (mostly web-based, with live interactive webcasts) for *Times* readers that are taught by its columnists. *The Guardian* launched a membership program in May 2010 that offers readers access to live events, expert briefings, and exclusive offers with commercial partners. Neiman's blog cited a job posting for a general manager of the Guardian Club, which said:

> Increasingly we believe our future resides at the centre of a community of engaged readers and users whose relationship with us will be much closer and more involved. The Guardian Club will be our transformational next step in bringing these customers to the centre of our business, rewarding loyalty while growing our reach and revenues. We want members of the Club to feel that they are genuinely part of our organisation, and as close as it is possible to get to the editorial heart of our company.

This is an interesting distinction: The paywall/subscription approach versus the notion that "Membership has its privileges." The debate around supporting professional news production has largely centered around free versus fee. And, given the abundance of free "good enough" sources for news, as well as the rise of reputable citizen- or blogger-based coverage from Topeka to Tehran, erecting a paywall in front of news content will do little to convince digital natives that your media brand is worth supporting.

Another aspect of this ad that makes *The Guardian's* approach sound promising is that it specifically mentions "rewarding loyalty." These content "clubs" have the potential to build readership from the inside out by identifying and promoting loyal readers, perhaps developing their position in the community as on-the-ground correspondents. These individuals could then become news hubs around which news would be further disseminated.

Membership certainly has a very different ring to it than subscription, particularly for those who demonstrate a great propensity for joining in social networks and the "conversation" online. Other ways to conceive of this concept might be to establish "spokesmen" or "advocates" in order to engage loyal readers as leaders who would then help promote the product or brand.

Simply changing the terminology won't suffice, of course. Yet, if media brands begin to conceive of revenue models around the notion of membership, concepts like community, participation, and perks immediately move to the forefront. Consider News International's move to offer Times+. The *Times* and the *Sunday Times* have launched a membership scheme offering their readers special offers and access to exclusive events in return for an annual fee. Katie Vanneck-Smith, the managing director of News International's Customer Direct division, was quoted by *The Guardian* (bit.ly/f3Sj1S) as saying, "We are moving away from the traditional model of volume in favour of developing more direct relationships with our customers based on their interests and passions."

## A New News Awakening

News organizations are beginning to realize that the best way to build a loyal reader base is to connect with readers. This sort of connection will become essential as digital natives become the dominant content con-sumers. Luckily, all over the world media brands large and small are experimenting with community involvement and interaction, and their experiences provide inspiration for further innovation:

**Gazette Live**

www.gazettelive.co.uk

Of Lindsay Bruce's work as the community editor at the *Middlesbrough Evening Gazette*'s website, online journalism blogger Paul Bradshaw wrote: "These 16–19s, known to have little or no interaction with their local newspaper, are signing up every day to offer their opinions, review gigs, diary events and most importantly, inform us and discuss local news issues." Top center on the site's homepage are "join the community" and "get involved" links, including the ability to send in stories and pictures.

The site also encourages users to "Shape the News" by contributing items such as job stories, music reviews, and opinions on ongoing news stories. It offers many opportunities to comment on and rate content, and in its Get Involved section, asks readers to send in stories, videos, or pictures, which are featured in the Your Videos & Pics section, and some of which are also used in the print edition. The gazette also hosts more than 20 community websites, which "aim to provide the latest local news, sport & events as well as details of anything and everything that's happening in your area. Please comment on local issues, or upload information from your schools, colleges, charities, pubs, clubs, churches, scout groups, nurseries, etc."

Takeaway: The gazette's approach demonstrates impressive digital native savvy in its engagement of the teen demographic through participatory journalism. It also leverages their desire to enhance its local coverage without adding staff.

**Digital Nation**

www.pbs.org/wgbh/pages/frontline/digitalnation

Despite its stuffy image, PBS has not shied away from digital initiatives. Consider its approach to developing a sequel to its documentary *Growing Up Online*. The documentary team created an area of the PBS site devoted to the sequel, *Digital Nation*, where the audience can help shape the project by contributing to Your Stories, in which they can share a story about life online. Access to this content is displayed as a vast array of contributors' faces. Mousing over them pops up intriguing six-word thoughts such as: "Crawl to laptop to Skype Grandma." Or "I emailed him. He deleted me." or "Dinosaur evolving. Fast enough? Who knows?" Click the thumbnails to view short user-uploaded videos providing nearly infinite insight into a topic *Frontline* will likely have to edit down to 60 minutes for television broadcast.

The *Digital Nation* area includes Rough Cuts—videos in progress, outtakes, interviews—that will factor into the final story. Pages boldly feature links to Write a Comment, Tweet, and Upload Video/Photo so that site visitors can provide a steady stream of feedback for the documentary crew. It is evident from the contributor thumbnails that engaged users vary in all aspects, not the least of which is age.

Takeaway: While making *Growing Up Online*, PBS listened to its subjects and responded by providing a vibrant, visual appealing site where almost any user will see a "familiar face"—and can add his or her own to the mix. It is clear from the contributions that this approach attracts a younger demographic than the stereotypical documentary viewer. Through the commenting process, the site also generates new ideas that will also appeal to its audience—since they contributed them.

### The Huffington Post
www.huffingtonpost.com

Web-native newspaper *The Huffington Post* recognizes that it needs to engage users where they live online. It teamed up with Facebook via its Facebook Connect API, to offer "Social News," which allows users to interact with its stories. According to founder Arianna Huffington, "Social media has fundamentally changed our relationship to news. It's no longer something we passively take in. We now engage with news, share news, react to news–news has become something around which we gather, connect, and converse. HuffPost Social News makes this more dynamic than ever."

Takeaway: Like America itself, our news media was founded on an "of and by the people for the people" foundation, yet as Huffington recognizes, the role of the media shifted over time and increasingly became a one-way channel. Her comments—while somewhat shortsighted—are reflective of the native's reawakening of news as discourse. Given that this site ranks 34th in the U.S. for web traffic (Alexa, December 2010), Huffington is clearly onto something.

## CNN

www.cnn.com

Established media brand CNN—which ranked 18 on the Alexa list—also leveraged the Facebook Connect API in CNN theForum, where users could find friends on CNN and discuss 2008 election issues. CNN was early in enabling sharing with RSS and continues to be so with its extensive use of Twitter. It provides a platform for user-generated content, iReport.com, and the site boasts unedited, unfiltered news (pointing out that only stories marked *On CNN* have been vetted for use in CNN news coverage). The About page says, "Lots of people argue about what constitutes news. But, really, it's just something that happens someplace to someone. Whether that something is newsworthy mostly depends on who it affects—and who's making the decision. On iReport.com, that is you! So we've built this site and equipped it with some nifty tools for posting, discovering and talking about what you think makes the cut." On the site, users rate one another and are ranked by a tally of their contributions, ratings, popularity, and site activity, with some earning the title *superstar*. However, all 30K or so iReporters are listed on the site.

Takeaway: CNN has demonstrated not only its ability to create a community around news but also its ability to tap this user-generated content to enhance its overall coverage and expand its audience engagement. Its focus on providing unfiltered news will certainly appeal to an audience that wants to decide for themselves what matters. However, considering the increasing force of individual social networks, incorporating personalized filtering will resonate further with the digital native.

### New York Times
www.nytimes.com

Big media poster child the *New York Times* has introduced its TimesPeople toolbar, which allows users to sync up to their Facebook profiles so that their activity within the TimesPeople network is visible on their Facebook page as well as on the *New York Times* site. TimesPeople users can build up Friends lists and can see a newsfeed of the stories their friends are recommending, sharing, and commenting on. *Times* online readers have been able to comment on stories, as well as rate reviewed restaurants and movies, for some time now, but the ability to recommend stories is new. Outside NYTimes.com, users can subscribe to an RSS feed of their friends' activities, or browse friends' updates with the iPhone interface. Readers are encouraged to build up their networks through the TimesPeople search box, by selecting from a list of "users you might know" or by importing contacts from various email services, Twitter, Myspace, or Facebook.

Takeaway: The *New York Times* has not shied away from putting its considerable weight behind tests of new business models and further demonstrates its experimental spirit with its many forays into social media. It is particularly interesting that it is taking the news to the native—users can see information on Facebook if that's where they "live"—while also showing readers their friends' activities on the *Times'* website, so that the filter of the social network remains part of the experience.

While major media players are able to invest in custom-developed applications, in some cases, it is the local news that is best equipped to engage readers as they are developing their news habits close to home.

## Metro Nordic

www.metro.se

Swedish newspaper *Metro Nordic*, part of the Metro International commuter newspaper chain, hired the five best-known bloggers in the country to provide content on its site. Michael P. Smith, executive director of Northwestern University's Media Management Center, said of this move, "They were already blogging and had their own audience, their own communities, and their own brand." He pointed out that the Swedish paper recognized that you need to go to where young readers are, "and you hope that by bringing them under the brand of the newspaper, they will see something that catches their eye that is more journalistic in nature. That is their new youth strategy" (bit.ly/egQ1jh).

Takeaway: Rather than try to launch its own blogs, the newspaper opted to bring successful bloggers who were already engaging young readers into its fold—and along with them, these youthful eyeballs. The real trick, then, is engaging them with the rest of the site's content.

## Bakersfield Voice

www.bakersfieldvoice.com

The *Bakersfield Voice* is a community-contributed publication and website designed to give its Bakersfield, California, readers a place to make their voices heard. "Whether you want to rant about a recent City Council decision, rave about your kid's sports team or share some of your favorite photos, if you're willing to post it, we're willing to publish it online and in our print publication delivered to 70,000 homes in Bakersfield and available on racks at a number of locations around town." Once users join the community, they can customize their profile, create their own blogs, and post articles, events, and photos. The site publishes all postings on its site (as long as they are "of good nature") and posts as many as possible in the weekly print edition. With features like "all star athlete" and "educator of the month," young readers in particular are drawn into the business of creating the local news.

Takeaway: Hyperlocal coverage provides one of the most promising applications of social media as journalism. At the local level, readers most want to see themselves in the news. This site is particularly adept at bringing young readers into its participatory mix, a great first step in engaging them as news readers for life.

## Properly Socializing the News

On her Groundswell blog, Charlene Li, co-author of a 2008 book by the same name, says, "In the future, social networks will be like air. They will be anywhere and everywhere we need and want them to be. And also, without that social context in our connected lives, we won't really feel like we are truly living and alive ..." She suggests that, among other things, developers compete on creating the most compelling social experience, integrate social networks into existing activities, and design business models that reflect the value created by people's social networks.

No one is likely to perish if a generation grows up without the news media writ large. Humans have always found a way to discover and share the information that they deem newsworthy. Ultimately, digital natives are at least as involved with information as every generation before them. They are literate, they are connected, and they want to know. Yet given their reliance upon the filter of their complex social networks, the way in which they vet information and develop notions of value, trust, and quality will be vastly more influenced by their social interaction than by brand name news. It is clear, therefore, that for the news business to stay in business, it needs to open itself up to developing a relationship with the next generation of content consumers on their own terms.

## About the Contributor

Michelle Manafy is the director of content of FreePint, Ltd., a publisher of sites and resources for the business information industry. Michelle previously served as the editorial director of the Enterprise Group for Information Today, Inc. In this role, Michelle was editor-in-chief of *EContent* magazine and the *Intranets* newsletter. She was also the chair of Information Today's Enterprise Search Summits and the Buying & Selling eContent Conference. Michelle's focus is on the emerging trends in digital content and how they shape successful business practices. She has written on a variety of technology topics including digital publishing, social media, content development and distribution, streaming media, and audio, video, and storage technologies. Michelle speaks at a variety of industry events and serves as a judge for many content and technology competitions. She has worked in book and magazine publishing for more than 20 years in areas ranging from pop culture to academic nonfiction, and holds a BA in Journalism from San Francisco State University.

## Recommended Reading

### *Books and Articles*

Anderson, Chris. *Free: The Future of a Radical Price.* New York: Hyperion, 2009.

Doctor, Ken. *Newsonomics: Twelve New Trends That Will Shape the News You Get.* New York: St. Martin's Press, 2010.

Li, Charlene. *Groundswell: Winning in a World Transformed by Social Technologies.* Cambridge, MA: Harvard Business School, 2008.

Postman, Neil. *Amusing Ourselves to Death: Public Discourse in the Age of Show Business.* New York: Viking Penguin, 1985.

### *Websites*

Neiman Journalism Lab, www.niemanlab.org/about

Media Shift, www.pbs.org/mediashift

Pew Research Center's Project for Excellence in Journalism, www.journalism.org

PoynterOnline, www.poynter.org

Readership Institute, www.readership.org

# Chapter 14

# T'écoutes quoi ti? Digital Natives as Music Consumers in Lille, France

Heidi Gautschi and Emilie Moreau

Over the past decade, the way music is produced, circulated, accessed, and consumed has undergone a fundamental change as digital storage has become both the industry and the individual's standard. It is now easier than ever before to access new music, and the listening experience has been revolutionized by the portability of the MP3 format.

As numerous studies have shown, digital natives' relationship with music has evolved in step with the technology available to them in their digital world. With a little patience and a few mouse clicks, you can download the latest hot single (or obscure remix) before it's been officially released, transfer it to your phone/MP3 player, and listen to it on the way to school, between classes, or on the way to work, or while chatting online, downloading more music, or updating your Facebook profile. It has become so easy to download music for free—thanks to specialized blogs, torrents, rapidshare, and various illicit programs that allow you to rip music from streaming sites—that at first glance it would appear that the digital native's music experience (listening, accessing, creating, and producing) has moved far past the anticipatory experience of past generations.

While it seems safe to assume that free and quick access to music has shaped digital natives' relationship with music products, we set out to determine more precisely how digital natives relate to music by comparing the consumption behaviors of two very different music formats: vinyl and MP3. While we could have chosen to look at CDs, too, we decided not to pursue this format. We felt that vinyl records and MP3s appeal to digital natives in very different ways, and better understanding the behaviors attached to each would add an interesting twist to the current debates about music consumption, or lack thereof.

Our study looks at the behaviors of a small group of digital natives in Lille, France (pop. 225,789, but more than 3 million for the greater Lille area), the main city in the North region of the country. As such, we do not purport that our observations hold entirely true in other countries, or even in France as a whole. Some of our findings, however, are in keeping with other studies, suggesting that there may be larger trends at work. Others will come as a surprise for American readers. Certainly, how different groups adopt technology depends on many factors. Culture, tradition, and institutional structures all play an important role. While French digital natives may be as well-versed in digital technology as those of their generation in other countries, their specific choices and how they use these technologies may vary due to their particular culture. Yet certain aspects will also carry through from country to country.

Undoubtedly, the internet allows for increased circulation of information across national borders and has resulted in a great deal of talk about globalization. However, like most of us, digital natives still prefer to access information in their own language. Obviously, people generally like to understand the lyrics to songs they listen to. French digital natives are not necessarily fluent in English, which means that certain music, as well as some music websites and services, will not be of interest to them or even on their radar. Case in point, it was only after Facebook offered a French interface that the French began joining en masse. Further, when it comes to music, we're dealing with something that touches people's emotions; music tends to be a very personal experience. The music you listen to reflects your personality, which may be multicultural, but is most likely dominated by your native language.

Since our aim is to understand the value music consumers place on vinyl and MP3s, we created a survey with both open and closed questions in order to elucidate Lillois digital natives' listening, purchasing, downloading, and sharing behaviors, as well as any music-creation activity they may participate in. Our survey was designed to collect both quantitative and qualitative data, an approach that allows researchers to build a more complete picture of the behaviors they are studying ("The man whose web expanded: network dynamics in Manchester's post/punk music scene 1976–1980," Crossley, 2009). We also conducted a series of semi-directed interviews. This chapter (which is part of a larger study that is not limited to a specific age group) mainly focuses on how digital natives listen to, purchase, and download music. Given the digital native focus, we had to eliminate a number of respondents because of their age. This is an ongoing study, and here we present preliminarily findings.

When we conducted this study, Heidi Gautschi worked at the University of Lille 3. Like all universities these days, Lille 3 is crawling with digital natives. After obtaining clearance from the department director, Gautschi asked her 45 master's students to complete the anonymous survey about their music consumption habits. Emilie Moreau ventured into the center of Lille and asked people in various music stores to fill out the same survey. She found 20 willing respondents. We then compiled and analyzed the results.

## Form and Function

Vinyl records and MP3s present obvious differences. One format is tangible, bulky, breakable; the other is intangible, modifiable, ephemeral. We were curious to know whether the disassociation of the object and the sound it traditionally contains lessens the intrinsic value of the music. The MP3 format is easy to access and easy to exchange, which might mean that it is more disposable and therefore less valuable than a vinyl record. On the other hand, MP3s are more easily modified (mashed) to create unique, exclusive products that are potentially more valuable than a vinyl.

For those unfamiliar with the term, a mashup—known in France as Bootleg or Bastard Pop—combines two or more songs to create a new listening experience. The songs selected often juxtapose two different genres that would under normal circumstances never be found together—Michael Jackson and Dolly Parton, Vanessa Paradis' *Joe le Taxi* with Nirvana's *Smells Like Teen Spirit*. While the first commercialized mashup we found dates from the early 1980s, the phenomenon became an underground sensation in Europe in the 1990s, thanks in large part to the Flying Dewaele Brothers' mixes. (The brothers are now known as 2Many DJs.) David and Stephen Dewaele see their work as mocking popular culture. They also use only vinyl records to create their mixes.

Lawrence Lessig, in his TED talk on laws that choke creativity (bit.ly/AY71h), places the remix and mashup phenomenon as a core component of the digital native experience. In his talk, he explains that mashups represent "an amateur, but not amateurish, culture where people produce for the love of what they're doing and not for the money. Kids these days are taking the songs of the day and old songs and remixing them to make them something new. It is how they understand access to this culture." Lessig makes clear that remixes should not be viewed as piracy. "Remixers use other people's content and digital technologies to create something new. It is how digital natives think and speak as they increasingly understand digital technologies and their relationship to themselves." He explains that professionals have been able to do the type of remixes found on bootleg and mashup sites and on YouTube for the past 50 years. However, he points out that technology has been democratized, so that this type of cultural creativity is now accessible to anyone with a decent computer and some patience. Thus, digital formats lend themselves to this type of cultural artifact.

## A Vinyl Revival?

Despite the incredible popularity of digital music worldwide, over the last two years or so, rumors have been flying about a vinyl revival. Kids may be buying fewer CDs, but apparently more and more of them are going old-school and starting to collect vinyl records. A 2010 Nielsen SoundScan report shows that vinyl record sales in the U.S. increased 14 percent in 2010. Late of the Pier, a British Indie band (all of whose members are digital natives) just founded its own label, Zarcorp, which only releases vinyl that you can purchase online or through the band's Myspace page (myspace.com/zarcorpinc). Tiga, Agoria, and Burial—all composers, DJs, and master remixers—have released or will be releasing vinyl records, often accompanied by digital versions that are issued post-vinyl release. And, in addition to digital releases, major artists such as Missy Elliot and the Beastie Boys have a long history of releasing vinyl that often includes instrumental versions of popular songs to actually facilitate mixing and remixing.

So it would seem that these rumors have some truth to them. However, given the Nielsen SoundScan figures, 2.8 million vinyl records sold and 443.4 million overall album sales, the revival is more of a niche market thing, targeted at DJs, remixers, and collectors. While a vinyl revival is not going to compensate for sales lost to piracy, it is a bit of positive news for both major and independent labels.

## Consumer Behaviors

### *Vinyl Records*

People of all ages who are relatively casual music consumers are sometimes surprised to learn that not only is it still possible to buy vinyl records, but that people continue to do so. Most major French music store chains do not have a wide selection of records, if any at all. The bins are hidden in a corner, or records are mixed in with other items. One exception is the Virgin Megastore on the Champs Elysée in Paris, which boasts a fairly broad selection of new releases and old standards on vinyl. It is probably safe to assume that most digital natives have never listened to a vinyl record, just as many in Generation X have never listened to an eight-track tape. It also would seem to make sense that digital natives would not be especially interested in buying vinyl records. Vinyl is, after all, an analog format.

This assumption was borne out in our research, as some of Gautschi's students had never even heard of "vinyl records." However, one-third of those surveyed have not only heard of, but actually buy vinyl. This is in keeping with the 2009 survey conducted by the University of Hertfordshire for UK Music, which found that "vinyl is making something of a comeback" though "interest in vinyl appeared to be more closely linked to the lack of availability of certain titles in digital format. It also carries a certain amount of retro-appeal kudos as a format." The digital natives we surveyed do not currently possess large collections of vinyl and for most, their interest in vinyl is relatively new.

Not surprisingly, the employees of the five record stores Moreau visited have been buying vinyl for the longest time of those we surveyed (between six and eight years) and possess the largest collections (more than 100 records). For the music industry, it must be heartening news indeed that the majority of vinyl buyers purchase their records in stores. The Nielsen 2009 SoundScan report also found this to be true: "Also notable is the fact that two out of every three vinyl records were purchased at an independent record store." We found that digital natives go to specialized stores because with this format, it appears that building a relationship with the sales force is important. Not only does it give the Lillois digital natives a sense of belonging to a community, it's also a way of getting advice and the latest news.

While there are online communities and ecommerce stores dedicated to vinyl, interestingly, none of our respondents mentioned being part of these specialized online vinyl communities. Some do turn to the web to purchase rare vinyl editions or hard-to-find releases. Most, however, purchase vinyl at concerts, at yard sales, and in specialized stores. None said that the web was the first place they turned to seek out new vinyl. This seems to contradict certain digital native behaviors, namely the importance of online social networks in their lives. That said, this study was undertaken in France, in an urban environment with a vibrant and diverse music community. The area boasts numerous independent music stores, specialized clubs, music-oriented neighborhood associations, and inexpensive live music venues. It is possible that French digital native vinyl collectors do not behave like their American counterparts. However, it is also possible to interpret this tendency to eschew the web in favor of offline communities as related to the tangible aspect of vinyl. A physical representation of music lends itself to physically present relationships. At the moment, we are unable to determine whether such a relationship exists. This is, however, something we plan to pursue.

Interestingly, it turns out that the digital natives we surveyed are motivated to buy vinyl by the same reasons as older music buyers: the beauty of the object and the sound quality—things absent from music delivered in the MP3 format. Being able to hold something in your hands, to read the liner notes, and to admire the cover art were all cited as important aspects. As Jeremy Eichler wrote in the *Boston Globe* on December 13, 2009, "A recording documents the presence of musicians who are no longer there, but the thing itself can stand in for them, can mediate our relationship to the music we are hearing" ("Untouchable," bit.ly/4pE9W5). The "warmer," "less perfect" sound of a vinyl recording appealed to the digital native buyer as well. One DJ we interviewed prefers to mix with vinyl precisely because of the imperfections. He claimed that computer programs correct the imperfections, making the sound less personal and less interesting. According to him, you can build a mix around the slight imperfections, which then makes the clubbing experience more intense. Another DJ said he leaned toward using vinyl because he preferred being able to *feel* what he was mixing and believed it added to both the production and listening activity.

However, the majority of native respondents to our survey do not purchase vinyl. According to our research, the most frequent reason digital natives did not buy vinyl was because they did not have the appropriate "material." The use of this word raises some interesting questions. We wonder if digital natives who used this term did not actually know what the device used to play records was called. Others explained their disinterest in records because they did not have a "turntable" or a "record player."

Our respondents brought to light other comparisons that affect digital natives' listening preferences: While not necessarily more expensive than an MP3 player, a record player takes up more space and is not portable. A record player implies a different listening experience: Unlike MP3s, vinyl isn't listened to on earbuds or headphones, anywhere and any time; it is a shared listening experience and rooted to one place. As compared with MP3s, records are neither convenient nor are they adapted to the native's expectation of how music fits with modern life. Some respondents simply didn't find vinyl appealing: "It's not a format that interests me" or "I don't see the point" or "It's not a format that is adapted to listening to music and it isn't practical." Others indicated that, if you can get all the music you want off the internet for free, then it doesn't seem worth bothering with vinyl. This reinforces our hypothesis that vinyl records are truly a niche market reserved for those, digital native or otherwise, who place a certain value on music and the object that contains it.

While vinyl continues to attract new consumers, it is simply not bringing in the same number of listeners as its digital counterpart. There is no longer a mass market for this music format, but those who buy vinyl are loyal consumers. They regularly go to the record store, after all. Based on our observations and discussions with vinyl buyers, the specialized record store is not just a store, but it also is a place to come and talk about music, listen to new releases, and generally "hang out."

## MP3s

Not surprisingly, of those questioned, more than 90 percent listen to music in MP3 format. Those who collect vinyl also tend to have large numbers of MP3s. Unlike a vinyl collection, however, no one was able to tell us the exact number of MP3s they had. There are a couple of reasons for this: MP3s are often free, or at the very least far less expensive than records, and therefore people pay less attention to the number they are accumulating; and MP3s are not tangible in the same way as vinyl records, so cognitively people have a more difficult time calculating the number they have. For the music industry, this is not good news. And yet, according to the 2009 survey carried out by the University of Hertfordshire for UK Music, music remains the most valued form of entertainment for people ages 18–24 and "ownership of music is hugely important—both online and offline." Ownership no longer necessarily means paying for something.

Most people we surveyed mentioned downloading more MP3s than they can listen to. In fact, hoarding MP3s seems to be a common behavior. Very few of our respondents ever deleted MP3s, even those they no longer listened to or even those they didn't like. Most claimed to download only music they like, which means they often don't download complete albums, rather just the songs they want to listen to. Since music in digital format can be easily posted or shared online, the MP3 could be construed as a vector for discovering new music. However, if digital natives are mainly downloading the songs they like best and not even bothering to listen to all the music they own, then perhaps MP3s are not so conducive to discovering new music. Deciding what to download looks suspiciously similar to getting your news solely from RSS feeds. There may be more choices out there, but there are also technologies in place that allow consumers to purposely restrict their options. What digital natives choose to download may actually narrow their perspectives and decrease the opportunity for serendipitous discovery.

MP3 consumption behavior turns out to be rather contradictory when looked at as traditional consumption behavior (i.e., as attempting to acquire something). We would argue, in fact, that our study participants' relationship to MP3s is closer to listening to the radio or watching videos on TV. In fact, 70 percent of those surveyed say they discover new music by listening to the radio. For the 63 percent who say they learn about new music on the internet, the most popular music website cited was the music streaming site Deezer (www.deezer.com).

Deezer is a music site that offers free and legal streaming. And much like a traditional radio, the artists and other copyright holders whose songs are played on the site receive payment; in this case, they got a cut of the advertising revenues. Deezer purchased the back catalogs of some major and independent labels, including Universal Music and EMI. That it was created by two French men and has been lauded far and wide in the French media goes far in explaining its popularity (15 million registered users) among French digital natives.

Streaming music rejoins our next point: the pros and cons of MP3s. There is no getting around the fact that the most commonly consumed digital formats, MP3s and MP4s, are of poorer sound quality than CDs, a much less compressed format. This was by far the most commonly stated negative point. Yet, the poorer sound quality doesn't deter anyone from listening to digital downloads because the positives outweigh any negative aspects. Because they are compressed, MP3s are small files, making them both convenient and portable. Digital natives, let's not forget, don't remember a time without portable music devices that can transport massive music collections, so being able to take your music with you is a given. Portable players let you regain control over one aspect of your environment by creating your own personal soundscape (R. Murray Schafer, *The Soundscape*, Destiny Books, 1993).

As Trevor Pinch and Karin Bijsterveld write in "Sound Studies: New Technology and Music" (2004), "The world since the industrial revolution has become more and more noisy." Not only has ambient noise increased, but the ways of creating personal soundscapes have multiplied. We have moved from car radios, boomboxes, walkmans, and MP3 players to the convergence of multiple technologies in one. The world we live in has become one of competing soundscapes. "Music technologies are tools for choice and control in the management of daily life" (Pinch and Bijsterveld, 2004). The convenience and portability of MP3s are a boon to digital natives. They are able to use music as it has always been used—to create and sustain an emotional response—wherever they want, thus blocking out the increasingly aggressive sounds of the outside world.

Through our research, we were able to shed light on natives' musical behaviors as related to both vinyl and MP3s in terms of how they relate to these two formats. In the next section, we seek to understand Lillois digital natives' downloading behavior as it relates to buying music.

## Making Music Pay

### Downloader = Freeloader

When people consider digital native behavior with regards to music, piracy is the number one issue that comes to mind. Downloading equals freeloading in most people's minds. In large part, this appears to be an accurate perception. According to our research, the majority of respondents download illegally (76 percent), 70 percent rip their own or their friends' CDs, and half get new music from friends and family. Only 9 percent actually buy digital music.

However, the situation isn't as dire as it might seem. Almost half of those surveyed purchase what they download in another format, most often as CDs. While downloading illegally remains the norm, the music industry can take heart that illicitly circulated MP3s serve to promote music to some extent. Some illegal downloaders do actually use this option to discover music *worth* paying for. This is a significant point: Now that digital natives can choose whether to spend their money on the latest hip new artist (as defined by a massive media blitz), music labels are in hot water.

In a review of Greg Kot's book *Ripped* in the *Christian Science Monitor* (June 2009), Lorne Entress writes how the major labels in the 1980s began focusing more on making profits and less on actually nurturing and producing *artists*. "Record companies abandoned their practice of patiently nurturing a musician's career, investing instead in pop acts with less talent and even less staying power. Success could be momentarily impressive. But the quick flame-out of artists such as Ricky Martin or the Backstreet Boys made for few lifelong fans and less profit in the long term. It also had another effect. Fed up with superficial stars and excessive CD prices, young people began to look for music that they could connect with—and they found it on the Web."

Digital natives are in the driver's seat because they now have the power to pick and choose exactly what they want to listen to and, more importantly, what they are willing to spend their money on. If the song they download isn't up to snuff, then they won't buy it in digital—or any other—format. This process also works the other way: Unsigned acts that garner massive numbers of downloads and listens online will be brought to the attention of record labels, as was the case with Kate Nash, The Black Kids, and SoKo. Some acts choose to sign; others opt for the DIY approach. Any way you look at it, digital natives are less susceptible to the recording industry's whims. What remains to be seen is whether the recording industry will stop focusing on diminishing sales and return to a focus on discovering and developing the caliber of music that people are willing to spend their money on. Everything has a price. Only now, record labels aren't the only ones deciding.

## Hadopi

According to the 2010 Nielsen SoundScan Report, the music industry continues to be in upheaval. Overall album sales decreased 12.8 percent during 2010. The good news is that legal downloading offers continue to present a glimmer of hope. Digital album sales were up 13 percent, and digital track sales increased 1 percent. Still, illegal downloading appears to many in the business of music to be "the root of all evil," and a number of mildly successful measures to combat it have been tried in various countries around the world. In France, President Nicolas Sarkozy's administration has taken a tough stance against illegal downloading, or *pirating,* as it is called in both the media and legal documents, and proposed a controversial law, called Hadopi, which was debated in the National Assembly in 2009. The law set up a three-step process to target illegal downloaders. First, downloaders would receive a cease-and-desist email from the government, followed by a registered mail letter. If, despite these two warnings, the person continued to download illegally, his internet service would be cut off from anywhere between two months to a year.

However, the European Parliament responded by passing a law stating that interrupting a person's internet service was an attack on freedom of expression and therefore illegal. Consequently, the National Assembly voted down the Hadopi law in April 2009. In addition, the general public and the media came out strongly against Hadopi. Despite the negative publicity it received, it was sent back to the National Assembly and this time, in May 2009, was voted into law. However, as is often the case with these kinds of measures, Hadopi is already obsolete, as it only covers file sharing through P2P programs and only on French territory.

Regardless, we were interested in knowing whether the digital natives we surveyed would continue to download illegally post-Hadopi. They responded overwhelmingly that laws such as these would not hinder their downloading behavior. The Lillois digital native response may, however, have something to do with President Sarkozy's negative image. This aside, digital natives' music consumption behaviors are well established and here to stay, for better or for worse. And this means making a place for free music.

### Circulating Knowledge

People who consider music an important part of their lives are part of networks or music scenes in which they circulate musical knowledge. However, even more casual music consumers are part of networks where music and music knowledge are shared.

Prior to the internet, there were already established ways in which music knowledge circulated, such as specialized publications, radio and TV shows, word-of-mouth, concerts and clubs, and localized communities based in music stores. All of these still exist to varying degrees and continue to provide spaces for the circulation and sharing of music knowledge. We found that the employees at specialized stores remained one of the major sources people turned to for recommendations, advice, and general conversations. In the small specialized stores we visited, employees knew many of their clients by name and took the time to talk with them and offer suggestions. Word-of-mouth, friends and family, and concerts also remain popular ways of learning about music, along with specialized print magazines and newspapers. The networks already in place continue to provide a wealth of information for music consumers.

Nowadays, of course, the internet is also a rich source of music knowledge. Most people we surveyed, however, used the internet to listen to music that they had read about, had heard on a radio station, or had been recommended to them by a friend (on or offline). The internet was not necessarily the first place they turned to for music knowledge but was used rather like an in-store listening booth.

Internet networks have been integrated into the pre-existing music networks. Both are richer for it. There is, however, a clear distinction between downloading music, discovering new music, and sharing MP3s. The majority of our respondents, as discussed earlier, use streaming sites like Deezer to listen to music they heard about elsewhere. From there, those who download use P2P networks, the most frequently cited being eMule and BitTorrent. When asked how they *shared* MP3s, however, very few considered P2P networks to be a vector for sharing. According to our survey results and our interviews, the concept of *sharing* appears to imply knowing the other person or people involved in the transaction. Therefore, when asked if they shared their MP3s, 43 percent said they did not, despite the fact that they used P2P networks. Of those who do share MP3 files, burning CDs for friends is the most popular behavior, followed by exchanging flash drives. Sending MP3s over email or while chatting online were low on the list. Facebook, Pandora, and other social networks weren't even mentioned.

The popularity of Deezer seems like good news for record labels both big and small since this type of site generates revenue for the music industry through advertisements and premium memberships. The Lillois digital natives neither seemed put off by the advertisements on the site nor the ads that interrupt the listening stream. Deezer offers ad-free listening for those who purchase Deezer HD and Deezer Premium memberships. The site also offers easy one-click access to iTunes so that you can purchase a legal digital copy of that great song your friend told you about the other night and that you just listened to on Deezer.

## The Band Plays On

Our study was small and local and is, therefore, difficult to draw general conclusions about digital natives as music consumers. That said, we believe that our results align with work that is being done elsewhere, which may suggest some broader trends for vinyl and digital music delivery.

There is a growth opportunity for vinyl, even if this format remains a niche market. Specialized stores with their knowledgeable sales staff and like-minded patrons have managed to stay afloat despite the recent difficulties the music industry has faced. We found that those who purchase vinyl turn to the internet only when they are unable to find that sought-after rarity at their local record store or flea market, so in-store opportunities will remain core to this market. Because vinyl aficionados continue to cite sound quality and the value of physical objects as key factors, marketing efforts that focus on an appreciation of these aspects may draw new consumers into the fold.

With regard to digital music, buying patterns have certainly changed, as has the way in which music is valued. Digital natives like the convenience and the portability of MP3s, and they enjoy being able to play their music on multiple devices in diverse places. They are accustomed to having easy access to the music they want to hear. They pick and choose their playlists according to their whims and not the predetermined preferences of a record label or radio station. The digital natives in our study download a lot of music, which appears to imply that possessing music remains important, though they don't necessarily feel that much of it is worth *paying* for. They are willing to view advertising in exchange for free streaming music and, when they've test-driven music and found it to be of sufficient quality, they are willing to purchase it in digital or CD format.

Despite their moniker, digital natives do still talk to people face to face, still shop in actual stores, and are still interested in listening to quality music. The good news is that digital natives are still willing to spend their allowances on their favorite music, despite their downloading expertise; desire for fast, flexible, personalized listening experiences;

and more hesitant purchasing behavior. They've just already listened to it before its release.

## About the Contributors

**Heidi Gautschi** grew up in France and the United States, and she continues to divide her time between these two countries. She has taught in the French university system since 2000, most recently at University of Lille 3. Her research looks at the relationship between society and communication technology with special emphasis on the comparative French and American contexts. She earned a BA in philosophy from Tufts University, an MA in health education from Teachers College, Columbia University, and a PhD in information and communication sciences from the University of Paris X.

**Emilie Moreau** lives in Lille, France. She is a musician, independent scholar, and school librarian. She has a PhD in information and communication sciences from the University of Lille 3. She wrote a groundbreaking dissertation on how the gay community was represented in the French print media. Her current research project focuses on music composition and new technology.

## Recommended Reading

### Books and Articles

Cavin, Susan. "Imaginary Social Relations." *Futures* 38 (2006): 875–885.

Crossley, Nick. "The Man Whose Web Expanded: Network Dynamics in Manchester's Post/Punk Music Scene 1976-1980." *Poetics* 37, no. 1 (2009): 24–49.

Flichy, Patrice. *Innovation Technique*. Paris: La Découverte, 1995.

Gautschi, Heidi and Emilie Moreau. "From the Record Store to Myspace: Sharing and Creating Music with Records and MP3s." Paper presented at the 6th Media in Transition Conference, April 24-26, at MIT, Cambridge, MA, 2009. web.mit.edu/comm-forum/mit6/papers/Gautschi.pdf (accessed October 18, 2010).

Gopal, Ram D., Sudip Bhattacharjee, and G. Lawrence Sanders. "Do Artists Benefit from Online Music Sharing?" *Journal of Business* 79, no. 3 (2006):1503–1533.

Perriault, Jacques. *La Logique de l'Usage*. Paris: Flammarion, 1989.

Pinch, Trevor, and Karen Bijsterveld. "Sound Studies: New Technologies and Music." *Social Studies of Science* 34, no. 5 (2004): 635–648.

Schafer, R. Murray. *The Soundscape: Our Sonic Environment and the Tuning of the World*. Rochester, VT: Destiny Books, 1993.

Serazio, Michael. "The Apolitical Irony of Generation Mash-up: A Cultural Case Study in Popular Music." *Popular Music and Society* 31, no. 3 (2008): 79–94.

Wendel, Evan Landon. "New Potentials for 'Independent' Music." Master's Thesis. Department of Comparative Media Studies, MIT, 2008.

## Websites

Deezer, www.deezer.com

eMule, www.emule-project.net

Nielsen SoundScan 2009 Highlights, bit.ly/58eMN5

Trax Magazine, magazinetrax.socialgo.com

Tsugi, www.tsugi.fr

U.K. Music, www.ukmusic.org/research

Zarcorp, myspace.com/zarcorpinc

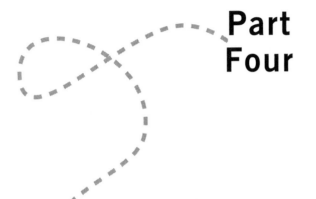

# Part Four

# Educating the Digital Native

# CHAPTER 15

# Making the Grade: Standards and Promoting Achievement Through Technology

Sarah Bryans Bongey

At home, the digital native may have spent his earliest formative years watching a parent using a cell phone and talking to or texting an "invisible" friend, or he himself may have had 24/7 access to television, computers, video games, MP3 players, and all manner of digital devices and resources—any or all of which will shape his world view and learning style. "Real life" is always-connected, always-entertaining, and endlessly interactive.

Contrast this with life at school, where the digital native spends a large part of the day sitting at a desk, listening to teachers, and fulfilling (even as a passive participant in) assorted programmatic and academic requirements, including an elaborate and evolving parade of standards and education reform initiatives described by acronyms such as NCLB (No Child Left Behind), ESEA (Elementary and Secondary Education Act), IDEA (Individuals with Disabilities Education Act), HEOA (Higher Education Opportunity Act), and ARRA (American Recovery and Reinvestment Act), among others.

Certainly, learning in a traditional school or university is sometimes a joyous and engaging experience, and at other times it is not. Regardless, for digital native students, the road to scholastic success involves meeting these myriad requirements and progressing to the next lesson, project, course, or grade level. This chapter will look at how digital technologies affect student engagement and success, and how a love of learning can be instilled in digital native learners. It will also examine how the use of these technologies can co-exist with—and even support and promote—the goals and standards of traditional education.

## A Never-Ending Education

When the end of the typical academic year arrives in June, the days of structure and guided learning come to an end. Having less autonomy than older, more self-sufficient siblings, younger children are more intensively exposed to whatever ready resources and parental prescriptions prevail. These can vary widely from one family to the next and, while some students may go on family vacations, attend interest-based camps, or spend time with friends, others—depending upon their age and situation—may wind up spending their time in a less stimulating environment in terms of exposure to new ideas, learning opportunities, or culture. Technology in general, and computer or internet-based resources in particular, has the potential to either alleviate or complicate this situation.

The concepts of inclusive education and universal design have emerged, and associated laws such as the Americans with Disabilities Act (ADA) have prompted and fueled the renovation and construction of accessible buildings in even the poorest schools and districts. Meanwhile, through the use of digital technologies and the increasingly complex network of computers and connections that has gradually developed, educational policy makers at the national, state, and local levels have developed an infrastructure that they hope will extend and promote learning among all learners, including (but not limited to) digital natives.

Recently, digital immigrants and digital natives alike have pointed to video games, television, and computers as possible culprits behind some of the challenges facing today's youth. Prior to the rise of digital technologies however, many of these challenges had already been noted. Back in 1983, *A Nation at Risk* (National Commission on Excellence in Education) concluded that "the educational foundations of our society are presently being eroded by a rising tide of mediocrity ..." Concerns relating to our country's ability to produce a work force that can innovate and compete in a world, that partly due to technology as a driver becoming "flat" (Thomas L. Friedman, *The World Is Flat: A Brief History of the Twenty-First Century*, Friedman, Farrar, Straus and Giroux, 2008), still seem valid. Technical and media literacy are and will continue to be increasing and essential factors supporting a capable and educated work force.

In educating the digital native, one must consider the system in which the instruction takes place. That system will establish the parameters of any teaching and learning activities. In the U.S., this necessitates taking a closer look at our K–12 public education system. To avoid the risks of a reduction in funding, the potential humiliation of published test score data and low ranking status, and possibly even being slated for closure, a school and its teachers must succeed in teaching all children a prescribed set of content and skills, regardless of how much foundational knowledge, family support, and ongoing resources these students bring to the table.

With its use of high-stakes testing and accountability to promote students' attainment of a pre-established set of content and performance standards, standards-based education (SBE) is a controversial reality (see Table 15.1 for a list of the main standards organizations). Title I funding, ARRA, grant programs, charter schools, and other programs are often attempts to offset the unequal funding of schools with operating

**Table 15.1   Standards and Guidelines Developed by Professional Organizations to Inform Standards Established by Individual U.S. States**

| Standards Content Area | Organization | Website |
|---|---|---|
| English | National Council of Teachers of English (NCTE) | www.ncte.org |
| | Teachers of English to Speakers of Other Languages (TESOL) | www.tesol.org |
| Mathematics | National Council of Teachers of Mathematics (NCTM) | www.nctm.org |
| Science | National Science Teachers Association (NSTA) | www.nsta.org |
| | American Association for the Advancement of Science (AAAS) | www.aaas.org |
| History | National Center for History in the Schools (NCHS) | nchs.ucla.edu |
| Civics and Government | Center for Civic Education | www.civiced.org |

*Note:* This is a partial listing. For a complete listing, please refer to ASCD and Mid-continent Research for Education and Learning (McREL).

budgets that depend on local tax revenues. In addition, poorer school districts reflect communities where social capital and family resources are likewise more impoverished than their affluent counterparts. This situation is particularly problematic in a nation where different school districts enjoy different levels of funding and support, and where state and federal funds must be used to supplement a funding formula that is dictated by the tax base of each school district. When applied in the K–12 classroom, national standards must be made to dovetail with prevailing state and local standards. By the time the professional teacher gets his turn to prioritize, prepare, and deliver curriculum, the pre-determined menu of requirements may leave little room for the development of local and responsive solutions. Systemically, for those who are designing and delivering education to digital natives in the K–12 setting, the role of standards—in terms of organizing and driving priorities and practices of states, districts, schools, and teachers—can represent either an opportunity or a threat to the kinds of technology-enhanced education that our digital natives need and expect.

## The Standards Struggle and Some Digital Solutions

Students who receive special education services are allowed accommodations based on their individualized education plan (IEP). However, they must still meet prevailing state content standards in subjects such as mathematics, English, and science. The good news is that there are tools and tactics being used by teachers today that not only can help meet these standardized objectives but that appeal to digital natives and better engage them in the learning process.

For example, to help her special education class of middle school students meet these essential standards in the area of math, Minnesota special education teacher Diana Vanasse uses Web 2.0 resources to spice up the effort to enforce more frequent drill and practice with multiplication tables and other foundational tasks. As Vanasse aptly explains, "Without knowing the basics, there's just no way that a student can progress to the next step."

Traditional flash cards, which often demand adult or sibling support during frequently required study sessions, just weren't doing the trick, and they were underutilized for a variety of reasons. As a digital alternative, Vanasse discovered that Web 2.0 tools like Brainy Math, A+ Math, or even the online games or explanatory videos provided by the textbook publisher had the potential to engage students in otherwise dull material, to extend the classroom to after-school hours, and to get kids who were at risk of falling behind to a place where they were ready to succeed. Six of the students in her resource room engaged in weekly three-minute "Skill Drills" and—graphing their own progress after each drill—they had the satisfaction of seeing visible proof of steady, and sometimes dramatic, gains in the number of correct answers obtained during these tests of basic math facts.

However, math is not the only subject area that can be supported through learning games and online resources. Many school media specialists and teachers view the internet as a rich resource to promote and support foundational attainment in other key content areas such as social studies, science, and English. Judicious use of these resources can help students attain key goals and objectives outlined in state content standards and generated by organizations such as the National Council of Teachers of English (NCTE), American Association for the Advancement of Science (AAAS), and others. When carefully selected and applied, online resources can also help teachers diagnose and address deficits.

Jane Sullivan, a third-grade teacher at Lowell Elementary School in Duluth, Minnesota, is a well-known advocate of using technology for education. Her three favorite technology tools are the SMART Board; document cameras for displaying images, text, or objects; and flip cameras (inexpensive iPod-sized video cameras with a built-in USB plug for easy transfer of video content to a computer).

Sullivan recalls how she first got her SMART Board six years ago through a Microsoft grant and how her teaching methods have never been the same since. Each day, third graders walk into the classroom to find a welcome message from their teacher projected on the large SMART Board display screen, along with colorful graphics and some guiding messages on what to expect for the day ahead.

Although the promise of grammar lessons has historically prompted reactions ranging from stifled yawns to gut-wrenching dread, Sullivan reports that her students now approach their grammar lessons alert and eager to participate, as the SMART Board allows them to engage via the technology. If a student's name is drawn and he or she knows the answer, the lucky grammar student gets to physically write her response on the big board using digital ink for all to see. Year after year—and crediting her success to her SMART Board and technology-enriched instructional methods—Sullivan sees test scores relating to grammar and other areas covered by benchmark exams rise steadily and dramatically. "The test scores in the fall are very low, but by the time I administer the third benchmark test in the spring, their standardized scores have not only improved, they have changed to very high," says Sullivan. "I think the students just blossom because of the engaging way the SMART Board presents the material."

During a math lesson on money, each student pulls out a bag containing plastic coins as the teacher fires up her SMART Board gallery and quickly generates movable coins that can be manipulated on-screen with the drag of an index finger. "This is the most powerful manipulative I've ever used in teaching math. I feel as though we're all on the same mental plane. They really understand the material."

And the greater world of people, places, and events outside is not ignored as Sullivan has perfected the means of integrating math, English, and performing arts through SMART Board-based guess-what or guess-who lessons. By adding an interactive button to the guess-who SMART Board display, she is able to link to multimedia clues on YouTube or other freely available resources on the internet.

Extending the classroom activities, Sullivan's website offers a section to support students in their efforts to practice for a standardized test known as the MCA (Minnesota Comprehensive Assessment). The website includes links to internet-based games such as A+ Math, Ghost Blaster, Spelling City, and Puzzle Maker to help students practice basic skills in reading, writing, and math.

One added benefit observed by many teachers who embrace digital teaching tools is that learning fluidly extends outside the classroom when students and parents are provided with vetted web-based resources. "There are many websites out there," Sullivan says, "but I screen and review everything before posting it on my site." Through the years, parents have particularly appreciated the web-based learning resources, as well as the option to email Sullivan through the website. Years after a child has moved on to the higher grades, parents and guardians remember and remark on how helpful the web-based resources were to their children.

Whether they provide free tools to generate mind maps, surveys, and puzzles or host blogs, wikis, video, podcasting, networking, and more, sites like Discovery School and Thinkfinity save parents and teachers time by providing annotated bibliographies and quality-screened links and resources. Many organizations, institutions, and individuals have expended considerable time, effort, and expertise designing and creating sites to promote learning among digital natives. These expert-generated resource sites can support the needs of our digital native learners to consume, create, and evaluate media and information. Natives have grown up expecting to use interactive and web-based media and tools, so Sullivan and other teachers who wisely guide students in their usage are able to capture students' attention and imagination, and help them achieve.

## Reaching and Teaching: Digital Opportunities to Extend the School Year

For states, districts, schools, and teachers seeking to close the achievement gap and to guide students toward the successful attainment of essential skills and knowledge, technology has the potential to serve as a stalwart ally. SMART Boards, internet resources, and similar technologies have become a ubiquitous form of support for many teachers. Teacher-moderated use of software, websites, and other tools can deliver interesting and appropriate educational activities for digital natives.

With the potential of digital technologies to enrich teaching and learning and extend the instructional day or year, educators and schools are still learning and developing ways to infuse the curriculum with (often free) resources never before available. Through the use of computer software, websites, and a learning management system (LMS), educators can extend learning far beyond the physical and temporal confines of the classroom for all students, including students at risk and those with special needs or gifts. It is now possible to construct universally designed learning environments that are always accessible, even after the school doors have been closed and locked for the day or for the year.

In their book *Teaching Every Student in the Digital Age* (Association for Supervision and Curriculum Development, 2002), authors David Rose and Anne Meyer discuss the importance of universal design for learning (UDL), stating, "First, it applies the idea of built-in flexibility to the educational curriculum. Second, it pushes universal design one step further by supporting not only improved access to information within classrooms, but also improved access to learning." In fact, undergraduate college students who were surveyed on their perceptions relating to the use of an LMS to support instruction and promote UDL reported high levels of engagement and satisfaction, with 98 percent saying that they would make a special effort to enroll in future courses that used the LMS in this way (Gerald Cizadlo, Lynn Kalnbach, and Sarah Bryans Bongey, "Blended Solutions: Using an LMS to Deliver Universal Design for Learning," 2009).

Using an LMS and other components of our rich and networked technological infrastructure, teachers have powerful new options to differentiate instruction, deepen and enrich content, and expand upon classroom-based instruction and information that—to students in a given classroom—may have represented a puzzle or an elusive topic of intrigue during the natural limitations of a typical school day. Whether through a simple website, blog, wiki, or a more advanced LMS like Moodle or Blackboard, students are increasingly empowered to extend their learning by accessing these prescribed resources from any environment that offers computer and internet access. This supplemental or web-enhanced approach to improving the educational process has been most prevalent at the college level, but it is now finding its way to the K–12 environment as well.

The promise of using technology to extend learning opportunities to after-school hours and the summer months has the potential to address serious educational challenges in the K–12 setting. In *Outliers: The Story of Success* (2008), Malcolm Gladwell describes a research study that explored the relationship of socioeconomic class (low, middle, and high) and reading scores in a Baltimore school district. The researchers discovered that a large proportion of the academic achievement gap between disadvantaged youngsters and their more advantaged peers can be explained by "what happens over the summer" (Karl L. Alexander, Doris R. Entwisle, and Linda S. Olson, "New Directions for Youth Development," 2007). Looking at the data provided by the researchers, Gladwell concludes that "virtually all of the advantage that wealthy students have over poor students is the result of differences in the way privileged kids learn while they are not in school."

It is clear that the judicious use of the growing digital infrastructure among students at home, as well as in schools and libraries nationwide, has the potential to enhance communication and provide instructional content and support on a year-round basis. Much of the excitement surrounding the digital age stems from its collaborative and constructive nature, and the fact that anyone can become a producer of information. However, no matter how slick or flashy the end product may appear, this ease of production does not mean that any given website, video, or blog will be reliable, comprehensive, and objective. The ease of production represents a great opportunity for students to become content creators; but at the same time, it places a huge burden on the school media specialists and teachers who have to select online resources and guide students in becoming qualified consumers of digital information. Selective judgment must be cultivated by the consumers themselves, as well as by those who teach or design curricula or individual learning experiences.

With the internet's plethora of free and already-prepared resources, those with foundational reading and computational skills need the ability to exercise judgment, as well as access to a fully equipped computer and an internet connection to avail themselves of training-on-demand resources and other educational opportunities. There is a philosophical tug-of-war between activists who call for year-round schooling and others who say that it would be disagreeable to students and families and too expensive to implement. However, our technology infrastructure has the potential to extend and enhance the typical, traditional school year at a lower cost and with a potentially less invasive impact on summer plans, jobs, discretionary time, and travel.

## From Brick and Mortar to "Brick and Click"

Meanwhile, in the world of higher education, colleges have often had to alter existing programs and develop new ones in order to respond effectively to the changing needs of students and society. Take the College of St. Scholastica, for example. Founded in the Minnesota northlands in 1912 by a group of pioneering Benedictine sisters, St. Scholastica was initially dedicated to providing much-needed undergraduate programs in the fields of nursing and education. Since then, its programs have evolved dramatically with the addition of high-tech offerings in healthcare informatics and information management and the establishment of a program in electronic health records. It's a far cry from the original programs envisioned by the college's founders. Yet remaining true to its mission, the college has built upon its century-old traditional programs as it moves into the world of online education.

"For several years, we have offered courses and even some graduate programs online, but now we have developed a comprehensive business plan and made substantial investments in new personnel and infrastructure to support this strategic venture," says college president Larry Goodwin. "St. Scholastica is not 'ahead of the curve' in the online world; some others have been involved in it for more than a decade. But our move to online education is not simply a way of grasping for straws in a tough economy. Indeed, our overall enrollment has never been stronger."

Online tools have much to offer parents and students in the K–12 environment as well, and many school districts have come to depend upon products like Digital Campus to keep themselves informed of grades and work submitted, thus helping with the organizational and motivational aspects of schoolwork. SMART Boards, websites, classroom clickers, tablet PCs, and document cameras, as well as electronic databases, media centers, and a vast range of Web 2.0 tools are also increasingly popular at the high school and the college level.

Beginning as a tool used by colleges, universities, private businesses, governments, and organizations, the LMS has also begun to take hold at the middle and high school levels. Leading LMS tools include several open source solutions such as Moodle and Sakai and commercial products such as Blackboard and Desire to Learn. An LMS can be used to organize and present course content in a fully online or hybrid format. Many teachers find that supplementing a face-to-face course with LMS components greatly improves student satisfaction and success.

A 2005 study by Sarah Bryans Bongey, Gerald Cizadlo, and Lynn Kalnbach, "Using a Course Management System to Meet the Challenges of Large Lecture Classes," found a statistically significant improvement in test scores of 156 college undergraduates based on their instructor's use of an LMS to provide his students with access to a range of tools and supports, including the syllabus, objectives, self tests, and grade information. Analyzing grade and survey information, the study concluded that the LMS "had a marked and highly beneficial effect on student achievement."

Individual course sites generated by an LMS come ready with a range of features such as an announcement mechanism, calendar, and assignment drop box. They also typically provide the ability to generate and grade tests, the ability to link files and multimedia content, and a grade book function that can provide individualized grade information privately to each student based on his or her login.

Technologies such as the LMS have also paved the way for the development of fully online high school and college degree programs. In this way, these technologies have not only been framed by traditional forces; their existence and power have promoted innovation and redefined traditional approaches to the delivery of instruction. The entire process continues to open doors for teachers and learners, although it also presents frustrations and challenges to those who are not yet completely comfortable with instructional technology.

## Converging Influences

At the college level, the LMS has enabled the design and delivery of courses that are fully online or that blend online and classroom instruction. Dr. Gerald Cizadlo, biology professor and a campus leader in his use of instructional technology, says he started out using the LMS to provide students with the course syllabus, objectives, self-tests, and lab schedule. Using a document camera or digitized images, Cizadlo (commonly referred to as "Doc C") orchestrates his lectures/podcasts and supplemental imagery with great care. "I believe that a lot of the trouble that students have with science is in visualization; they just can't make pictures in their minds of these atomic or molecular or cellular objects and processes. If I constantly give them pictures, in addition to my descriptions of my mental images, they can build a framework that will allow them to fit new ideas in later on in their lives."

While Cizadlo stresses the need for any delivery method to assist students in developing a "visual framework," he is also quick to disparage publishers and instructors who create and distribute illustrative material of poor quality—solely to include some visual interest. "In my classes, we're better off with accurate verbal descriptions than inaccurate, full-color, moving images. So, in that way, the technology that allows easy animation can be a hindrance, and, to tell you the truth, that is mostly what I see today. The potential is fantastic, but the reality is extremely disappointing."

Although his original intent was simply to provide podcasts of his lecture for his students, Cizadlo has inadvertently established a place on the worldwide digital stage through his podcast channel on iTunes. He supplements his podcast lectures with a website providing a course outline and slides from a "digital blackboard" that displays illustrations generated during each lecture. Audio links are also provided directly on Doc C's website (faculty.css.edu/gcizadlo), making it easy for those without MP3 players to supplement the slides and to see and hear the material.

"I'm a strong believer in an oral tradition. We have learned for thousands of years by listening to explanations by someone who is more knowledgeable ... Our non-verbal clues that are embedded in our voices add tremendously to the impact of the ideas. Students everywhere would much rather listen to good oral presentations rather than read books stating the same facts. And, the internet allows that mode of transmission, painlessly."

In welcoming our digital natives to college, faculty find that these students are very comfortable with web-based collaborative activities, virtual worlds, game-based simulations, video production, and all manner of flashy high-tech interactions. However, many of these students are emerging from high schools where filtering is the norm. Despite the increasing need for student instruction in media literacy, intellectual property, and research strategies, school media programs are often the first to be cut, meaning that many students may lack essential training and skills in these areas. As a result, many colleges are finding it necessary to integrate research and media literacy instruction into foundational courses such as English composition or other freshman-level classes.

Technology has revolutionized education for digital immigrants as well, and they are increasingly finding themselves sharing the same learning environment with their digital native counterparts. Undergraduate college students are often drawn to the convenience of an occasional online course. At the same time, online programming is convenient for working professionals, full-time parents, or those living in remote areas, extending their opportunities to take classes and pursue a variety of certificates and advanced degrees with little or no need to attend face-to-face classes. In response to the changing market, many colleges such as St. Scholastica, which may have traditionally catered to an undergraduate population of students just out of high school, are experiencing major changes in their student profile as they establish new web enhanced or online programs for students at the graduate level.

Since online education shatters traditional parameters and environments for learning, it likewise includes students with varying comfort levels in using technology. Thus, the composition of the online or blended class challenges the educator or instructional designer to develop an online learning environment that can support and engage students with a wide range of technical skills and abilities. Strategies for managing an online course in an LMS or other forum are therefore essential. One simple support strategy might involve including a digital Getting Started folder with links to websites, orientation materials, user manual, welcome message, online office hours, and technical support resources for the novice. Additionally, a second Enriching Resources folder might include optional online interactivities and resources for students who are (or who eventually become) quite comfortable with the online environment. An increasingly diverse population, with growing numbers of English language learners (ELL) and students with disabilities, requires responsive instruction, the application of UDL approaches, and the support of an active disabilities resource center.

## National Technology Standards

*Advancing excellence in learning and teaching through innovative and effective uses of technology.* —Mission of ISTE

In addition to the many standards guiding fundamental curricula such as mathematics, language arts, science, and social studies, today's teachers also have access to national technology standards. In its mission to promote effective use of technology in education, the International Society for Technology in Education (ISTE) has established standards for administrators, teachers, and students. Specifically developed to support and inform teacher education and stakeholders in pre-kindergarten through 12th grade, ISTE's standards reflect, respond to, and drive instructional technology and how it is implemented. As shown in Table 15.2, the ISTE's National Educational Technology Standards (NETS) address three key roles in education: student, teacher, and administrator. It is important to note, however, that the ISTE NETS are only *suggested* national technology standards. While teachers do not necessarily need to contend with them, many in education turn to ISTE standards for resources and guidance.

ISTE standards—and success by the instructional leaders that deploy them—will continue to encourage the application, exploration, and constructive use of digital tools to achieve the stated content standards that have been so widely adopted by various U.S. states. Additionally, the ISTE standards help frame the educational use of digital tools to promote rigorous learning, beyond mere "edutainment," and the construction of a meaningful framework by which these tools can be ethically and effectively used.

The ISTE standards, as well as the real-world experiences of native and immigrant alike, make it clear that if administrators, teachers, and learners are to fully benefit from the technology resources at hand, it is essential that they develop skills and knowledge to use these tools strategically and ethically. Students need to become qualified producers, consumers, and evaluators of media messages and information to ensure that they can communicate, create, and survive in the digital jungle. Teachers need to use technology effectively and inclusively to ensure that all students can learn. Administrators need to cultivate excellence and a shared vision for transformation, overseeing a responsive infrastructure in which all learners will be able to access, benefit from, and contribute to the best of what the digital age has to offer.

## Table 15.2   NETS Established by the ISTE (Source: ISTE, www.iste.org)

ISTE National Educational Technology Standards (NETS)

| Students | Teachers | Administrators |
|---|---|---|
| **1. Creativity and Innovation** Students demonstrate creative thinking, construct knowledge, and develop innovative products and processes using technology. **2. Communication and Collaboration** Students use digital media and environments to communicate and work collaboratively, including at a distance, to support individual learning and contribute to the learning of others. **3. Research and Information Fluency** Students apply digital tools to gather, evaluate, and use information. **4. Critical Thinking, Problem Solving, and Decision Making** Students use critical thinking skills to plan and conduct research, manage projects, solve problems, and make informed decisions using appropriate digital tools and resources. **5. Digital Citizenship** Students understand human, cultural, and societal issues related to technology and practice legal and ethical behavior. **6. Technology Operations and Concepts** Students demonstrate a sound understanding of technology concepts, systems, and operations. | **1. Facilitate and Inspire Student Learning and Creativity** Teachers use their knowledge of subject matter, teaching and learning, and technology to facilitate experiences that advance student learning, creativity, and innovation in both face-to-face and virtual environments. **2. Design and Develop Digital-Age Learning Experiences and Assessments** Teachers design, develop, and evaluate authentic learning experiences and assessments incorporating contemporary tools and resources to maximize content learning in context and to develop the knowledge, skills, and attitudes identified in the NETS. **3. Model Digital-Age Work and Learning** Teachers exhibit knowledge, skills, and work processes representative of an innovative professional in a global and digital society. **4. Promote and Model Digital Citizenship and Responsibility** Teachers understand local and global societal issues and responsibilities in an evolving digital culture and exhibit legal and ethical behavior in their professional practices. **5. Engage in Professional Growth and Leadership** Teachers continuously improve their professional practice, model lifelong learning, and exhibit leadership in their school and professional community by promoting and demonstrating the effective use of digital tools and resources. | **1. Visionary Leadership** Educational administrators inspire and lead development and implementation of a shared vision for comprehensive integration of technology to promote excellence and support transformation throughout the organization. **2. Digital-Age Learning Culture** Educational administrators create, promote, and sustain a dynamic, digital-age learning culture that provides a rigorous, relevant, and engaging education for all students. **3. Excellence in Professional Practice** Educational administrators promote an environment of professional learning and innovation that empowers educators to enhance student learning through the infusion of contemporary technologies and digital resources. **4. Systemic Improvement** Educational administrators provide digital-age leadership and management to continuously improve the organization through the effective use of information and technology resources. **5. Digital Citizenship** Educational administrators model and facilitate understanding of social, ethical, and legal issues and responsibilities related to an evolving digital culture. |

## Standard Education and Limitless Promise

The first generation of digital native learners are growing up, graduating, and making inroads in the workplace. New cohorts of natives are entering our classrooms every year. While these students may seem very comfortable with the technology used in the classroom, they will need solid skills to help them wisely navigate the use of digital technologies and truly be in a place where they can constructively and reliably leverage the continual and lifelong learning opportunities that the digital age offers. It will be exciting to see how some of these natives develop the skill and the dedication needed to join the ranks of instructors who can produce, select, evaluate, and deliver world-class learning experiences to new and emerging generations of digital natives in turn.

Of course, basic reading, writing, analytical, and computational skills will continue to provide an entry into realms of learning. However, one exciting area of growth with the always-connected native is that the ability to collaborate with others will manifest itself in new ways and with new benefits.

Another quality of digital learners that inspires hope is their positive recollection of their early exposure to technology. "As a child, growing up with educational computer games gave me a new conduit through which to practice creative skills. They have also allowed me to learn scholastic concepts with more ease and fun," claims one digital native. It may just be that his early exposure to math game software like Jump to Learn and Math Blaster helped form his positive attitude toward mathematics, which in turn helped him master a multitude of academic prerequisites leading up to his current status as a geology major at Beloit College.

Basic subject areas such as math, science, and English will remain foundational keys to advanced study in emerging fields such as nanotechnology, game design and geographic information systems (GIS). Meanwhile, new technology tools and techniques are on the horizon.

However, as they are subject to the same whims as other fashion and technological fads, these tools may or may not "take hold." Educators and administrators must continue to apply their own expertise, as well as ongoing research and scholarly practice, to assess which tools will appeal to digital natives' interests and best achieve educational objectives.

Educational standards remain controversial and challenging, as there are a multitude of goals and objectives for each core content area, and teachers are left with inadequate time to cover them all. However, educational strategies that include a well-planned and positive partnership with digital technologies offer great promise. Creative use of technology in supplementing and delivering instruction can poise our entire educational system to extend learning, provide struggling students with needed scaffolding, and offer all students access to a relevant, trackable, and adjustable array of learning supports and catalysts.

We need to achieve these goals if we want all students to succeed later in life. However, research data from sources like Malcolm Gladwell, Karl Alexander, and the U.S. government's Center for Education Statistics reveal that student achievement is often associated with family resources, socioeconomic status, and social capital. Thus, as we peer into the depths of this achievement gap, we must recognize that digital tools have the potential to help level the playing field through potentially year-round and digitally delivered learning opportunities based on the universal provision of needed and ubiquitous access to learning opportunities. Educators must recognize the challenges digital natives present as learners but also the overwhelming opportunity that digital tools provide. These are exciting times for teachers and learners everywhere, and it is our responsibility to be open to these tools and teach students to use them well so that they can achieve to their fullest potential.

## Acknowledgments

I would like to thank my advisor, University of Minnesota professor Dr. Trudie Hughes, for reviewing this chapter and offering expert suggestions and resources.

## About the Contributor

**Sarah Bryans Bongey** is a licensed teacher and K–12 media generalist with experience in face-to-face and online instruction of both K–12 and college-level students. She currently serves as an adjunct instructor for the School of Education and holds a full-time position as academic technology coordinator of the College of St. Scholastica in Duluth, Minnesota. In this capacity, she works with college faculty to facilitate the effective integration of instructional technologies for online as well as traditional face-to-face courses. She received her MEd in educational media and technology, and she is currently pursuing her EdD in teaching and learning at the University of Minnesota. Recent presentations include an informational session on "Addressing Multiple Intelligences in the Online Course Environment" (at the 24th Annual Conference on Distance Teaching and Learning), a poster session UDL at AHEAD, and an informational session describing UDL research at the Sloan-C Conference. She has published articles on instructional technologies in *Campus-Wide Information Systems* and *Teaching & Learning Magazine*. Professional memberships include ISTE, SLOAN-C, and EDUCAUSE.

## Recommended Reading

### Books and Articles

Conrad, Rita-Marie and J. Ana Donaldson. *Engaging the Online Learner: Activities and Resources for Creative Instruction.* San Francisco: Jossey-Bass, 2004.

Pink, Daniel. *A Whole New Mind: Why Right-Brainers Will Rule the Future.* New York: Berkley Publishing Group, 2006.

Rose, David, and Anne Meyer. *Teaching Every Student in the Digital Age: Universal Design for Learning.* Alexandria, VA: Association for Supervision and Curriculum Development, 2002.

## Websites

Big 6: Information and Technology Skills for Student Achievement, www.big6.com

California State University Lesson Plans and Teaching Strategies, csun.edu/~hcedu013/plans.html

Council for Exceptional Children (CEC), www.cec.sped.org

Department of Education Office of Educational Technology (OET), www2.ed.gov/about/offices/list/os/technology/index.html

Discovery School, Kathy Schrock's Guide for Educators, school.discoveryeducation.com/schrockguide

Educational Freeware, educational-freeware.com

Education World, www.educationworld.com

Educator's Reference Desk Lesson Plans, eduref.org/Virtual/Lessons

Edutopia, www.edutopia.org

Filamentality, www.kn.pacbell.com/wired/fil

Microsoft Education, www.microsoft.com/education

MultiMedia & Internet @ Schools, mmischools.com

SMART Exchange, exchange.smarttech.com

TeacherLINK Teacher Resources, teacherlink.ed.usu.edu/tlresources/index.html

Teachers Helping Teachers, pacificnet.net/~mandel

Thinkfinity, www.thinkfinity.org

WebQuest.org, webquest.org

# CHAPTER 16

# Quest to Learn: A Public School for Today's Digital Kids

Robert J. Torres, Rebecca Rufo-Tepper, and Arana Shapiro

The writing is on the wall: Kids have moved and reside comfortably in the 21st century even as schools continue to lag behind. Led principally by the digital practices of today's kids, a new school for grades 6–12 called Quest to Learn (Q2L) has been carefully designed to capitalize on those practices to engage students in deep forms of learning. Drawing from contemporary research and theories of learning as a socially and technologically mediated endeavor, a design group at the Institute of Play, made up of game designers, learning scientists and content experts, spent two years architecting Q2L, which opened its doors in September 2009.

Q2L was created in an attempt to change the conversation about school reform from one traditionally focused on ensuring students acquire basic numeracy, reading, and writing skills to one that creates conditions in which students are challenged to help solve the invention and innovation challenges of our time. To meet this goal, Q2L uses a "systems thinking "framework as a core curricular and pedagogical strategy within carefully designed game-like, immersive environments. By "systems thinking," we mean a holistic perspective that sees the world as increasingly interconnected and seeks to understand it systemically, from elemental components to complex systems of activity. We define systems broadly to include social, natural, and technological systems that can be studied and understood as having certain crosscutting commonalities, such as rules, goals, and particular behaviors. Our games-based curriculum is designed by teachers, professional game designers, curriculum directors, and other content experts to create 10 week-long "missions," each of which is unique and creates an immersion environment in which students take on various identities—ranging from cartographer to architect to nature ecologist—to solve design and systems-based problems.

Q2L opened its doors in September 2009 to an ethnically and economically diverse group of New York City sixth graders. Entry into the school is based solely on interest: Students and families must attend an information session, but no student is denied admission based on merit or prior performance in school. The inspiration for Q2L comes from two observations: the seismic gap that exists between traditional schooling and the digital practices of youth today; and the alarming and persistent rates of high school dropouts in the U.S. A number of recent in-depth accounts by scholars like Mimi Ito, John Palfrey and Urs Gasser, and Craig Watkins have not only documented the extensive worlds youth have created in digital spaces, but they have highlighted the highly social, collaborative, and interest-based learning taking place in these digital environments. A few studies have quantified the rates at which youth are increasingly accessing digital media. For example:

- Studies by the Pew Internet & American Life Project report that 97 percent of youth are playing video games (bit.ly/hbAKyc, 2008), 57 percent of youth (or about 12 million) are creating content for the internet (2005), and 93 percent of teens go online (bit.ly/h8G4QS).

- Palfrey and Gasser (2008) claim that about 50 percent of YouTube's registered users are under the age of 20.

- As of 2009, the Child Trends Data Bank reported that 93 percent of American youth have access to a computer at home (bit.ly/eYNhMC).

In the meantime, a typical day in today's middle and high schools sees lethargic teenagers exercising varying degrees of patience as they endure the same low-tech delivery of information practices we've had in place since at least the 19th century. This may explain in part why 50 percent of students in urban areas drop out of high school, and 30 percent do so nationally. A March 2006 report called "The Silent Epidemic" (funded by the Bill and Melinda Gates Foundation) tells us that 81 percent of students who drop out say school is not relevant to their lives. Q2L's designers are keenly aware of these realities and have drawn inspiration from digitally mediated and collaborative practices that mirror those in most professional industries from business, health, and medicine to government and the arts. These practices are marked by participatory, co-creative processes and social engagements that exemplify what contemporary learning scientists have been saying for some time: Learning is not an individualized, lone-ranger endeavor but a highly social and collaborative achievement.

## A New Way to Learn

Scholars who look to the affordances of digital media technologies (like Mary Kalantzis and Bill Cope at the University of Illinois) have appropriated the term *new learning* to describe the promises of using these technologies for learning purposes. But what digital media—especially games—are making possible is the creation of participatory, socially mediated environments; immersive contexts; exploration; identity experimentation; and recursive learning through trial and error. These are the markers that have defined human learning forever. It is only since the creation of the Industrial Era school in the early 1900s, designed to maximize sorting for a one-size-fits-all efficiency, that we have moved away from this model.

We stress this point so as to place a special focus on our work, which is not a wholesale promotion of the use of games and digital media technologies (though many of these platforms are proving to support deep learning) but rather an exploration of fundamental questions regarding human development and cognition—questions, ironically, that we as educators have seldom found to drive activity in schools: How do people learn? What is the role of context? If social relationships are central to our human experiences, what is the role of social interactions and the cultures they give rise to, especially for youth? How do we design the kinds of immersive and social experiences that are conducive to human learning? How do games help us do this? And can we take social and technological contexts into consideration when we assess learning?

Our quest to seek out research-based approaches and to continuously gain deeper insights into how children learn has led us to develop a notion we call *nodal learning*. Central to this notion is the belief that to learn anything deeply, learners have to experience the content (be it science, art, music, or a sport) in a variety of different and distinct spaces, in and out of school, that allow for redundancy and predictability of content. Take for instance the way in which a high school basketball player becomes a masterful player. Solely playing basketball with her high school team will likely not grant her mastery. She will need to *be a basketball player* in other nodes as well, such as (a) with friends on a local court on the weekends, (b) on the phone at night with friends critiquing her game and those of others, (c) with her coach during one-on-one drills, (d) when reading magazines or online blogs about basketball, (e) when watching a professional team play on television, (f) when attending a summer basketball camp, and (g) when competing against other teams in her region. In school, most students are given opportunities to learn in one node (and in most instances, they are learning *about* something, a point to which we shall return in a moment).

As never before, we are now able to create distinct learning spaces (nodes) through the use of social technologies that blur the boundaries between in- and out-of-school spaces. As part of one of our research projects, we piloted a game with sixth graders called Gamestar Mechanic, which generated seven distinct learning spaces. The game, designed to teach players the basics of game design as an outcome of playing it, is a social technology that instantiates a community where players design and post games, rate games, and receive feedback from other players. At the time of our pilot study, the community was 600 players strong. The "nodes" generated by Gamestar Mechanic included the online game itself, an in-school game design workshop space that met three times a week over 16 weeks, meetings with professional game designers at their game design offices, out-of-school engagement with the games where students shared their designs with family and friends, and daily lunch meetings where students met with each other voluntarily. (Indeed, this last instance was a robust node created by students, which emerged out of their interest in meeting beyond the time allotted during workshops.)

Our nodal perspective is largely influenced by social network theory and from research on learning, identity development, and communities of practice. We believe this notion has significant implications for the design of learning spaces, most of which currently provide students only one node for practicing their understanding of new skills and content. For this reason, we make every attempt to design curricula that allow students to travel through an ecology of nodal in-and-out-of-school experiences that reinforce content in predictable and redundant ways.

## The Learning Program

While keenly interested in the question of how deep learning occurs, we are also guided by a particular preoccupation with *design* and *invention*. A driving question for us is: What are the learning conditions necessary to help develop the designers and inventors of this new century? Ensuring that we integrate the digital media practices of today's youth has been a leading design principle. Other principles have included the need for 21st-century learners to account for and cope with systemic complexity, to synthesize increasingly large bodies of knowledge and data, to develop a design perspective, and to see themselves as global citizens. Nine design competencies (see the Appendix at the end of this chapter) currently frame our curricular and assessment program. Among these is "designing for innovation," which requires students to design projects in which they account for the history and contexts of past innovations regardless of the field in which the new design will occur. Students are asked to innovate at the design methodology level (e.g., approaches for play testing and feedback) and at the level of design representation and aesthetics.

Systems thinking underpins our core curriculum. Stephen Hawking and other prominent scientists have said that we are living in the era of complexity, and that complexity itself will form the science of the 21st century. Similarly, Heinz Pagels has claimed in his book, *The Dreams of Reason: The Computer and the Rise of the Sciences of Complexity* (Bantam, 1988), that those who master this science will form the economic, political, and cultural superpowers of this new century. Understanding and mastering these so-called sciences of complexity requires systemic thinking, which has been identified by a growing number of researchers and learning scientists as a critical 21st-century skill. And though research has shown that systems thinking is a difficult skill to acquire (Linda Booth Sweeney and John D. Sterman, "Thinking About Systems: Student and Teacher Conceptions of Natural and Social Systems," 2007), game scholars like James Gee and Katie Salen and scientists at a

2006 Federation of American Scientists conference have claimed that video game play and game design may be useful means of developing this essential skill.

To be sure, an approach that engages public school students as systemic thinkers and charges them with designing their own world and social futures requires new methods of teaching and learning. We are humbled by the ambition of this project while also keenly aware of the challenges of reform. Change in the way we fundamentally conceive of learning and school design has been a long time coming. We are hopeful that this project will help to serve as a viable model in a sea of much needed game-changers. Here we offer some specifics about the model. The school—envisioned as a complex learning system—has many more elements and subsystems than these, but we offer here the core features of the program. Before continuing, however, we'd like to make one more general point about our learning program. Our game-based teaching and learning program is based on the principles that characterize good games (e.g., they are rule-based, immersive, and often highly social), which research is showing are also the principles that characterize deep learning. This does not mean that students play commercial games to access our standards-based curriculum, but that our students' learning experiences are carefully designed to embody the principles of games. In this way, we are not advocating for the use of games (although many off-the-shelf commercial games are useful learning tools), but rather that our game designers and teachers work to create learning experiences (explained in more detail later) that are game-*like*.

## A 21st-Century Curriculum

The core architectural structures of Q2L's learning program illustrate how we have capitalized on kids' digital practices while preparing our students for success in the 21st century. The curriculum is interdisciplinary, follows national and local content standards, is design-focused, and is relevant to the culture of today's students.

The five critical features of our curriculum are:

- A systems thinking focus
- A philosophy and practice of technology integration
- A blending of new literacies and traditional literacies in a set of interdisciplinary domains
- A game-based pedagogy
- An innovative approach to teacher development and curriculum design

## Systems Thinking in Practice

As mentioned earlier, the curriculum at Q2L is geared toward helping students develop systems thinking skills. Each grade focuses on an essential question and specific knowledge structured around systems, which we have separated into three phases (see Table 16.1).

The curriculum is designed to facilitate student understanding of systems and their structures. Students create, take apart, analyze, and innovate on models of many different types of systems, including (but not limited to) academic systems, natural systems, and interactive systems. Our goal is to help students develop the skills to cope with, understand, and navigate an increasingly complex world. Our hope is that this will allow them to be productive and active citizens at Q2L and beyond, as well as allow them to choose from a wide variety of college and career options.

Within the classroom, systems thinking skills are connected to the key content, core skills, and big ideas of each domain. For example, when sixth grade students study simple machines, they are asked not only to develop an understanding of levers, pulleys, and energy transfer but also to consider how the simple machine works as a system.

**Table 16.1   Systems Learning Trajectory, Grades 6–12**

| Phase I: Understanding the structure of systems | 6th grade | What is the architecture of a dynamic system? |
|---|---|---|
| | 7th grade | How do we use dynamic systems? |
| | 8th grade | How do we contribute to and transform dynamic systems? |
| Phase II: Understanding the disciplines as systems | 9th grade | How is disciplinary knowledge created and used? |
| | 10th grade | How do communities organize around systems of knowledge? |
| Phase III: Transforming systems | 11th grade | What practices emerge from the way a discipline organizes knowledge? |
| | 12th grade | How do we *transform* disciplinary knowledge? |

Students explore essential questions and fundamental knowledge related to mathematics and science, as well as those related to systems shown in Table 16.2.

## The Five Knowledge Domains

At Q2L, student learning is organized into five knowledge domains rather than traditional classes. While these knowledge domains integrate traditional content, the primary purpose of this structure is to foster students' abilities to make connections across domains and to "real world" learning. *Being, Space and Place* integrates English language arts (ELA) and social studies. Students are challenged to see how they are influenced by and relate to the world around them, as they look at different systems such as social systems, political systems, and economic systems, as well as systems of writing and communication. In *The Way Things Work,* science and math come together to give students hands-on experiences with how the things that make up their world work. Students spend time taking things apart and putting things back together to understand the systems all around them, such as natural and biological systems. In *Codeworlds,* students examine how ELA and math are both systems of representation. They create, manipulate, and deconstruct the

**Table 16.2   Content- and Systems-Related Essential Questions and Understandings**

| Content-Related Essential Questions | Systems-Related Essential Questions |
|---|---|
| • Why do humans create machines?<br>• What is work?<br>• What is simple about simple machines? | • What are the qualities and elements of a system?<br>• Can a system exist without a goal?<br>• If the components of a system are changed or modified, can the system still achieve its goal?<br>• How do the rules of a system allow it to behave in a particular way? |
| **Content-Related Understandings** | **Systems-Related Understandings** |
| • A system is composed of elements. Elements of a system have different attributes and characteristics that determine what the system can do.<br>• A goal is an element of a system. The goal defines what must be accomplished and can be composed of sub-goals.<br>• Rules are an element of a system. The rules of a system organize relationships between elements. The rules of a system allow it to behave in a particular way.<br>• Components are an element of a system. The components of a system are the pieces of the system that interact. | • Technology (machines) is created out of a need to make a task or tasks easier.<br>• Newton's Laws describe the general principles that guide the pattern of motion of objects.<br>• Force applied in a specific direction is essential to doing work. Force applied must move an object for work to be done. Machines are devices that make the doing of work easier. |

English language and mathematics as code. In *Wellness,* physical education, social emotional learning, and health come together to help students understand how a healthy body system contributes to a healthy mind system and vice versa. Finally, in *Sports for the Mind,* students take on the identity of designers to learn media arts and technology skills. Students play and author their own games as a way of looking at games as systems.

Key values for each domain are:

1. Helping students develop a systems perspective of the world, by which we mean enabling students to see and

understand the world as a set of dynamic relationships among parts of a whole.

2. Allowing students to explore diverse modes of accumulating, creating, understanding, and using knowledge.

3. Fostering targeted assimilation and synthesis of data, theories, and hypotheses of traditional academic disciplines, as well as habits of mind. A student's thoughts and actions demonstrate progressive understanding and personal growth.

4. Defining a set of socially acceptable norms, values, knowledge, and ways of validating and creating knowledge.

5. Defining clear trajectories to mastery. Offering opportunities for students to consider and design structured, physical models of complex problems.

## Game-Based Pedagogy and Curriculum

At Q2L, all curricula are developed by teachers in collaboration with game designers, curriculum directors, and content experts. The Institute of Play, the anchor partner of the school, has a staff of five game designers and two full-time curriculum directors. Game designers bring the expertise and understanding needed to create immersive, social environments, while teachers bring content knowledge and pedagogical skills. The merging of game designer and teacher expertise creates a powerful context for student learning. The curriculum director's role is to ensure that the integrity and vision of the curriculum is maintained. He or she guides the process of curriculum development while also ensuring that each Mission and Quest helps students uncover and explore the trimester's key systems concepts. Outside content experts are brought in to support the curriculum development team when needed.

The collaboration among game designers, curriculum directors, and teachers allows for games to be used in a variety of ways and for the curriculum to be developed in a game-like manner. Games offer concrete examples of systems and allow students to process, reflect on, and practice their understanding of systems. In addition, games provide highly immersive spaces where students are asked to take on roles and solve complex problems. At Q2L, students play and design games in their domain classes in order to develop knowledge and skills, and grasp the big ideas of the knowledge domains while developing systems thinking skills. Games are used in many different ways within the classroom to support learning. For example, during a Mission that deals with geography, middle school students may play Civilization IV (a commercial digital game) to learn how geography affects the development of a civilization. They might also play Sculptionary (a game designed by the Being, Space and Place teacher, game designers, and curriculum directors), where they have to sculpt different land formations within a given amount of time with pieces of clay.

Like games, the curriculum is immersive, participatory, allows for social engagement, and provides a challenge-based context for students to work within. We believe that students learn best when they are focused on a goal and are given continuous feedback on their performance. Students are given immediate and constant feedback and don't progress unless they have mastered certain knowledge and skills that are needed to complete the Mission (for example, they may be asked to multiply fractions, collect a set of evidence cards, or complete a set of journal entries on a blog). Students must show adequate progress in these areas, or they won't be allowed to enter the next Quest within the Mission. Additionally, we believe that learning is more meaningful when it is driven by a *need-to-know*. In order to create a need-to-know condition, the curriculum gives students purposeful and relevant opportunities to master a skill or seek specific knowledge. As is the case in most forms of game play, a game-like curriculum also creates a condition of *learning to be* rather than *learning about.* This requires students to step into and take on identities such as cartographers, archaeologists, engineers, international relations experts, mathematicians, or game designers, rather than *learning about* the content of these fields, which is the norm in traditional school settings.

## Missions and Quests

The Q2L curriculum is organized around a series of Missions and Quests. Every trimester, students try to complete five 10-week Missions, one in each of the five knowledge domains. A Mission provides students with a complex problem they need to solve and casts them in a role of some sort. Within each Mission, there is a series of Quests. Each Quest helps the students move toward completing the Mission and provides feedback as they progress. For example, in The Way Things Work domain (math/science), middle school students participate in a Mission called Invisible Pathways. This Mission asks students to consider the essential systems question: How do the relationships between elements in a system create a dynamic? The challenge of this Mission casts students in the role of scientists and communication specialists, tasked with the job of revealing a message hidden in a beam of light. They study how light and matter interact (refraction, absorption, scattering, and reflection) using digital cameras to document the results. They use a 3D simulation to model the movement of light through space, thus applying understandings gained through direct observation in the real world to a virtual representation. They do data analysis to understand the colors of light and study the eye as an optical device. Throughout the Mission, students use the scientific method to propose and test theories, observe and gather evidence of outcomes, and then apply this understanding to the development of new theories. The Mission culminates in a scientific challenge requiring students to collaborate in small teams. The challenge: Construct a pathway for a beam of light to travel to a target, changing direction a minimum of five times. The resulting pathway will require students to apply their understanding of the different ways light interacts with different materials, how it is filtered, strengthened, and changed.

Within the Invisible Pathways Mission, there are several Quests:

1. **Quest I.** The Problem of the Oar (week 1): Students develop an inventory of behaviors for Photon, a beam of light that has lost its way.

2. **Quest II.** Enigmo (weeks 2 and 3): Having compiled an inventory of behaviors describing Photon's interaction with different forms of matter, students are challenged to apply this knowledge within a 3D simulation tool called Enigmo 2.

3. **Quest III.** Can You Believe What You See? (weeks 4–6): Students work with a digital model of the eye. Using "light-boxes," they establish the conditions for sight: a light source, object, eye, and straight, unimpeded path.

4. **Quest IV.** Invisible Pathways Challenge (weeks 7–10): The Mission culminates in a Quest that requires students to collaborate in small teams to complete a challenge: Construct a pathway for a beam of light to travel to a target, changing direction a minimum of five times.

## Technology Integration at Q2L

The Partnership for 21st Century Skills has identified the ability to apply technology effectively as a key skill for students. At Q2L, technology is used for clearly defined purposes intended to add breadth and depth to the educational experiences of all students. Priority is placed on providing a personal laptop for every student. With this one-to-one laptop program in place, teachers and students determine when technological tools are needed to increase learning and productivity. With the proliferation of technology in students' lives, Q2L teaches students how to decide which tools are appropriate and when to use them. For example, students may decide to write physical persuasive letters to city government officials regarding local issues or concerns but may reach out via Skype to debate issues with students abroad.

Digital tools today allow for the development of structured collaborative environments unlike any seen before. The Q2L team has developed collaborative design and social network environments that fit the needs of our curriculum. Gamestar Mechanic, as explained earlier, is an online game through which players learn to design games as a result of game play. Through an online social network, the game players take on the identity of game designers as they design games, post them, and offer each other feedback. Yet another social networking environment designed specifically for the school is called Being Me. This environment focuses on creating and sustaining a healthy social/emotional community and gives students opportunities to interact digitally in a safe space. Students are given the space to communicate casually and are given prompts to discuss their feelings and emotions. They also are charged with the challenge of keeping their community healthy by constructing positive and supportive interactions.

## Teacher Support and Professional Development: Teachers for the 21st Century

In order to prepare students for success in the 21st century, we need teachers who are able to teach in innovative ways. Though many teacher education programs now emphasize the importance of effective use of technology in the classroom, they do not prepare teachers to plan a curriculum and teach in a manner that is game-like and systems thinking-focused. At Q2L, we have developed a professional development program called Studio Q to support teachers in developing the knowledge, skills, and understandings needed to be effective teachers in the Q2L

**Table 16.3   Six Dimensions of Teacher Development at Q2L**

| | |
|---|---|
| Systems thinker | Teachers understand the architecture of dynamic systems and are able to think systemically. |
| Practitioner | Teachers exhibit exemplary pedagogical practices in areas such as differentiation, integrating content expertise, classroom management, communicating with parents, lesson planning, engaging students in learning, and maintaining an effective learning environment. |
| Designer | Teachers co-design, implement, and revise game-like curriculum with game designers and curriculum directors. |
| Assessor | Teachers design and implement embedded assessment, use data from assessments to evaluate student learning, make adjustments to curriculum based on assessments, and help students set learning goals. |
| Wellness integrator | Teachers understand dynamics among their students and with other members in the school community. They are able to act on understandings of interpersonal and group dynamics to address student emotional, academic, physical and nutritional needs. |
| Technology integrator | Teachers are able to seek out, identify, and use technology to enhance student learning. |

model. Through Studio Q, teachers are supported along six dimensions of teacher development (listed in Table 16.3) that we have identified as critical for successful teaching and learning at Q2L.

Studio Q, as an integrated and well-supported professional development plan, is a key component of Q2L. Our professional development philosophy is centered on the core design-based values and practices of the school. The foundation of Studio Q rests on an awareness of how members of a school community can best support both the effectiveness and satisfaction of its teachers. Our philosophy is informed by current academic literature and research, which, as indicated by the National Staff Development Council (NSDC), shows that professional development is most effective in changing teacher practice when it is collaborative, school-based, focused on student learning, continuous, and embedded in the daily work of teachers.

The Q2L design team has created and implemented the following structures to support teachers in Studio Q:

1. Mission Lab: Staffed by the Institute of Play, the school's founding partner, the lab serves as a site within the school for collaborative curricular work among teachers, curriculum directors, and game design experts. Mission Lab staff hosts sessions in game design, systems thinking, and mission planning. Teachers attend formal weekly sessions with Mission Lab's directors of curriculum, game designers, and researchers.

2. Teacher induction: Regardless of their prior experience, teachers entering the school attend a series of "induction" sessions, held in late spring and summer. These sessions continue throughout the year and serve as an ongoing professional development space.

3. Public sharing: Teachers are supported and encouraged to give papers at conferences, publish, and share their work with other professionals in the field as a way to build, grow, revise, stabilize, expand, and share their approach and methods.

4. Peer review: All Q2L teachers engage in a peer review process. The purpose of this process is to provide teachers at Q2L with peer-level support. This process is in addition to reviews mandated by the Department of Education and is used to identify teachers' areas of strength and areas that need extra support.

Studio Q exists in a variety of contexts: It crosses into different times and spaces during the school day and throughout the year. Most importantly, the school's schedule is designed to allow teachers not only to attend the formal weekly Studio Q sessions during the normal school day but also to meet individually with their domain teams, which include game designers and curriculum directors.

## Conclusion

Q2L has emerged at a time when the nation's education crisis has reached its peak. In an unprecedented move, the Obama administration is investing nearly $4.5 billion to fund educational innovations. At Q2L, we argue that educational innovation should be about creating learning opportunities that are relevant to the lives and practices of today's youth. Equally important, learning experiences should reflect the learning practices that contemporary research has shown to be natural and necessary—nodal, participatory, social, immersive, and embodied—since we began to make meaning together. Research shows that not only are youth increasingly immersed in digital media spaces, including games, but that games create the kinds of learning environments that support deep learning. Much more design, implementation, and research are necessary to understand the potential of games and game-like environments in supporting learning, but as two of our students, Kees and Aviv, tell it, "We do a ton of work, and it's really fun. It's not like any other school, it's totally new" and "I really enjoy it—I think every other kid does too."

Ultimately, Q2L is about two things: meeting youth where they are and using the most up-to-date understandings of learning. It has been an extraordinary journey thus far. Each day we have more questions than answers, but the sheer excitement and intensity with which our kids are engaging in deep thinking and design tells us that something magical is happening here.

For more information about Quest to Learn, please visit our website (www.q2L.org). For a more detailed overview of the design of Q2L, please refer to our white paper, "Quest to Learn Planning Document: Growing the School for Digital Kids" (MIT Press).

## Acknowledgments

First, we would like to thank our courageous leader and master designer Katie Salen, the executive director of Institute of Play. Katie has been the leading force behind Q2L. We'd also like to recognize the amazing staff of teachers, games designers, and administrators at Q2L who make this project possible. As well, we are tremendously grateful to the pioneering work of James Gee, whose ideas and guidance have closely informed our work. A very special thanks to Connie Yowell and the MacArthur Foundation, whose support has shepherded this project. Finally, and most especially, a warm and heartfelt thank you to our students, who are the true trail blazers in this new era of digital media and learning, and to their parents for their trust and invaluable support.

## Appendix A

### *Quest to Learn Design Competencies*

Created by Q2L design team members Robert Torres and Loretta Wolozin.

### Systems Thinking

Systems thinking combines conceptual knowledge (knowledge of systems properties, structures, and reoccurring patterns of behavior) and reasoning skills (the ability to locate situations in wider contexts, see multiple levels of perspective within a system, trace complex interrelationships, look for endogenous or "within system" influences, be aware of changing behavior over time, and recognize "homologies"—recurring patterns that exist within a wide variety of systems), as defined by Sweeney and Sterman, 2007.

### Digital Media Tool Use

Students incorporate the use of digital media, including programming, using it as a tool to communicate, design, write, collect data, analyze, and do calculations to solve problems.

310 Dancing With Digital Natives

## Iteration

Design is a cyclical, iterative process of moving through multiple versions of any idea or solution by tinkering, prototyping, playtesting, and redesigning, constantly reflecting, and integrating feedback.

## Representation

The creation of multiple types of representations such as diagrams, graphs, tables, sketches, illustrations, or physical forms that enable students to structure, record, and express ideas. Use of multiple representations is a critical design thinking strategy.

## Communication

Use of oral, written, performative, and visual forms of language to formulate, exchange, present, and reflect on ideas. Shared understanding is the aim of communication.

## Intelligent Resourcing

Intelligent resourcing is the process whereby a learner researches and merges current and past information with prior knowledge to form a new idea, perspective, opinion, or validation to generate insight. Intelligent resourcing taps into expertise in any form, requires discernment, and is an ongoing process. As new sources of support or knowledge are acquired, these are synthesized with prior knowledge to generate new ideas toward iterative design.

## Designing Play

Designing play entails the ability to design meaningful and deep interactivity within a game-based context.

## Designing for Innovation

Students act on creative ideas to make tangible and useful contributions to the field in which the innovation will occur.

**Participation in Interest-Driven Communities**
Students pursue their own interests, explore their own questions, and push their imaginations as they share expertise in teamwork with peers, mentors, and experts. Participatory membership requires that pro-amateurs participate in such things as clubs, associations, or informal online groups in which they are innovating design, constantly training one another, and seeking venues and opportunities for developing themselves in their chosen interest.

## About the Contributors

**Robert J. Torres** is the chief research officer at Institute of Play in New York City and is completing a post-doctoral program at the Social Science Research Council. He has worked as a teacher, school principal, and education consultant since 1988. He taught fifth grade as a Teach for America (TFA) teacher, served as a school director as part of TFA teacher induction programs, and eventually became president of TFA's national faculty. Robert designed a spin-off of TFA, the Learning Project One Middle School, and served as its principal from 1995 to 1999. Since 1999, Robert has focused mostly on school design and currently runs a not-for-profit, Design by Design (designbydesign.org), which has supported the creation of more than 30 small progressive schools across New York City and Connecticut. Robert has a BA from Oberlin College, a master's in policy and school administration from Bank Street College of Education, and was a Stanford University Research Fellow. He recently completed a doctorate in immersive game technologies at New York University.

**Rebecca Rufo-Tepper** has been working in the New York City public school system for more than 10 years. After receiving a master's degree in English education from Teachers College, Columbia University, she taught high school and middle school English and social studies for seven years in Brooklyn and Manhattan. In addition, she was a literacy coach at East Side Middle School, a District 2 public school in Manhattan, for two years. She was a professional development facilitator for the Holocaust Educators Network in New York City and the Folger Shakespeare Library in Washington, D.C., and her research has focused primarily on professional development and school reform. Rebecca was an adjunct instructor of English education in Hunter College's Curriculum and Teaching Department for two years and completed her PhD in urban education in May 2009 at The Graduate Center at The City University of New York. She is currently a director of curriculum and instruction for the Institute of Play in New York City, where she works with the faculty and students at Quest to Learn.

**Arana Shapiro** has been working in the field of education since 2000. Her first teaching position was in the Inglewood Public School District, where she taught for three years. In Inglewood, Arana served on the district curriculum review team, helping to develop and implement new curriculum in this small district. Upon moving to New York City, Arana began working at Teachers College (TC), Columbia University's Early Childhood Education Program. At TC, Arana helped develop the Early Childhood Education Department's new student teacher program by visiting New York City public school classrooms and finding appropriate placement and mentorship for TC students. It was during her work at TC when Arana began working with a group of educators to develop curriculum for a new school, The School at Columbia University, and subsequently became a founding faculty member of The School in 2003. Arana's desire to bring new media technologies into the classroom prompted her to migrate from the classroom to the technology team at The School and later to the lead educational technologist position at the Ross Institute, where she integrated technology into K–12 classrooms at both The Ross School in East Hampton and Ross Global Academy Charter School. In addition, Arana was a reading specialist for Groundwork for Youth in East New York Public Schools. She has presented research at many national education conferences, including the

American Educational Research Association (AERA) and National Council of Teachers of Mathematics (NCTM). She received her master of arts in education with an emphasis in Second Language Learning and Acquisition from Pepperdine University and is currently pursuing her master's in school leadership from Bank Street. Arana is currently a director of curriculum and instruction for the Institute of Play in New York City, where she works with the faculty and students at Quest to Learn.

## Recommended Reading

### Books and Articles

Gee, James Paul. *What Video Games Have to Teach Us About Literacy and Learning.* New York: Palgrave Macmillan, 2003.

Ito, Mizuko, Sonja Baumer, Matteo Bittanti, Danah Boyd, Rachel Cody, Becky Herr-Stephenson, et al. *Hanging Out, Messing Around and Geeking Out: Kids Living and Learning with New Media.* Cambridge, MA: MIT Press, 2010.

Palfrey, John and Urs Gasser. *Born Digital: Understanding the First Generation of Digital Natives.* New York: Basic Books, 2008.

Salen, Katie and Eric Zimmerman. *Rules of Play: Game Design Fundamentals.* Cambridge, MA: MIT Press, 2004.

Salen, Katie, Rebecca Rufo-Tepper, Arana Shapiro, Robert J. Torres, and Loretta Wolozin. MacArthur Foundation White Paper. *Quest to Learn Planning Document: Growing the School for Digital Kids.* Cambridge, MA: MIT Press, 2010.

Sawyer, R. Keith. "Introduction: The New Science of Learning." In *The Cambridge Handbook of the Learning Sciences,* (ed.) Keith Sawyer. Cambridge, England: Cambridge University Press, 2006.

Squire, Kurt. "From Content to Context: Videogames as Designed Experience." *Educational Researcher* 35, no. 8(2006): 19–29.

Sweeney, Linda Booth, and John D. Sterman. "Thinking About Systems: Student and Teacher Conceptions of Natural and Social Systems." *System Dynamics Review* 23, no. 2/3(2007): 285–312.

Torres, Robert. J. *Learning on a 21st-Century Platform: Gamestar Mechanic as a Means to Game Design and Systems Thinking within a Nodal Ecology.* New York University: ProQuest Dissertations, 2009.

Watkins, S. Craig. *The Young and the Digital: What the Migration to Social-Network Sites, Games, and Anytime, Anywhere Media Means for our Future.* Boston: Beacon Press, 2009.

## Websites

Epistemic Games, epistemicgames.org

Games for Change, gamesforchange.org

Gamestar Mechanic, gamestarmechanic.com

Partnership for 21st Century Skills, www.p21.org

Quest to Learn, q2l.org

Waters Foundation (systems thinking resources), watersfoundation.org

CHAPTER **17**

# Teaching Digital Literacy Digitally: A Collaborative Approach

Jami L. Carlacio and Lance Heidig

*As little as we know about the future for which we are preparing our students, it is clear that it will be a place that is governed by information. Accessing, processing, building with, and communicating that information is how we will all make our livings.*

—David Warlick

*In recent years, digital storytelling has turned college and university classrooms into spaces of creative critical production. Digital stories have proven to be a powerful medium for students to represent a theoretically informed understanding of texts and contexts in a form other than "traditional" writing.*

—Michael Coventry and Matthias Oppermann

## Introduction: Multiple Literacies in the 21st Century

No one would argue with the fact that today's students need more than alphabetic literacy to communicate effectively in a world increasingly

315

suffused with digital media and information. We expect them to be adept not only at translating what comes to them via screen, through image, and across the page but also at interpreting, evaluating, and critically assessing information in print and digital environments—and doing so ethically and responsibly even as the terrain underneath them is shifting constantly.

We are not suggesting, of course, that today's students come to us as digital tabula rasae. Quite the contrary. These digital natives, born after 1980, have grown up in a world that for them was "never not markedly digital." As John Palfrey and Urs Gasser explain, students today are adept at crafting identities in online environments and at creating new relationships there as part of their social network. They commonly use networked public spaces as environments for socialization as well as identity development (*Born Digital: Understanding the First Generation of Digital Natives*, Basic Books, 2008). Moreover, as persons born in an era in which access to an abundance of information is as easy and as quick as the click of a key, these digital natives—or "Net Geners" as Susan Gibbons dubbed them in *The Academic Library and the Net Gen Student: Making the Connections*—are nevertheless confronted with the challenge of sifting through that information to discern what is and is not valuable. "For digital natives," Palfrey and Gasser continue, "much turns on one's ability to navigate through information of varying qualities, and those who come to understand the dynamics of information production in the digital era will be better prepared than anyone else to thrive in the integrated digital world." And this is why digital literacy and the ability to critically assess and evaluate information are so important.

We want to emphasize that our students are literate to a large extent in that they are already avid text messagers, bloggers, and (post-2007) Twitterers; they socialize on, embed videos in, and share photos and links on their Facebook or Myspace pages; and they are experts at finding information (or so they believe) via Google. At the same time, we must ask, to what extent do these abilities demonstrate critical literacies? How do we create curricula to engage students in what they know, with the information resources and communication tools that they commonly use, and translate these skills into critical abilities for exploring, interpreting, and participating in our increasingly complex and globalized community? How do we teach students to use and to cite information properly and ethically when materials are so easy to download and often don't appear to be proprietary? How do we teach digital literacy digitally?

We offer some answers to these questions by way of a discussion of a writing class that we co-taught at Cornell University in spring 2008. As a writing instructor (Jami Carlacio) and a reference librarian (Lance Heidig), we collaborated to develop and teach a first-year writing seminar (FWS) titled "Writing and Research in the University: Writing in the Twenty-First Century" that focused on helping students develop not just the writing skills they would need throughout their undergraduate years but also the long-standing *information* competency that they would need as both students and professionals.

FWS instructors, a mix of advanced graduate students and professorial faculty, will often ask a reference and instruction librarian to offer a 50- or 75-minute overview of research resources at the library early in the fall or spring semester as a prelude to a research assignment. Though some students later return to the library to seek help on one or another of their (research) papers, many do not. In subsequent semesters, these students are expected to know how to use the library—both its print and digital resources—in much the same way that expert researchers do. The class we co-taught was a response to what we perceived was a gap between the brief overview offered to students in their first or second semester of college and the lack of information competency follow-up that inevitably ensues as these undergraduates pursue their majors.

Since we wanted to immerse our students in a digital and information-rich environment, we taught the class in a networked, PC-equipped library classroom, where students had access to the internet as well as to our own resources including digital cameras, voice recorders, and moviemaking/editing software. Since the chief aim of the course was to enhance students' literacies across the board, we trained them on this equipment as well as explained how to navigate and contribute to the course websites, which we describe in more detail later. In the spirit of Web 2.0, (Tim O'Reilly, "What Is Web 2.0: Design Patterns and Business Models for the Next Generation of Software," September 30, 2005), we used both Cornell's Confluence wiki and Springshare's LibGuides software to manage our course content and to encourage two-way communication. LibGuides is a Web 2.0 content management and publishing system designed specifically for libraries that combines the features and functionality of social networks, wikis, and blogs in one easy-to-use software package (Springshare, "LibGuides Features," www.springshare.com/libguides/features.html). With "literacy" as our broad theme, we structured the curriculum so that students began in familiar territory (writing personal essays about themselves) using familiar study habits (looking for information with Google and Wikipedia). From here, it was fairly easy to transition to more complex subject matter and to use the technology in more sophisticated ways.

## The Chosen Course and Constituents

Despite the fact that our students possess some degree of digital literacy, we would not characterize it as the kind of critical literacy they need in order to participate fully and ethically in a complex digital environment. As we already noted, our students appear to be tech-savvy: They bring their sophisticated cell phones and PDAs to class, enabling them to text their friends; check their email accounts; download attachments; keep up-to-date on the latest news, entertainment, or stock reports; and find out who's doing what for dinner that night. But the complexity of the integrated digital world requires more than this. Our response, therefore, is to include in our curricula information specialists, or translators, as Gibbons call them, who are versed not only in the intricacies of information storage and retrieval but also in particular subjects, whether English, math, history, anthropology, or biology. Residing in both the information and the academic worlds, librarians are perfectly situated to guide students through the labyrinthine data universe they encounter as they navigate their assignments.

The goals for our course, then, were twofold: First, we wanted to help our students develop a more robust understanding of literacies, particularly those that occur in hybrid spaces: online, on paper, and in sonic form. Second, we wanted to enable our students to be more sophisticated information gatherers and evaluators as they worked on their assignments, whether they were using the library's resources—digital and print—or searching the web.

On the one hand, the students' affinity for technology made it easy for us to introduce them to the concepts of the course; on the other, they came to the course with specific and naïve expectations (and assumptions) about how to gather, work with, translate, and share information. In other words, their use of Google, Wikipedia, Facebook, Myspace, YouTube, and Flickr did not represent critical digital literacy as we have defined it. In fact, despite their status as digital natives, they still had much to learn about how to navigate the digital universe, particularly about how to manage the information overload and sift through it for what they needed, and how to make strategic (or wise) connections through social networks. Although we are referring mainly to students here, we realize that all of us find ourselves in unfamiliar waters when it comes to navigating a Web 2.0 culture. We designed our course to bridge these crucial gaps in literacies.

## The Library Setting and First Literacy Assignment

Beginning with the first week of class, we introduced more complex concepts of information and digital literacy through a series of in-class exercises and discussions. Starting with a general overview of where to look for different kinds of information, we then integrated seven additional library sessions into our syllabus that addressed the specific resources and skills students needed to complete class assignments. Just as our students are wont to do, we started with Google and Wikipedia, and then discussed their utility and their limitations. We wanted them to develop a habit of thinking critically about the information they were retrieving and to evaluate its content in terms of objectivity, timeliness, and accuracy. Our objective was not to discredit these tools—in fact, we wanted the students to begin their research and information gathering with the web sources they were familiar with—but rather to get students to use these sources in a more "scholarly" way. Therefore, we posed questions about these resources: Did the Wikipedia entry have a bibliography of books and articles? How does a resource with an ".edu" in the URL differ from a source with a ".com" or ".org" domain? What is proprietary information? After starting where they were, we introduced them to Cornell Library's website and encouraged them to take advantage of the wealth of resources contained there and to compare and contrast what they found using the library catalog with what they discovered through a general web search.

The information and activities we covered in these library sessions are preserved on the course's LibGuide, which grew both systematically and organically through the semester. Each week (and sometimes daily), we added new pages and boxes of information within pages, including links, embedded videos, and research tips, to correspond with our lesson plans and as a response to student inquiries and suggestions. As previously mentioned, the LibGuide software enables a user to comment on any element of the guide (individual boxes, whole pages, or the entire guide) and features a librarian profile box containing contact information to promote communication with library staff.

Several of our in-class exercises included having students supply answers to research questions in the LibGuide comments boxes, thus sharing them with the class. The idea behind these exercises was, of course, to parallel the environment with which they were already familiar—an intertextual and collaborative one that makes the learning and doing more transparent and communal. We agree with Palfrey and Gasser when they caution readers that digital technology should not be used in the classroom for its own sake but instead to support or enhance the pedagogical goals of the instructor or curriculum.

Complementing our instruction on information literacy, we also asked students to think more broadly about literacy, with the first writing assignment focusing on traditional (alphabetic) literacy. (Due to space constraints, we won't review all course materials here; please visit the Writing 142 wiki site at tinyurl.com/yc8grdt for access to all readings, assignments, student work, and so on.) After discussing the models in class, we asked students to craft a three- to five-page literacy narrative re-telling or analyzing one important scene, incident, experience, or character in their development as readers, writers, or thinkers. We wanted them to devote equal time to dramatizing the memory and to pondering its significance. We expected them to reflect critically on what literacy means to them and how they saw this notion operating in American (or college) culture. We included some specific questions to get them started, including these: 1) What are your earliest memories associated with learning to read and write? 2) How do you currently approach reading and writing tasks? and 3) How do you feel about yourself as a reader and writer?

In the context of writing essays and conducting preliminary research, we needed to ensure that students felt at home using the class wiki, and so we instructed them on the basics: how to log in, create and edit wiki pages, and use the comments boxes to provide feedback on each other's writing. None of the students was familiar with using a wiki interactively (although all were familiar with and had used Wikipedia as a resource). With all writing assignments, we expected students to post drafts of their papers to their wiki homepages and to be prepared to review them as a large group. Although we made the wiki public by the end of the course, early in the semester we limited access to course members only to help prevent students from feeling self-conscious about their works-in-progress.

However, we encouraged students to think of the class wiki as a public site insofar as their work, comments, in-class responses, and discussion leads were available to all members of the class. We wanted them to see themselves as writers for a public audience and to become accustomed to the idea that they could use digital spaces to publish their work, get feedback, and then revise and resubmit it. Though many digital natives are already comfortable writing in public spaces (e.g., composing "wall posts" on Facebook or Myspace and contributing to blogs or commenting on YouTube videos), we wanted them to view their writing for this course as something more than the casual post—something more formal and ostensibly accessible to a broad but invisible audience. As a result, our peer-review sessions were productive because we projected papers from the computer onto the large screen. As students offered comments on a given paper, one of us would type, highlight, or delete text as a way of demonstrating the writing process. Students found this method to be useful for improving their writing, remarking for example in their final evaluations, "I thought using the wiki was such a good idea; it really did help me communicate" and "I really liked the large-group peer reviews. [They were] useful because I got very diverse feedback from different perspectives."

## The Digital Literacy Assignment

In preparation for the next assignment, which was to prepare a *digital literacy narrative*, we wanted students to search the web for blogs with postings on the topic of digital media and literacy, so we developed a guide page specifically devoted to the "how-tos" of blogging, including a Anton Zuiker's 2004 blog post titled "Blogging 101" (www.unc.edu/~zuiker/blogging101); how to use RSS feeds; and how to use blog aggregators, such as Technorati, to locate blogs specifically related to their final projects. We devoted some class time to explaining what RSS feeds are, how and when to use them, and why blog aggregators can be helpful as a way to make a complicated search for information on the internet much easier than it otherwise might be. We also previewed and discussed Michael Wesch's video, "The Machine is Us/ing Us" (bit.ly/1TcgXr), as well as read excerpts from core texts including Marshall McLuhan's *Understanding Media: The Extensions of Man* (McGraw-Hill, 1964) and Sherry Turkle's *Life on the Screen* (Simon and Schuster, 1997), which served as springboards for class discussion. Students took turns leading the class in a conversation about the texts and posting notes to the class wiki a day ahead of time for their peers to view so they could prepare follow-up questions. Such discussions gave students enough of a background on digital environments that they could consciously begin to think of themselves as digital natives, even if they had never used that epithet to describe themselves. We believe these sessions helped them to consider the critical cultural function of the technologies themselves—from the hardware to the wiki to the LibGuide to the search engines and so on.

Once they had completed the written component of their digital literacy narrative, we asked them write a one-paragraph summary of it, focusing on their main point, and then to imagine how they might construct a visual interpretation of this point, drawing on the same examples using only images and music. We explained that the purpose of the second half of the assignment was to help them become more rhetorically aware of the myriad ways we produce knowledge—through written, visual, and aural media. How, we asked, can you represent your ideas in multiple modes? How would you choose to narrate, without talking, a "story" about blogging, creating, or watching YouTube videos, or communicating with friends on Facebook? For this assignment, the students also needed to know where to find, how to cite, and how to credit multimedia items—images, music files, and video clips—available for "free" or labeled as fair use on the web. Students were directed to Creative Commons.org (another surprise for them), where they could find music, images, movie clips, and so on, that were not restricted by copyright. They were also given the option of using their own digital images or scanning images from other media. We expected them (and showed them how) to cite all sources properly in their paper bibliography as well as in their video credit section.

As a prelude to this first video assignment, we took time to discuss what other outcomes we expected of students. First, we introduced the concept of digital storytelling, which we define as narrative that combines texts, images, and audio files into a short film clip. Initially, students were comfortable consuming digital stories (hence the popularity of YouTube) but not producing them; however, this quickly changed. We led them to UC Berkeley's Center for Digital Storytelling website as one exemplar that appealed to us, and we shared some multimodal narratives that students from another class had completed for their final projects. (Interested readers may visit the final projects page for Jami's course entitled Women's Activism in the U.S. at tinyurl.com/yknb7yb). Once students felt comfortable with the assignment, we provided them with ample class time to complete their videos.

We were confident at this point in the semester that students were ready for their debut in video storytelling—and we were right. They performed remarkably well. One student, for example, wrote about (and then crafted a video on) her Facebook experience as a college freshman, confirming at least one of Palfrey and Gasser's observations: "In these online social networks, many good things are happening: Participants learn what it means to be friends, to develop identities, to experiment with status, and to interpret social cues." Like other digital natives, she initially saw Facebook as an opportunity to meet new people since she found the prospect of being new at a large university such as ours intimidating. She explains that she had blithely accepted invitations from people who "friended" her, whether or not she knew them. After realizing what she had done, she began to reverse this process, particularly when she saw that she had exposed herself to strangers with whom she was not comfortable sharing her profile. Her essay functions as a warning to those who would uncritically participate in a social network without first asking themselves what their motives are as well as what they hope to achieve. Palfrey and Gasser would not dismiss our student's experiences, but they would put her fears to rest by reminding her that sites like Facebook "are working on ways to use technologies to help young people learn how to pick up on the social cues that they need to understand in order to stay safe." The authors go on to say that it is not the technology *per se* that should concern us but rather, the "root causes" of problematic behaviors, which may occur in digital or real environments. This reassurance notwithstanding, our student's message warrants respect.

Another student, Kun Yi—whom we profile in this chapter—wrote an essay and crafted a video titled "Beyond Google Generation: A Proper Point of View of Search Engines Needed" (tiny.cc/2yvVG), delivering a cautionary message based on his own experience and his knowledge of others' heavy reliance on Google as their main (or only) method of researching a topic. Being a self-proclaimed member of the "Google Generation," he warns of the ways in which he and others like him "find" information without considering the many other places where information resides or without carefully evaluating the information found. According to him, "many teenagers of [the] Google Generation do not, as many believe, acquire a competent information literacy even though they [a]re familiar with … new media, especially the internet, from an early age. It is important for them—and all of us—to distinguish search engines, tools that require literacy to handle, from actual resources of information. Otherwise, if the user does not have the information literacy needed to search, a search engine can easily be a source of distraction rather than information." He goes on to suggest that we are all members of this Google Generation, and it is incumbent upon us to consider not just how we retrieve (or locate) information but also what we do with it.

Building a digital story out of the written product was initially difficult, since students were unused to thinking about what it means to compose in image and sound and to relying very little on text (slides with minimum text were allowed, for quoting purposes). As we have indicated, digital native students are comfortable as consumers and even to some extent as producers, of web content; but do they consider the interdependent relationship between the medium, the content, and the producer? To help students craft a product they would be pleased with and proud of, we developed guidelines—a rubric—that established clear criteria for evaluation. We developed questions such as these: How well does the video's overall message communicate clearly—does it have a central message or thesis? Will an audience unfamiliar with the topic and who has not read the corresponding print essay be able to follow your line of reasoning? Indeed, the videos students produced—a completely new task for all of them—exceeded our expectations. The student who wrote about the Google Generation produced what we deemed to be a superior digital interpretation, not simply because it demonstrated a clear understanding of the assignment but also, and perhaps more importantly, because we felt that he had vindicated our reason for the course. Kun's work, "Digital Literacy in the Google Generation," posted on YouTube (tinyurl.com/yjfg2lx), clearly demonstrates what we had been emphasizing in the course: Google is a great search engine that contains a plethora of useful information, but it pays to evaluate that information, and it behooves us to consider libraries, books, and other resources in our research.

## Combining Traditional Print Research With Digital Composing

It is important to reiterate the point we have been making throughout this chapter. That is, we see digital storytelling as part of, not separate from, the larger process of making meaning. As Michael Coventry and Matthias Oppermann explain in "From Narrative to Database: Multimedia Inquiry in a Cross-Classroom Scholarship of Teaching and Learning Study" (*Academic Commons,* March 5, 2009), "There is a somewhat familiar relationship between research and writing which underpins student work; however, because students are working towards a digital end, they are already thinking about their work as being different—more visual, more compressed, and more public than traditional writing products." We believe this to be true of their first digital videos, but since the final project was more research intensive, we want to emphasize here the value of combining traditional print research with digital composing, since these meaning-making activities are reciprocal rather than mutually exclusive.

With this philosophy guiding us, we led students toward their final project, a research paper and corresponding video on a topic of their choosing. By the end of the third week in the term, students were to have decided on a topic or issue they would pursue for their final project, and in the fourth week, we guided them through the process of writing a proposal as a way of thinking their project through, from crafting a good research question to examining the relevance of their chosen subject or issue to contemplating its implications and consequences in the longer term. Over several weeks' time, once the proposal was completed and the topic approved, students built their annotated bibliographies a few citations at a time as a prelude to the traditional research paper they would eventually write. When there were about four weeks left in the term, students began mapping out their digital stories, just as they had done for the previous digital video.

Since this second digital video was similar to the first one, students were able to move more quickly toward their goals, but unlike the previous assignment, they were expected to include (voice-over) narration, which turned out to be the most difficult part of the project. (One student directed us, in his/her final evaluation, to "reduce the amount of work in this class. The visual essays actually take a lot of work.") Because they had spent so much time on their final projects and we wanted them to keep in mind the public nature of their work, we asked students to deliver a final oral presentation introducing their work, explaining what prompted this particular research and describing in brief what their research process involved. (These were similar in most respects, but each student's project also featured enough unique dimensions to warrant some discussion; moreover, we wanted to give students practice in oral delivery, since most students at Cornell do not take courses in public speaking and may not otherwise have the opportunity to hone this important skill.) Despite the complaints—which were indeed legitimate—students shared many positive insights in their final evaluations, for example: "I learned that composing in new media [is] very closely related to writing. When composing through digital multimedia [sic], it was exactly like writing an essay but explaining my arguments through pictures, music, etc., rather than words."

## Conclusion: Digital Natives and New Cognitive Maps

We believe that there will always be a place for the traditional research paper in the college writing classroom, and we have certainly not jettisoned this, as a glance at our course wiki and class syllabus demonstrates. But more and more, we see that new media technologies undergird every aspect of our lives. By combining the print with the digital, our digital native students were able to think more broadly about their work—how it would look and how it would sound—and to translate their ideas into a complex mixture of words, images, and sound. Further, the fact that students knew they were producing a digital project made them more aware of their multiple audiences: those of us in the immediate space of the writing classroom as well as those in the vastly larger and ambiguous space of the internet who might come upon their work while surfing and browsing. As the 2009 Horizon Report, titled "The

New Media Consortium," makes clear, "increasing globalization continues to affect the way we work, collaborate, and communicate … Increasingly, those who use technology in ways that expand their global connections are more likely to advance, while those who do not will find themselves on the sidelines (bit.ly/ei1rJh)." In 2010, Horizon reported that "Digital media literacy continues its rise in importance as a key skill in every discipline and profession" (bit.ly/hL9ZaG). We hope that our collaboration in the networked writing classroom will have given students the critical literacy tools they need to participate fully in this global environment to truly become digital natives.

## About the Contributors

**Jami L. Carlacio** is currently the managing editor of the *Industrial and Labor Relations Review* at Cornell University. Prior to this, she taught writing and literature courses for more than 15 years, with most of her courses including some form of technology or, more recently, new media. She has edited a volume of essays on the teaching of Toni Morrison and has published work on the history of women's rights and abolition. She engages her students' interest in pioneering women by teaching them how to craft original digital media compositions that recapture their subjects' lives in new ways. As a member of Cornell's faculty, she collaborated with Lance Heidig in combining information and alphabetic literacy in both first-year and upper-level writing courses.

**Lance Heidig** has worked as a reference and instruction librarian at the Cornell University Library since 1984. His work there has concentrated on the integration of traditional and digital library services, with a focus on web-based instruction and information literacy. He also blogs in support of Cornell's New Student Reading Project (cornellreading. typepad.com), and in 2010, he curated the library's exhibition, "Known to Everyone—Liked by All: The Business of Being Mark Twain."

## Recommended Reading

### Books and Articles

Coventry, Michael and Matthias Oppermann. "From Narrative to Database: Multimedia Inquiry in a Cross-Classroom Scholarship of Teaching and Learning Study." *Academic Commons* 5 (March 2009). bit.ly/fDpyDF (accessed January 18, 2011).

Darnton, Robert. *The Case for Books: Past, Present, Future.* New York: Public Affairs, 2009.

Gibbons, Susan. *The Academic Library and the Net Gen Student: Making the Connections.* Chicago: American Library Association, 2007.

Jenkins, Henry and David Thorburn (eds.). *Democracy and New Media.* Cambridge: MIT Press, 2003.

Johnson, L., A. Levine, and R. Smith. *The 2009 Horizon Report.* Austin, Texas: The New MediaConsortium. 2009. wp.nmc.org/horizon2009 (accessed December 7, 2010).

Kress, Gunther. *Literacy in the New Media Age.* New York: Routledge, 2003.

McLuhan, Marshall. *Understanding Media: The Extensions of Man.* New York: McGraw-Hill, 1967.

Morville, Peter. *Ambient Findability: What We Find Changes Who We Become.* Sebastopol, CA: O'Reilly, 2005.

O'Reilly, Tim. "What is Web 2.0: Design Patterns and Business Models for the Next Generation of Software." O'Reilly. September 30, 2005. oreilly.com/web2/archive/what-is-web-20.html (accessed October 20, 2010).

Rodriguez, Richard. *Hunger of Memory: The Education of Richard Rodriguez.* New York: Bantam, 1982.

Selfe, Cynthia and Gail Harwisher (eds.). *Gaming Lives in the Twenty-First Century: Literate Connections.* New York: Palgrave Macmillan, 2007.

Turkle, Sherry. *Life on the Screen: Identity in the Age of the Internet.* NY: Simon and Schuster, 1997.

Weinberger, David. *Everything Is Miscellaneous: The Power of the New Digital Disorder.* New York: Times Books, 2007.

"Writing for Web 2.0—Best Practices." The Rockley Group. October 25, 2007. rockley.com/blog/?p=28 (accessed October 20, 2010).

Yi, Kun. "Kun's Home." Writing and Research in the University. March 26, 2008. tiny.cc/2yvVG (accessed October 20, 2010).

Zuiker, Anton. "Blogs: A Short History." Blogging 101. February 27, 2004. www.unc.edu/~zuiker/blogging101 (accessed October 20, 2010).

## Websites

Final Projects—Amazing Activist Women, tinyurl.com/yknb7yb

"Digital Literacy in the Google Generation," tinyurl.com/ccg43j

"The Machine is Us/ing Us," bit.ly/1TcgXr

Springshare LibGuides, www.springshare.com/libguides/features.html

Warlick's Colearners: Contemporary Literacy, bit.ly/bN8Hem

Writing and Research in the University, tinyurl.com/yc8grdt

Writing and Research in the University Library Guide, guides.library.cornell.edu/writing142

# French Lessons: How France Is Educating Its Digital Natives

Heidi Gautschi

Digital natives, those who have grown up in a society permeated with information and communication technology, don't live just in the United States. They're popping up everywhere. As in the U.S., countries across the globe have been integrating digital technologies into the social fabric. That said, information and communications technology (ICT) consumed in different places around the world bear a physical resemblance, but the complex relationship between technology and society plays a large role in determining the behaviors, uses, and social imagination attached to these technical objects and interfaces. This means that while digital nativity is a global phenomenon, there are still fundamental differences in how digital natives respond to the digital culture in which they are growing up. Digital natives' needs, therefore, must be analyzed and met in their local environments, and schools provide one such environment.

This chapter looks at how the French educational system is responding to the increasing presence of ICT in all facets of society and the way it is educating its digital native student population. The French response piqued my interest for a number of reasons. I have lived in France for almost half my life and am in part, a product of the country's educational system. Due to my background, I believe I am able to place the French response in a larger context that should provide a clearer understanding of the French approach. Beyond a personal interest, however, France presents an interesting case because it is so different from the U.S., which should serve to illustrate the importance of local, homegrown approaches to the educational challenges and opportunities presented by the digital native.

Since this chapter deals with a country many readers may not be familiar with, I will begin with a brief overview of the French digital native and France's educational structure. This should provide the context needed to understand and appreciate the second part of this chapter, which outlines the major steps the French have taken to address digital literacy and educate the digital native. To better grasp the practical challenges educators face, I also visited a local middle school for a first-hand look at how it was addressing both the governments' directives and its students' needs.

## History and the Future

Historically, French governments have had a conflicted relationship with communication networks. "For fear of the power others might acquire against them, ruling elites have often kept knowledge secret, limited public discussion, and controlled religion, education, and science so as to prevent their subjects from acquiring sensitive information and dangerous ideas" (Paul Starr, *The Creation of the Media: Political Origins of Modern Communications*, Basic Books, 2004). And even today, the relationship between political powers and communication systems can be fragile. As Thierry Gaudin in *De l'Innovation* (1998) and Joel Mokyr in "Technological Inertia in Economic History" (*The Journal of Economic*

*History,* 1992) make clear, France also has a more conservative approach to technological development. Given this historical precedent, the current communication landscape is surprisingly robust. The need for such a pragmatic approach is clear, however, as digital natives not only have a need to develop effective technological skills to succeed but also have a relationship with technology that affects their learning expectations and style.

There has been far less research undertaken specifically on the digital native phenomenon in France than there has been in the U.S. However, a number of French agencies do track the general public's internet, computer, and cell phone use, which is then broken down by age. One such agency is the Centre de Recherche pour l'Étude et l'Observation des Conditions de Vie (CREDOC). In December 2010, it published a report at the request of the General Council for Industry, Energy, and Technology and the Regulation Authority for Electronic Communications and Posts on the distribution of ICT in French society. Among other things, this report offers a snapshot of 12–17 year olds' digital behavior. Not surprisingly, this group is highly "connected." The report found that 94 percent of this population have a landline mainly to connect to the internet, 94 percent have an internet connection, and of those 98 percent have a high-speed ADSL connection. Additionally, it found that 96 percent of French digital natives have access to a computer at home and 80 percent at school. Seventy-seven percent of digital natives use the internet every day overwhelmingly as a source of entertainment. Not surprisingly, cell phones are also popular, with 84 percent of digital natives owning cell phones and 97 percent using them to send text messages (182 per week on average). French digital natives are unconcerned about privacy online, unlike older generations, who see this as a major worry.

These statistics from CREDOC provide some insight into the behavior of the digital native in France. Clearly, this population relies heavily on computers, cell phones, and the internet. The French government has worked hard to reduce its internal digital divide, which is also evident here. In terms of overall connectivity, France ranks about average for the EU. That said, income level is still a major factor for digital access in France. Only 44 percent of households that earn 900 euros a month or less have internet access.

## French Education Primer

While the saying goes "All roads lead to Rome," in France, all roads lead to Paris, the heart of the country. The seat of the government is there, as are all of the country's major institutions. The transportation and communication networks all radiate from Paris into the "provinces," as all areas beyond the Paris region are pejoratively called. There has been a recent move to decentralize the system, and the various French regions have been given more and more responsibility. However, the overall plan has been met with general discontent.

The French educational system follows the same centralized structure. In theory, this means that a student should be able to change schools partway through the year and not be lost. The Ministry of Education in Paris governs the school system, and there are 30 academies roughly divided along regional lines that are in charge of implementing the Ministry's directives on a local level.

Each village with more than the minimum number of school-age children has a primary school, which teaches children ages 6–10. In small villages, as in the region where I live, these are often one-room schools. Children are required to begin attending school at age 6, though France offers free, national nursery schools as of age 2. There are almost 59,000 primary schools, 7,000 middle schools, and 4,300 high schools.

Since 1881, primary school has been free for all students. In 1933, secondary school also became free. The Jules Ferry law of 1882 made school obligatory for all children between the ages of 6 and 13, and the mandatory age was extended to 16 in 1959. French students are required to complete a ninth grade education, after which point they can choose to continue with a traditional high school program, follow a vocational program, or enter the work force.

Education is nationalized in France, as is teacher training, so that students throughout the country learn the same thing, often in the same manner. As Maryline Baumard writes in a 2008 special report on digital natives in *Le Monde de l'Education,* "Teachers are trained to rigidly pass on what they have learned." This means that all students who attend a French school anywhere should leave school knowing the same things and also view the world in a similar way. This may strike some as rather Big Brother-ish. France, unlike the U.S. and the U.K., for example, follows the integration model. The thinking goes that by offering all students the same education, the system ensures that they are then on an equal footing when they leave school and that all adhere to the basic tenets of French citizenship: liberty, equality, and fraternity. To paraphrase Baumard, school is also seen as a way of connecting past, present, and future generations through class content but also through a shared learning experience.

As with any centralized institution, the French educational system is not the most adaptable or reactive. Centralized institutions evolve more slowly and show more resistance—but less vulnerability—to technological change than decentralized ones. This protects these systems from chaos and helps maintain the status quo (Mokyr, 1992). Without doubt, the French school system is by nature conservative and resistant to innovation. Case in point, when I was in 10th grade (many years ago), one of my friends used her mother's 10th grade textbooks in French class. There's an argument to be made that the French language (and the textbooks used to teach it) is uniquely resistant to evolution. This continuity could be seen as a strength, but if France wants to prepare its kids for the future, some changes are desperately needed.

## Leveling the Playing Field

The world is changing and new developments, such as the proliferation of communication tools, need to be addressed by teaching institutions. As Baumard writes, "These evolutions and the debates surrounding them are asking a fundamental question about the meaning of school. Should it adapt, or resist? Should it follow society's mutations or guard tradition? Does it have a right to transmit, or adapt?" (2008). Ultimately, what role should school play in today's digital society?

From the CREDOC research, it is clear that the majority of French digital natives are familiar with digital tools and the internet. They use them on their own, in their homes, and at school. Yet, while digital natives are often assumed to be tech-savvy, they still require education to use technology effectively. In "The 'Digital Native' Debate: A Critical Review of the Evidence," Sue Bennett, Karl Maton, and Lisa Kervin warn that "there appears to be a significant proportion of young people who do not have the levels of access or technology skills predicted by proponents of the digital native idea ... With this comes the danger that those less interested and less able will be neglected" (*British Journal of Educational Technology*, 2008). If, as seems to be the philosophy in France, school is meant to produce citizens with a similar level of basic education, it must be assumed that despite the proliferation of computers, not all school-age children are equally skilled in their use.

The second point that needs to be considered is also raised by Bennett, Maton, and Kervin. They write that "students' everyday technology practices may not be directly applicable to academic tasks, and so education has a vitally important role in fostering information literacies that will support learning" (2008).

Barbara Combes echoes this point in her article, "Digital Natives or Digital Refugees? Why We Have Failed Gen Y?" (*International Association of School Librarianship. Selected Papers from the Annual Conference*, 2009), in which she writes, "Members of the Net Generation may be tech-savvy, if by this we mean they are confident and disposed to use technology." However, Combes points out that "they are definitely not information literate." She also points out, "Members of the Net/Gen Y are teaching themselves how to use the internet at a relatively young age (average of 10 years), which has led to the development of an 'entrenched culture of use.'" This doesn't mean that they are also developing judicial use of these technologies. According to Combes, "Using the internet for information seeking and developing information literacy skills needs to be embedded in curriculum programs in the early primary years if educators are going to impose a different culture of use on this generation of users" (2009). Perhaps then, assumptions about digital natives' innate familiarity with digital technology need to be rethought. A school-based program is one way of addressing different levels of familiarity as well as the more serious question of inadequate/ superficial information literacy.

## The B2i

In response to the unquestionable importance of, but unequal access to, digital technology in French society, the French Ministry of Education has developed a new program aimed at giving all of the 3 million or so digital natives enrolled in middle school the same basic technology skills and the digital literacy they'll need to be successful members of the digital world. The Ministry's program is in keeping with the institutional and traditional model. It is a *French* response to perceived *French* needs. The program neither fully adapts to digital natives nor does it ignore them or their requirements. The Ministry has tried to find a balance between the new and the old ways of teaching and learning.

The French program is named the *brevet informatique et internet*, aka the B2i. Since 2008, the B2i has been part of the *brevet,* a first cycle certificate received at the end of ninth grade. Since, as I mentioned previously, school is not obligatory after ninth grade, the *brevet* is proof that students have acquired a certain level of education. Without the *brevet,* a French person is basically unemployable. The *brevet* is like a mini-baccalaureate and, like the SATs stateside, is a nerve-wracking experience. Students are evaluated based on their work during the school year, their computer/internet skills (the B2i), and their foreign language skills; they take national exams in French, history-geography, math, and civics. By making the B2i an integral part of this certificate, the Ministry of Education is attempting to provide all students with the opportunity to learn the necessary skills to succeed in the future. As Combes writes, "How the citizen of the future functions in society will depend on how well schools prepare the next generation to be information literate. At the moment schools worldwide are at a crossroad" (2009). Given the social, cultural, and political context found in France, the B2i is certainly a move in the right direction.

The B2i measures 29 criteria divided into five categories. Each category aims to give the student appropriate knowledge and skills to help digital natives make sense of the mess of tools and practices they are regularly confronted with. In order for a student to pass the B2i, he or she must fulfill a minimum of 23 of the 29 criteria. For each category, the Ministry establishes both the aim and what the student must be able to accomplish or must have assimilated.

The B2i, as outlined in the Ministry's *Bulletin Officiel* No.45 defines the objectives as:

**Category 1:** Master a computer work environment (6 criteria)
*Aim:* A computer environment allows one to acquire, stock, and treat coded data to produce results. Computer environments can communicate with one another, especially in networks.
*Skills/knowledge to acquire:* Use and manage the storage at one's disposal. Use the available peripherals. Use the available programs and services.

**Category 2:** Adopt a responsible attitude (7 criteria)
*Aim:* The laws and regulations governing ICT use.

*Skills/knowledge to acquire:* Know and respect the basic rules relative to one's practice. Protect one's person and one's data. Able to analyze and process information critically. Participate in collective projects, understand the stakes and follow the rules.

**Category 3:** Create, produce, treat, and exploit data (7 criteria)
*Aim:* The appropriateness of the nature of the data and the type of program used determines the relevance of the results.
*Skills/knowledge to acquire:* Input and lay out a text. Process images, sound, or videos. Compose a document and anticipate how to present it depending on what or who it is for. Differentiate a simulated or modeled situation from a real one.

**Category 4:** Keep oneself informed and conduct research (5 criteria)
*Aim:* Search tools use information classification and selection criteria.
*Skills/knowledge to acquire:* Consult information retrieval databases. Identify, sort, and evaluate resources. Search for and select from the information requested.

**Category 5:** Communicate and exchange (4 criteria)
*Aim:* There are communication tools that allow for direct and differed communication.
*Skills/knowledge to acquire:* Write, send, disseminate, and publish. Receive a comment, a message including attachments. Exploit the specificities of different communication situations—real time and deferred.

Evaluating these laudable B2i skill objectives, however, is where things get complicated. Unlike with standardized testing in the U.S., there is no final B2i exam. Two teachers must evaluate each criterion for each student. The 29 criteria are to be assimilated between grades six and nine, and it is up to each school to determine how this is done. For example, the criteria can be confirmed by teacher observation, by having students present their work in class (for example, a presentation that uses information found on the internet), by having students explain how to do a certain action, by giving students tests, and so on.

One of the major roadblocks is the teaching staff's own computer skills. Just like their students, teachers vary widely in terms of digital literacy and computer skills. Since the French school system is a slow-moving institution, many of the pedagogical approaches, let alone the programs, haven't changed much in decades. New teachers are required to learn basic technology skills, but those who are already in the system are not required to learn these skills. Asking French teachers and administrators suddenly to evaluate their students' digital competency can be a frightening prospect and largely ineffective.

As we have seen, the French are keen on top-down organization. In keeping with this tradition, in an effort to help schools master the B2i, the Ministry has set up numerous websites that provide further explanations about each criterion and evaluation suggestions as well as both printable and online lesson plans and exercises that can be integrated into the regular subject programs (bit.ly/gOKnxT). The special B2i page on the Educnet website (www.educnet.education.fr/secondaire/ b2i) also offers links to websites for schools that have put in place exceptional B2i programs. The Lille Academy, which governs the school system where I live, has also set up an online forum dedicated to B2i questions. So far, there are only three messages. Again, expecting a group of educators who are far from well-versed in digital literacy to turn to the internet for help may not be the most effective strategy.

After reading the documentation—and there's a lot of it—I was still unclear as to how exactly the B2i worked on a local level. I can only imagine that administrators and teachers confronted with all of the information floating around on this subject must feel equally lost. I was perplexed that the Ministry didn't offer more precise directives and was left wondering how schools truly put the B2i into action. Thus, I decided to talk to the vice principal at the middle school in Avesnelles, the Collège Renaud-Barrault, to get a first-hand view of how he and his team approach the B2i.

## Going Local

Before delving into one school's experience with the B2i, I want to provide a quick sketch of where exactly I live to illustrate some of the specific challenges the Collège Renaud-Barrault (bit.ly/eE7wZU) is faced with. I live in one of the poorest *département* of France—the North. The region was depicted more or less accurately in Emile Zola's novel *Germinal*, which was required reading in my ninth grade French class. The North was once known for its mines, its textile mills, and its rainy weather. The mines are now closed, and the textile industry collapsed after most of the mills were destroyed during World War I, but it still rains a lot. Unemployment is high, and all the social ills that accompany poverty are evident.

As stated earlier, income is the major determining factor for whether a French household will have access to the internet. Based on this, it can be assumed that many of the students at the Collège Renaud-Barrault do not have easy access to the internet. They are digital natives in that they have grown up in a digital culture, but they may not be as tech-savvy as this group is generally assumed to be.

The Collège Renaud-Berrault is in Avesnelles (pop. 2,555), the next village over from where I live. It serves the 14 surrounding villages (some with as few as 100 inhabitants) and has a student body of 600. Despite both its rural location and its students' often difficult backgrounds, the school is committed to helping its students succeed.

The vice principal, Olivier Cornille, has been at Collège Renaud-Berrault for six years, and he recognizes that providing students with good computer skills and a basic level of digital literacy is one way to prepare them for the world of tomorrow. I met with Cornille to discuss the school's B2i program, as well as any other measures he and the staff were taking to adapt to the digital native's learning style and learning needs.

The B2i has been a required part of the curriculum for less than three years, but the Collège Renaud-Berrault recognized the role computers could play in the classroom more than 10 years ago. In fact, the school was the first in the region to ask for a computer classroom. This first classroom, because of the way it is set up, is now used as a study hall. Instead of looking like a traditional classroom with rows of desks facing a board, this room has a center island of desks and computer stations against the two side walls. According to Cornille, the administration decided to stop using this room as a classroom because teachers found that it was more difficult to control the students and because students had to share computers. This illustrates the traditional, unchanging aspect of French education. When I mentioned that this setup would allow for group work and require students to move around, which can help the learning process, I was met with mild surprise. Knowing that I have university teaching experience, Cornille conceded that this may work with older students but not with 11-year-olds. It is generally recognized that different learning styles exist and that the environment we work in influences the learning process. A nontraditional classroom, where students would have to share computers and therefore collaborate, could actually provide new opportunities for students to learn not only from the teacher but from each other as well.

The school also has two computer-equipped study halls, each staffed by a room monitor. During their free periods, students can come to these computerized study halls to work on class projects, do homework, and probably goof off a little. The Academy of Lille provides the school with a special internet connection that comes with filters and various other security measures.

Because the school was an early adopter of computer equipment, it lost out on the next wave of offers. In order to receive equipment, computer or otherwise, a school must respond to an offer by following a complex proposal procedure. Depending on what equipment the school already has and the number of credits the academy has, the proposal may or may not be accepted. However, Cornille explained that the school was able to take advantage of the more recent opportunities. There is a computer classroom in the special education section that is very popular but somewhat outdated. Recently he, along with the teaching staff, put together a proposal for new equipment, which was approved by the academy. Cornille admits that the request process is a slow one. It takes about a year from the submission deadline to actual installation of the equipment. However, Cornille pointed out that this lag time does provide time to prepare the teachers and offer them special training sessions.

The school now has a brand new computer classroom set up like a traditional class—desks in neat rows facing the board. Each desk is also a computer station. The teacher is able to control the students' computers, and each student can print on the central printer. The classroom is not yet equipped with an overhead projector, but Cornille assured me that was the next step.

Instead of assigning the classroom to one teacher or one grade, the school opted to let teachers sign up to use the classroom when they want. In theory, this gives the whole student body the opportunity to use computers and to discover educational applications for the skills they may have developed outside of the classroom, such as using search engines to find specific information, communicating with others online, or even watching videos on Dailymotion (www.dailymotion.com). Cornille says that so far only the same three or four teachers are using the computerized classroom, which means that certain students are missing out on this opportunity. Cornille is hoping that as other teachers become more comfortable with computers, they too will take advantage of this new teaching environment.

The other new development at the school this year was that half the school's classrooms (18) were equipped with a computer, each with internet and a projector. Cornille says that this caused some grumbling among the teaching staff. However, despite their initial hesitation, almost all of the teachers have now started using the new equipment. All of these efforts by Collège Renaud-Berault help pave the way to better meet the B2i objectives. This particular school starts working on the B2i in eighth grade. Cornille explained the logic behind this decision. Moving from elementary school to middle school is a big change: The school day is longer (8:30 AM to 5:00 PM), there are far more classes than in elementary school, and kids begin to learn their first foreign language in sixth grade. Therefore, it was felt that starting the B2i in sixth grade would be a bit too much for the new students.

However, teachers who use the computer classroom can begin to integrate B2i criteria into their programs as of sixth grade even if students are not being officially evaluated. They are also able to check whether the students have accomplished the various criteria. And now that 18 classrooms have computer and internet access, teachers are able to verify students' digital competency as well. However, the B2i measures far more criteria than can be addressed in one computer-based classroom or with intermittent computer access and the use of a projector. To circumvent this lack of resources, the Collège Renaud-Berrault, like many other French schools, uses specially designed computer programs provided by the academy to evaluate students. These are step-by-step programs that take students through different activities. If they are able to correctly complete the exercise, then the corresponding B2i criteria are validated. This begs the question though whether students actually assimilate what they are meant to be learning. Students use the special B2i program to evaluate those criteria not covered in class. If the student successfully completes the necessary tasks, then those B2i criteria are not revisited.

Ultimately, this is where the practicality of the B2i comes into question. It is all very well for the Ministry of Education to have recognized that it is necessary to evaluate students' digital knowledge. Putting it into practice is complicated to say the least. If Cornille must fight for a limited amount of resources to get his school to slowly creep into the 21st century, what of those administrators who are not interested or have not yet recognized the importance of providing students with solid digital skills? The B2i is a good first step in tackling this complex problem. It is in keeping with the basic tenets of the French education system (universal, basic education for all). It also attempts to provide students with basic information literacy, something that while not necessarily a new phenomenon (Neil Postman raised this point in *Amusing Ourselves to Death*) is an increasingly crucial literacy to have, as both Combes (2009) and Marilee Sprenger ("Focusing the Digital Brain," *Educational,* 2009) mention in their articles on this subject. As with many top-down organizations, however, the decisions made at the top look good from a distance but prove problematic to put into practice.

## Future Tense

Like many of its counterparts worldwide, the French school system is trying to come to terms with its digital native student population by striking a balance between new and old learning and teaching methods. France has a long history. According to Pierre Musso ( *Télécommunications et Philosophie des Réseaux,* 1998), this creates a society where memory rather than communication (the American model) dominates. Furthermore, the state produces the dominant ideology, unlike in the U.S. where private enterprise fulfills this role. This means that a non-French program for educating digital natives would most likely fail.

The Ministry of Education has recognized that in order for French kids to be successful nationally and internationally they must be given the skills to succeed, and these include knowing how to use digital technology effectively and responsibly. The B2i is one possible response to this conundrum. This program corresponds to perceived needs in a specific context. In short, it is a local response to a global phenomenon. It is also an institutional response that is requiring schools to modify traditional approaches to education. Without proper teacher training and organizational backing, the French answer meant to address local digital natives' needs may prove to be extremely difficult to put into place.

While the French system might be difficult to fathom for outsiders, it is good to see efforts being made to evolve a system that has been historically inflexible. The B2i is an illustration of just how high the Ministry's hopes are. I'm hopeful that teachers and administrators will not opt to take the easy way out but will rather show their commitment to this generation and future generations of *petits* digital natives by embracing digital technologies in classroom settings and recognizing the importance of fostering information literacy.

## About the Contributor

**Heidi Gautschi** grew up in France and the United States, and she continues to divide her time between these two countries. She has taught in the French university system since 2000, most recently at University of Lille 3. Her research looks at the relationship between society and communication technology with special emphasis on the comparative French and American contexts. She earned a BA in philosophy from Tufts University, an MA in health education from Teachers College, Columbia University, and a PhD in information and communication sciences from the University of Paris X.

## Recommended Reading

### Books and Articles

Baumard, Maryline. "Apprendre Avec un Cerveau Numérique." *Le Monde de l'Éducation* (April 2008).

Baumard, Maryline. "Dissertation Contre QCM, Résister Ou S'adapter." *Le Monde de l'Éducation* (April 2008).

Bennett, Sue, Karl Maton, and Lisa Kervin. "The 'Digital Native' Debate: A Critical Review of the Evidence." *British Journal of Educational Technology* 39 no. 5(2008): 775–786.

Bijker, Wiebe, Thomas P. Hughes, and Trevor Pinch (eds.). *The Social Construction of Technological Systems: New Directions in the Sociology and History of Technology.* Cambridge: MIT Press, 1989.

Combes, Barbara. "Digital Natives or Digital Refugees? Why We Have Failed Gen Y?" *International Association of School Librarianship. Selected Papers from the Annual Conference* (2009): 1–12.

Musso, Pierre. *Télécommunications et Philosophie des Réseaux,* Paris: Presses Universitaires de France, 1997.

Perriault, Jacques. *La Logique de l'Usage.* Paris: Flammarion, 1989.

Postman, Neil. *Amusing Ourselves to Death.* New York: Penguin Books, 1986.

Sprenger, Marilee. "Focusing the Digital Brain." *Educational Leadership* 67, no. 1(September 2009): 34–39.

Starr, Paul. *The Creation of the Media: Political Origins of Modern Communications,* New York: Basic Books, 2004.

## Websites

B2i Documentation, www.b2i.education.fr/college.php

Collège Renaud-Barrault, www.4b.ac-lille.fr/~rbarrault

CREDOC, La diffusion des technologies de l'information et de la communication dans la société française, www.credoc.fr

Educnet, www.educnet.education.fr

Extracurricular B2i Online Practice, www.nathan.fr/b2i/eleve

Le Guides des Égarés, www.guidedesegares.info

Ministry of Education, www.education.gouv.fr

Parliamentary Mission: Modernizing Schools Thanks to Digital Tools, www.reussirlecole numerique.fr

# Native Knowledge: Knowing What They Know—and Learning How to Teach Them the Rest

Mary Ann Bell

Remember back in the day when the hardest technology grown-ups faced was programming the VCR? The adage was: "Just ask any kid." The notion that youngsters have a natural affinity for all things new and technological goes back at least that far. There is a certain amount of verity to this idea, and the assumption that young people know a lot about technology is even more widely held today. Even the term *digital native* carries an inherent connotation that youngsters who were born into the Internet Age, since around 1980, are inherently confident and adept at all things digital.

So true! And also, so wrong!

Both responses are appropriate, which is what this chapter will address. Because I have worked in education all my life, both as a teacher and librarian for public schools, and as a professor working with adults who will be school librarians, I have a perspective as to what adults think school- and college-age students know, what youngsters actually do know, and how these two sets of information differ in potentially dangerous ways.

## Smart Kids

In July 2009, I queried school librarians and technology teachers, and asked how they keep up with technology in today's fast-moving digital world. One of the most frequently offered answers was, "Keep a kid around!" The responses included comments such as this one: "I know this sounds flippant, but the best way I know to keep up with technology is to hang out with kids. They really are the digital natives, and they take things that start out hypothetical and adapt them to real life usage. And if you can't use it in real life, what good is it really?"

Certainly, younger users, ranging from their earliest exposure through their 20s, tend to exude confidence about technology. While many adults are tentative about approaching a new gadget or application, younger people usually proceed without such apprehensions. The young are also unconstrained by the caution (or lack of imagination) that may keep adults from finding loopholes in filters or firewalls, sharing files or software "illegally," or using a device in ways not intended. So yes, if you want to know how to do certain things or keep up with certain aspects of technology and popular culture, you would be wise to "keep a kid around."

Unlike their elders, digital natives have little or no fear when handed a new device or gadget. They know from first-hand experience that most gizmos today are fairly intuitive and not particularly delicate. Consequently, a youngster is much more likely to pick up a new device and simply start out trying to use it without the slightest thought of opening the instructions, either print or online. As a rule, digital natives have an innate expectation that they can learn by doing, and most of the time they are right.

Most parents would agree that with sufficient motivation, their children can do amazing things. Back when I was a kid growing up in the 1950s and 1960s, I knew boys who were walking encyclopedias when it came to sports statistics. By the same token, today's youth are often experts at pastimes that involve technology. If a device, game, or social networking program captures their imaginations, kids of all ages can and will spend inordinate amounts of time sharpening their skills.

Gaming is a particularly good example of this. Whether the fascination is with X-Box, Wii challenges, online role-playing games, or handheld devices, many kids find gaming a major source of fun and recreation. The Entertainment Software Alliance found that, as of December 2010, the average gamer is 34 years old and has been playing for 12 years. Twenty-six percent of game players are over the age of 50, an increase from 9 percent in 1999 (bit.ly/erRAr2). In fact, Pew's Amanda Lenhart reported that game playing is universal (every generation plays to some extent), yet it is significant that almost all teens play games and at least half play games on a given day ("Major New Study Shatters Stereotypes About Teens and Video Games," 2008, bit.ly/fV2ubr).

According to Marc Prensky, who coined the term *digital natives*, people born into the era of the internet are wired for digital games, and by the time they graduate from college, they will have spent twice as much time playing digital games as they have reading books. In fact, Prensky has asserted that since 2001, the amount of time natives spend in digital pursuits has been changing the very way they think and possibly even their brain structures.

Prensky and other fans of digital gaming for learning are pressing for teachers and parents to recognize that playing online games is more than a pastime and has great learning potential. Sadly, in today's high-pressure test-driven environment, such pleas often fall upon deaf ears. Since games are an important part of many youngsters' lives, adults need to be tuned in to them as well. Whether the games are designed for learning or geared for entertainment, parents and educators must not ignore them or brand them as irrelevant. The learning potential of gaming is receiving increasing attention in formal studies. One such project was conducted in 2007 at Miami University (Ohio) that explored the use of massively multiplayer online role-playing games (MMORPG). Examples of MMORPGs include World of Warcraft for older users, ToonTown for children, and a host of others. In her paper "Game Design and Learning: A Conjectural Analysis of How Massively Multiple Online Role-Playing Games (MMORPGs) Foster Intrinsic Motivation," Michele Dickey concludes: "MMORPG design may provide a flexible model for creating engaging interactive learning environments which foster intrinsic motivation by providing choice, control, collaboration, challenge, and achievement. There is much in contemporary game design to be explored and annexed to support different types of learning" (*Education Technology Research and Development*, 2007).

Video games specifically designed for learning lag behind commercial games where design is concerned, but they are a growing phenomenon. This may be because of their obvious intrinsic appeal, which is demonstrated by the amount of time youngsters use online games when not in school. Further, though, there is increasing pedagogical support, spearheaded by Prensky and others such as Jill Olthouse ("Video Games: Why Kids Play and What They Learn," *Meridian: A Middle School Technologies Journal*, 2009) who have long touted the learning potential of electronic games. James Paul Gee asserts that school-age youngsters expend more time and effort, and consume more information, during their time spent playing video games than they do in the traditional classroom. His challenge is for educators and those who construct educational materials to recognize the power of games for learning and increasingly incorporate it in school life and learning ("High Score Education," *Wired*, 2003).

Other areas where digital natives derive a lot of enjoyment are music, video, animation, and combinations thereof. Young people under the age of 30 have always been driven by the latest fads and artists in music, yet the fact that music today is digital, both in format and in delivery, has radically transformed users' relationship with the content. iPods, smartphones, and myriad portable music devices make it possible for people to have their favorite music with them at all times. However, digital natives are much more than just listeners. They are active in creating their own music and adapting creations of others.

The name most commonly applied to creations where multiple works are combined and remixed to produce new derivations is *mashups*, and digital natives are in the forefront when it comes to these new creative products. According to Brian Lamb, in his 2009 article "Dr. Mashup; or, Why Educators Should Learn to Stop Worrying and Love the Remix" (*EDUCAUSE Review*, bit.ly/eEOHsO), combining online content and works of art to make new creations is something educators ought to support and encourage, while at the same time teaching that attribution of the original works is important.

The digital native's interest in do-it-yourself media goes beyond audio, of course. Today's young people are also devoted observers, collectors, sharers, and creators of video productions. The ubiquity of cameras in phones, digital cameras, and so on makes it possible for people to film just about any where, any time. The rise of YouTube, with its wide variety of selections garnering millions of hits, is a testament to the popularity of video today.

Creating videos, whether simple recordings of family events or sophisticated productions for school assignments or competitions, can provide opportunities for adults and youngsters to work together. One of the most popular new gadgets in recent years is the flip cam, a small video camera that can plug into a computer USB port and instantly upload content. These inexpensive and easy-to-use cameras have put video capability into the hands of thousands of users. Further, with the advent of the latest generation of phones with video capacity, more and more people have a video camera in their pockets at all times. In "How Executives Perceive The Net Generation," Karine Barzilai-Nahon and Robert M. Mason write that "Members of the net generation are perceived by executives and others as using information technologies in ways that differ significantly from those of prior generations ... In many cases these behaviors are viewed as inefficient, ineffective, or even unethical by those already in the work force." The authors conclude that "few organizations currently are set up to accommodate these behaviors" (*Information, Communication & Society*, Vol. 13, No. 3., 2010). In his article "Digital Natives' Lead Enterprise IT," Stan Gibson warned the business world to be ready for digital natives in the work force, where they will change the way things are done in fundamental and far-reaching ways (eWeek, 2006, bit.ly/hn94Ca). In his words, "Generation Y is invading corporate America and bringing with it personal technology that will create a revolution in corporate technology departments." He stressed the impending explosion of technologies such as video and audio productions, podcasts, and blogs, and urged older users to welcome the coming changes and the future leaders who will bring them. Those of us born before the digital age will do well to keep up with changes in order to stay current at work (and also young at heart).

## Don't-Know-It-Alls

However, while it is true that digital natives have a great degree of comfort with technology, it must be remembered that they do not know everything about it. In fact, there are crucial areas where they lack important skills and knowledge. Failure on the part of parents, educators, employers, and others in leadership positions to provide guidance and instruction is a woeful abdication of responsibility. Areas in which young people need guidance include respect for intellectual property, internet searching skills, evaluation of internet information, and online safety. Yet, they are currently getting little or no guidance in these areas. There are two main reasons for this. First, adults assume kids know it all (or at least more than they do) because, after all, they are digital natives. Second, in far too many cases, the adults that digital natives encounter, both at home and at school, are also uninformed about these important issues.

Even without turning attention to the myriad challenges involved in helping digital natives learn to be responsible and savvy internet users, it is instructive to consider basic computer use and ask how capable kids are in actuality. Youngsters can claim and appear to be experts at using any and all computer applications, but it should be noted that there are areas where this is not the case.

It is not enough for digital natives to be masters of their sophisticated cell phones, social networking sites, and gaming devices—the three primary areas where many young users concentrate their interest and use. Teachers and professors assume too much if—upon witnessing the speed with which a student can thumb a text message—they take it for granted that students are experts at using all of the applications available at school such as office suites, mind-mapping software, graphics tools, and so on. Granted digital natives are likely to be quick learners, but they do still need instruction and guidance to maximize their productivity with these digital devices, communities, tools, etc.

## Learning What They Don't Know

My own experience with adult students in the Master of Library Science program at the university where I teach—the youngest of whom are digital natives themselves—is that far too few of them are adept at the most basic computer applications, including office suites and other programs that are ubiquitous in academic and workplace settings. Consider some shortcomings I regularly observe: Most of my students come into our introductory computer class professing a great deal of confidence in using office applications, particularly word processing. They are, however, surprised and thrilled to see demonstrations of such basic features as drawing tools, charting and graphing tools, and advanced formatting options. They are thrilled because they do not, in fact, know how to use many of these features. If they do not know the capabilities of these programs, how can they teach students about them?

While word processing is commonly used, people frequently do not use spreadsheet applications such as Excel before they enter the work force. I am a big fan of Excel and find I have to provide a basic introduction to this useful and versatile application. Younger business and information professionals will certainly find that Excel is useful for delivering all kinds of great graphs, timelines, tables, and other deliverables, but only if they are exposed to the full potential of the software.

Though widely used in schools, presentation software such as PowerPoint is often employed at only the most rudimentary level, with little or no interactivity. This results in the many glorified slide shows that teachers and students produce. Again, the native may show a ready ability to dabble with the tool but lacks a deeper understanding of how presentation software can be leveraged to create products that use it to its limits for school assignments or other uses.

This is not to imply that educators should cease to recognize and appreciate what their students do know. There are some tools with which the native may have vastly more experience and may be able to teach older users a few things. For example, even though Paint, a simple drawing program, is available free on all PCs, many teachers never use it, and some have never even seen it in use. This is one great tool that many kids do already use and that is readily at hand at no cost. If educators know to tap into kids' interest and ability in Paint and other easily accessed (often free) programs, they will find further common ground on which to base educational experiences and may well discover some powerful tools along the way.

Again, digital immigrants need to increase their interest and skill in modeling the use of digital tools and helping students become confident users of computer technology in their future work and leisure activities. Yet, however lacking digital natives may be in some basic office applications, the gap between what they really know and what they truly understand is even greater in the realm of internet use.

## The Search for Information

When we examine what digital natives do and do not know about using the web, we should start where most people do online: with search. Yes, Google is great and everybody uses it—and rightly so. It is an excellent tool, though only one among many that we should encourage (and properly train) students to use. Certainly, it is a mistake to just turn kids loose and say, "OK students, here is your assignment: Ready ... set ... Google!" Yet, all too often I fear that is what happens. Any teacher or librarian who really watches students as they seek information on the internet knows that they lack sophisticated search skills. In fact, they often lack the most rudimentary skills.

Something I used to notice when I worked in libraries was that many patrons, whether adult or teens, simply went to the browser address line and typed in a word or two, thus bypassing search engines altogether. With today's smarter browsers, this tactic can actually bring a degree of success; most browsers now assume that people will do this and have been designed for that event, with words in address lines being automatically searched by Google or other tools.

However, this lapse is a small problem in the larger scheme of things. There is a bigger problem: When I did a little preliminary reading regarding kids and search habits, I came across a term that I had not heard before for another problematic behavior: *bouncing*. Dr. David Loertscher used this very appropriate label to describe what many searchers, both young and old, might admit is a common practice.

Moving quickly from one resource to another without closely reading any material is the culprit ("What Works with the Google Generation?" *Teacher Librarian*, 2008). Granted, this type of skimming may be used early in a search to find promising information, but it is not productive if it is not followed up with careful reading.

Bouncing's older cousin might well be named *printout mania*. During my days as a junior high librarian and also as a community college librarian, I saw lots of examples of people printing out massive amounts of text, far more than anyone could ever plan or need to read. This wasteful and pointless activity gives the user a sense of getting work done, when little is actually being accomplished.

Even if students move beyond the very basic step of actually using a search engine, many never leave the comfort of Google-land, and fewer employ search techniques such as varying search terms or using Boolean logic. As they bounce around the internet, often skimming and printing indiscriminately, youngsters display almost no reflection. There is far too little thinking about what they find and in trying to assimilate or evaluate the material. Of course, the problem is exacerbated by the fact that too often adults do not know how to search either. Thus, it falls to those educators who do know to offer training and resources to help colleagues, parents, and the general public become savvy searchers. The best resources around are often those found in libraries, whether they are public or school. Parents and other interested adults, as well as educators, should take responsibility first for their own learning and then for offering guidance to youngsters.

Earlier in this chapter, I mentioned posting a question to several message boards for K–12 educators about how to keep up with technology and reported that many people replied that kids were the know-it-alls about all things digital. I began to wonder just how accurate this generality really was. In an effort to learn professionals' opinions about school kids and searches, I decided to delve into the topic more deeply. To that end I posted a survey at SurveyMonkey, an online tool that makes it easy to conduct surveys. I invited participants via Twitter, Facebook, and three major educator message boards: LM_Net (Librarian-Media Director Network), TLC (Texas Library Connection), and EdTech (for technology teachers and supervisors). What I learned reinforced my impressions. My survey garnered more than 130 responses from librarians and teachers (bit.ly/kidsearch).

Here are some of the things I learned:

- Yes, indeed, kids still put search terms in browser address lines. Well over half of the respondents replied that this happens at least some of the time, with 18.5 percent calling it a frequent practice. Again, it is true that such a habit can produce results, but it certainly is not the route we want our students to take.

- Google does indeed rule. Less than 1 percent reported that their students never use Google. I suspect these responses were from a few schools that actually block the use of Google. As well, 19.7 percent said students always go to Google, with the rest reporting frequent use.

- Subscription databases are not getting the attention that I would have hoped. Only about 25 percent reported that they are used often or frequently.

- Educators seem to be fighting an uphill battle to get students to use the databases, with more than 75 percent reporting that they try to promote the use of these resources. A depressing 16 percent say students never use databases. Alas, I do not know if this is because none are available.

- The practice of bouncing from one site to another without close examination of any is epidemic: More than 90 percent of survey takers agreed that students are doing this.

- Indiscriminate printing was a concern on the part of more than half of those providing information.

As I worked on this survey, I began to wonder if efforts are being made to actually teach students safe and smart search skills. Educators must ask themselves to what extent they are addressing the shortcomings that the survey reveals. Most certainly youngsters need to be learning how to conduct smart searches. While students do display some search skills, there is certainly room for improvement. Even the simple process of varying search terms is not common among many young searchers. In my survey, 10.2 percent responded that kids *never* do this, with 71.2 percent giving the weak response of "sometimes." Only 2 percent of respondents could boast that their students always knew to do this.

Narrowing a search is another simple skill that is far too seldom used, with 20 percent reporting this never happened. As to Boolean searching, where users employ the operators AND, OR, and NOT, the gap was the greatest: 56.2 percent said students *never* use these methods, which suggests to me a lack of instruction. No one reported that students always know to employ these techniques.

While these responses do not surprise me, I do find it worrisome that teachers are not aware or concerned about their students' lack of search skills. I asked how many librarians/technology teachers observe other faculty giving students guidance regarding how to search. More than one-third (36 percent) reported that teachers leave students to their own devices when it comes to searching, offering no instruction or guidance about the process.

The information I was able to garner from librarians and teachers by means of my online inquiries caused me to remember an old cliché: *Never assume.* Teachers should never take for granted that their students know how to search and find accurate online information. By the same token, librarians, technology teachers, and administrators should not assume that all their teachers know what is necessary to help students seek information online. Staff development covering internet use is a continuing and unmet necessity. Additionally, parents should be encouraged to join in at home when their children are searching for information and to work together with them to construct smart searches.

## Assessing Information Quality

Making sure that kids are capable searchers is only half the challenge facing adults who want to help them learn to navigate the internet. According to John Palfrey and Urs Gasser in the seminal book *Born Digital*, the ever-growing glut of information flooding the internet defies assimilation. "In 2003, researchers have estimated the world's information production to be around five billion gigabytes. Current reports predict that there will be 988 billion gigabytes of information in 2010" (2008). Given this impossible morass of material, how does one become a discerning and thoughtful user?

Never before has the need been so great for people to evaluate the information that they encounter. Since anyone can publish to the internet on any possible topic, there is a plethora of information, much of which lacks credibility. While a good deal of this information is relatively harmless, some sites are deliberately misleading and even downright dangerous. One of the most infamous examples is Martin Luther King: A Historical Perspective (www.martinlutherking.org). This is one of the most insidious hate sites on the internet, and it directly targets youth. It is sponsored by Stormfront, a radical racist organization with ties to the Ku Klux Klan. A November 2009 visit yielded information that the site is growing in popularity and moving to larger and more powerful servers, "due to resistance to the Obamination." Because this site is blocked at most schools, the hosts actively recruit users to access it at home. There, all too often lacking parental guidance, youngsters can have plenty of time to peruse the site without adult supervision.

Clearly, kids need guidance when searching the internet, not just in finding information but also in assessing their results. Students need to know how to find and recognize quality information that is authoritative, current, unbiased, and relevant. Teaching website evaluation is, in my opinion, one of the most important responsibilities of educators today. There are bountiful resources available to help people learn to be discerning consumers of information. One of the best, most easily found, and most useful of these is Kathy Schrock's Guide for Educators (school.discoveryeducation.com/schrockguide). This site offers a number of training tools, checklists, and other resources for educators and parents who want to teach youngsters to be smart searchers. Sadly, though, my experience is that many long-time educators are unaware of this and similarly valuable resources. Again, lack of training is largely to blame.

## Appropriate Information Usage

Once a youngster finds material that seems useful and appropriate, far too often he or she does not know how to use it in an ethical manner. A major problem is the "cut and paste" syndrome, in which students simply lift large sections of text or even entire articles and submit them as original work for school assignments. Sadly, they sometimes are enabled or even encouraged in this practice by teachers who do not follow through and provide instruction that makes it clear that plagiarism is not acceptable. And even if kids know it is "wrong" to plagiarize, it is so easy to do that the temptation is hard to resist.

Secondary and college students know all too well that they can easily find ready-to-submit papers at cheat sites such as schoolsucks.com. They can even choose papers that are in line with their usual level of work. A "B" student, for example, can get a paper that is adequate but not so sophisticated as to arouse suspicion by being markedly better than his previous work. Many of these papers are free, with more sophisticated and customized offerings available for sale. The old scare tactics that I remember from my own school days didn't work then and are even less likely to now. I can remember being told, "If you copy someone else's words and call them your own, you are as much a thief as if you steal a loaf of bread from the store."

It is possible to teach kids to respect copyright and responsible use of information, though. One of the most powerful arguments for giving credit where it is due is to relate the issue to how the youngster would feel if someone took his or her work. In today's world of online creating and publishing, this argument actually resonates even more than it did in the past. Another powerful antidote to plagiarism is the creative assignment. Asking kids today to write a report about a topic, with no further clarification, is essentially inviting plagiarism. Creative teachers know how to craft challenging tasks that require students to assimilate information and then give it back along with their own reactions in inventive ways, often involving technology in the process.

The lack of respect for intellectual property affects digital natives' recreational as well as their educational use of media. The desire to build media collections, especially music collections, has given birth to the epidemic of file sharing, both legal and illegal, and kids know how to do it all. Part of the problem is that today's copyright laws have not kept up with the rise of digital media. The laws are both confusing and overly strict, and thus do not deter kids from file sharing. At the same time, though, kids are disregarding intellectual property rights and making it difficult for musicians and artists to be able to earn what they deserve from their creations.

The flipside of this free and loose approach to intellectual property is the digital natives' propensity for creating and sharing their own works—or remixing the works of others into their own unique interpretation. A 2007 Pew Internet & American Life Project study, "Teens and Social Media," found that many teens were at that time actively creating content and posting their creations online, and it is certainly likely that the numbers have increased since that time. In this national telephone survey of 935 youngsters between the ages of 12 and 17, more than one-half of those contacted (57 percent) reported that they were creating content and sharing it online (bit.ly/fS8sGw). Creations included artwork, photographs, videos, blogs, webpages, and other offerings. Interestingly, girls were more active than boys in creating online content in many areas, with 35 percent of girls and only 20 percent of boys posting blogs, and 54 percent of girls uploading photos as opposed to 40 percent of boys. The one area where boys led was in posting videos, with 19 percent of boys active in this pursuit as opposed to 10 percent of girls. As mentioned previously, mashups are made by combining two or more existing digital works, whether text, audio, video, animation, or other formats. The survey found that 26 percent of the boys and girls contacted reported remixing works in this fashion.

When it comes to mashups, who gets credit? How is it attributed? This is one of numerous issues that need to be addressed by revising copyright laws and moving them into the 21st century. Further, because youngsters are much more prone to share content online via social networking, they are less and less inclined to subscribe to the older beliefs that view intellectual property as static, unchanging, and not available for sharing or tweaking. This desire for more generous interpretation of copyright law is the driving force behind the internet phenomenon called Creative Commons.

Lawrence Lessig is an outspoken proponent of a more lenient interpretation of the concept of intellectual property and copyright laws. In his widely read *US News and World Report* article (December 2008, bit.ly/fzV8FE), he calls for more lenient interpretations to allow sharing and remixing of published works. To that end, he collaborated with other intellectual property experts to found Creative Commons in 2001. This large and growing online community is a place where people can post their own creations and define the rights for use as they wish, and they can also use works that are shared by others. Adults who work with digital natives need to rethink old notions about copyright and intellectual property, and find ways to combine creativity with attribution to those whose works they adapt and change.

Those in leadership roles must keep aware of the issues involving intellectual property and help youngsters understand how to decide what is appropriate usage. Parents and teachers need to instill in younger people the importance of giving credit where it is due for borrowed work and providing compensation to creators for their works so as to allow them to continue with their work. Too often adults turn a blind eye to the situation, offering neither guidance nor advice.

## Safe Surfing

Perhaps the most pressing concern about digital natives using the internet is the fear that kids do not know how to stay safe and smart when online. A great deal of concern has been generated about online safety. Indeed, the topic has generated as much hype as substance, with fear-mongering leading some parents and educators to believe the internet is, in and of itself, dangerous and a place to be avoided.

Many educators seem to rely on filters as the "final solution," and some families have home filtering applications to keep kids safe there. The notion that filters keep kids safe is not accurate and, I am convinced, actually conspires to make kids less safe. Because filters offer a false sense of security, the teaching of safe internet searching and communicating is often given short shrift. After all, the filters are keeping out all the bad stuff, right? Wrong.

There are several problems with this line of thinking: First of all, filters both over and under block. Even the "tightest" filter can sometimes let objectionable material pass through. At the same time, a great deal of valuable information can be blocked. The day before I wrote this paragraph, a librarian member of the LM_Net listserv reported that the word *specialist* was blocked at his school for reasons unknown. Finally, it was determined that the problem was the fact that the word contained *cialis*, a word blocked because it was the name of a popular drug for erectile dysfunction. I have within the last year asked graduate students to search for terms such as *triggerfish, sperm whale,* and *breast cancer* at the schools where they teach, and they have verified that these words are often blocked as well.

Just as important, though, is the fact that filters often give teachers, administrators, and even parents a false sense of security. Because filters are in place, they do not actively teach students about safe internet use. Then when these youngsters access the web on a cell phone, use a public terminal at the library, or simply venture forth into the world, they may be babes in the woods due to lack of instruction about safety. That is why I assert that filters can cause students to be less, rather than more, safe.

Finally, the law that seeks to protect students, Children's Internet Protection Act (CIPA), is very specific and limited. It only mandates that sites with obscenity or extreme violence should be blocked. Most schools and districts block far more than these, and thus are in violation of the letter as well as the spirit of the law. Internet safety is definitely an area where adults should not just assume that kids know what they should and should not be doing online. The best filter is a vigilant and informed adult, whether at school, in a library, or at home.

## Native Knowledge

Digital natives do not have some sort of innate ability regarding all aspects of technology by virtue of the fact they were born into a digital world. It is true that they cannot imagine a world without cell phones, powerful computers, mesmerizing video games, and the internet. However, it is always important to consider the sizable group of youngsters who do not have the means to enjoy these things. We need to remember that there are many people of all ages who do not even have electricity at home, much less multiple computers and internet access. Surely everyone concedes that youngsters from these homes need extra assistance and access at school. However, putting aside this group, parents and educators need to face up to our responsibilities to teach even the most tech-savvy kids. What should be done?

For starters, we need to continue promoting greater awareness of the areas where students need instruction and better instruction for both faculty and students. I do not particularly subscribe to the line of thinking that says that if someone admits to having a problem, he/she is well on the way to a solution. Lots of people have been trumpeting the need for greater awareness and improved computer skills among digital immigrants in order for them to provide guidance to natives for a long time. Recognizing a shortcoming is a positive step, but the big leap is to then take steps to solve it.

There is a crying need for systematic, comprehensive teacher training. How to provide such instruction is a subject for other articles and books but lack of training must be addressed. For as long as I can remember working with technology and learning, I have personally observed that far too many schools and districts will spend thousands of dollars on equipment and software, and then fail to provide time and resources for training. Alas, the problem persists. But passively waiting for training is no longer an option for the adult who wishes to learn what is needed. Responsible adults should seek out information on their own if none is offered to them. Again, this is an area where we can take a cue from the natives' instinct to turn to their online community as a resource: The internet abounds with tutorials, online resources, and even communities where people can communicate online as they seek to gain the knowledge and skills they need to keep up with the emerging challenges and opportunities in educating digital natives. All adults who work or live with digital natives should step up to this responsibility.

## Native Insights

What can we expect from these digital natives in the future? In addition to specific skills and techniques, are there some other ways that kids outshine their elders? Their ways of thinking about technology and the internet are different. Indeed, if we are to believe what Prensky has been saying since early in this century, their very brain structures have been altered by immersion since birth in digital media.

Here are some ways they have moved ahead: First, they are ready to redefine the use of intellectual property. The predisposition of the native to network, collaborate, and share, as well as build on previous works with mashups and other adaptations, contributes to their willingness to rethink copyright and plagiarism. At the same time, they need guidance regarding how to proceed and still honor the creator. Next, digital natives have different ideas about privacy than their elders. Natives are willing to concede more openness in order to get what they want. Whether digital immigrants like it or not, our lives today are much more public than they were in the past. Post-911 security is one reason for this, and the proliferation of online activities such as banking, shopping, and social networking have brought most of our lives online. Digital natives have less fear of divulging details about their lives and are willing to share information in order to get the things they want online. More often than not, convenience trumps privacy. Like it or not, this is the wave of the future. Finally, they are hardwired to collaborate and share. The concept of every man for himself is much less valued. The lone writer or artist, toiling away in his garret, is no longer the artistic ideal. Today's youngsters are much more likely to seek out others' opinions every step of the way in their creative endeavors.

Those of us who have chosen to venture into today's digital world are called digital immigrants. No matter how hard we try to assimilate, we will always have what Prensky calls an "accent." There will always be things about the way we express ourselves, go about our work, and enjoy our leisure time that differ from the ways of the natives. But we immigrants are important. We are the people who need to become actively involved in teaching our young charges about smart and productive use of technology and the internet. We can teach classes, present at conferences, write articles, blogs, and other missives, and otherwise share our concerns with friends and co-workers. Most of all, we can move forward through direct and personal contact with colleagues and students. With our young native students, offspring, and acquaintances, we must be willing to be followers as well as leaders. Whenever possible, we should be partners. If we don't do these things, who will?

## About the Contributor

**Mary Ann Bell** is an associate professor in and chair of the Department of Library Science, Sam Houston State University, where she teaches classes related to technology and librarianship. She is the author of *Internet and Personal Computer Fads* (Haworth Press, 2004) and *Cybersins and Digital Good Deeds: A Book About Technology and Ethics* (Haworth Press, 2006). She has also written numerous journal articles and presented at conferences on the topics of information ethics and creative teaching with technology. She is active in the Texas Library Association, American Library Association, Texas Computer Education Association, Association for the Advancement of Computing in Education, and Delta Kappa Gamma. She received her BA from Baylor University, her MLS from Sam Houston State University, and her EdD from Baylor University. She enjoys nature photography, hiking, and reading.

## Recommended Reading

### Books and Articles

Bell, Mary Ann, Bobby Ezell, and James VanRoekel. *Cybersins and Digital Good Deeds: A Book About Technology and Ethics.* New York: Haworth Press, 2006.

Goodstein, Anastasia. *Totally Wired: What Teens and Tweens Are Really Doing Online.* New York: St. Martin's Press, 2007.

November, Alan. *Web Literacy for Educators.* Thousand Oaks, CA: Corwin Press, 2008.

Palfrey, John and Urs Gasser. *Born Digital.* New York: Basic Books, 2008.

Richardson, Will. *Blogs, Wikis, Podcasts, and Other Powerful Web Tools for Classrooms.* Thousand Oaks, CA: Corwin Press, 2009.

Willard, Nancy. *Cyber-Safe Kids, Cyber-Savvy Teens: Helping Young People Learn to Use the Internet Safely and Responsibly.* San Francisco: Jossey-Bass, 2007.

## Websites

21st Century Educational Technology and Learning, 21centuryedtech.wikispaces.com

3D WiredSafety, 3dwiredsafety.blogspot.com

Around the Corner, www.mguhlin.org

The Blue Skunk Blog, doug-johnson.squarespace.com

Bud the Teacher, budtheteacher.com/blog

Cyber-Safe Kids, Cyber-Savvy Teens, www.cskcst.com

Digital Natives Blog, blogs.law.harvard.edu/digitalnatives

From Now On: The Educational Technology Journal, www.fno.org

Marc Prensky, www.marcprensky.com

NeverEndingSearch, School Library Journal, blog.schoollibraryjournal.com/never endingsearch

Pew Internet & American Life Project, www.pewinternet.org

Weblogg-ed, weblogg-ed.com

# About the Editors

**Michelle Manafy** is the director of content of FreePint, Ltd., a publisher of sites and resources for the business information industry. Michelle previously served as the editorial director of the Enterprise Group for Information Today, Inc. In this role, Michelle was editor-in-chief of *EContent* magazine and the *Intranets* newsletter. She was also the chair of Information Today's Enterprise Search Summits and the Buying & Selling eContent Conference. Michelle's focus is on emerging trends in digital content and how they shape successful business practices. An award-winning columnist, Michelle has written on a variety of technology topics including digital publishing, social media, content development and distribution, streaming media, and audio, video, and storage technologies. She speaks at a variety of industry events and serves as a judge for many content and technology competitions. She has worked in book and magazine publishing for more than 20 years in areas ranging from pop culture to academic nonfiction and holds a BA in journalism from San Francisco State University.

Michelle's interest in the distinct differences and opportunities presented by the digital native generation was triggered by her experiences working with interns. Each summer, as a new mound of bright shiny clay turned up in the office, Michelle increasingly sensed subtle changes in texture that began to affect the shape of the mentoring experience. Michelle found that while digital natives bear a striking resemblance to their predecessors, their approaches to work, information interaction, and many other aspects of life are profoundly influenced by their digitally empowered world view. As these young team members began to participate in story creation and collaborative projects and to leave the office to enter the world of work, it became increasingly clear to Michelle that as a lifelong publishing professional who hadn't used a computer until college, she had a lot to learn about—and from—them.

**Heidi Gautschi** grew up in France and the United States, and she continues to divide her time between these two countries. She has taught in the French university system since 2000, most recently at University of Lille 3. Her research looks at the cultural, social, political, and economic implications of communication technology, with special emphasis on the comparative French and American contexts. She earned a BA in philosophy from Tufts University, an MA in health education from Teachers College, Columbia University, and a PhD in information and communication sciences from the University of Paris X.

Heidi's interest in digital natives arose from her observations in the classroom and during her commute. She noticed mobile technology taking on more and more importance among teenagers and young adults, both in social situations and during classes, and wanted to better understand this phenomenon. In parallel, Heidi has also begun experimenting with different technology applications in the classroom to see if her students would learn more effectively by using the tools they are comfortable with.

# Index

## A

*The Academic Library and the Net Gen Student: Making the Connections* (Gibbons), 316
ACT! contact management software, 109–110
ADA (Americans with Disabilities Act), 270
adult use of social networks, 98, 134–135, 155, 160
advertising. *See also* marketing
  as content, 120–121
  conversations, initiating, 206
  crowdsourcing for, 127–128
  to digital natives, 122–126, 135–136, 147–148, 197–200, 205
  of executive-level jobs, 89
  failures, 204
  on mobile devices, 124, 125, 137, 148
  role of trust, 205, 206
  social, 176
  successes, 48, 49, 199–200, 201–202
  traditional, 135–137, 198
Ahonen, Tomi, 118
airplanes and property rights conflict, 217
Alcatel-Lucent, 124–125

alerts tools for detecting conversations, 161–162
Alpine Access, virtual work force, 26
Alterian, 162
always-connectedness, 74–75
Amazon.com review feature, 44
"American College Survey" (Anderson Analytics), 230
"Americans and Their Gadgets" (Pew Internet), 149
Americans with Disabilities Act (ADA), 270
*Amusing Ourselves to Death* (Postman), 230, 231, 347
*The Anti 9-to-5 Guide* (Goodman), 28
anywhere-everywhere work practice, 7, 9–12, 17
Apple, advertising successes, 199–200
"Are We Having Fun Yet?" (Labash), 24
*Asia's New Crisis* (Richter & Mar), 213
audio blogging, 166
Autodesk 3D-design company, 45–46
"Automotive Industry Survey—Millenials' Technology Preferences" (Microsoft), 146
awareness tools, 161–162

# B

B2i (brevet informatique et internet), 339–342, 344–348
Baby Boomers, 98, 134–135, 155
BackType, 162
*Bakersfield Voice* (newspaper), 245–246
Basotect resin foam, 47
Bastard Pop, 252
Baumard, Maryline, 337, 338
the Beamer, 51
Beastie Boys (band), 253
BEINGGIRL.com, 121
Being Me social network, 305
Bell, Mary Ann, 351–352, 371
Bellamkonda, Shashi, 170–171
Berners-Lee, Tim, 39–40
"Beyond Google Generation: A Proper Point of View of Search Engines Needed" (Yi), 325–326
Bhargava, Rohit, 153–154
billboard campaigns, Generation Y views, 136–137
BitTorrent P2P network, 263
blip.tv, 169
Blocher, Joseph, 186–187
"Blogging 101" (Zuiker), 322
blogs, 118, 144, 162, 165–167, 195, 229, 233–234, 322. *See also* individual blogs
Blowtorch Media & Entertainment, 209
Blyk, 123
Bongey, Sarah Bryans, 288
bookmarking, 165–166
Bootleg, 252
*Born Digital: Understanding the First Generation of Digital Natives* (Palfrey & Gasser), 316, 363
bouncing, 359–360
Bradshaw, Paul, 240
"The Brand Called You" (Peters), 81
branded utilities, 125–126
branding, 76–78, 88, 92, 125–126, 141–142, 199–202, 204–205. *See also* personal branding

brand loyalty, Generation Y lack, 144
"Brave New World of Digital Intimacy" (Thompson), 13
*brevet,* 339–340
brevet informatique et internet (B2i), 339–342, 344–348
Brisbourne, Nic, 238–239
Brown, Adam, 101
Brown, Graham, 121–122
browsers, development of early, 57
Buck, James, 168
bursty work, 8, 9, 10–11
businesses. *See* companies

# C

Cadbury, 198–199
Calanis, Jason, 88
cameras, 64, 77, 355
Canton Car Wash, 159
Capgemini consultancy, 177, 179–180
Capitol Media work environment, 31–32
career advancement, personal branding as tool for, 88
Career Builder, 82
career status, influence on personal brand, 87–88
Carlacio, Jami L., 317, 329
Carroll, Dave, 197
cell phones, 116–119, 136, 148–149, 217, 335, 355–356
centralized institutions, character, 337
Centre de Recherche pour l'…tude et l'Observation des Conditions de Vie (CREDOC), 335
Cerf, Vint, 39–40
change, digital natives' influence on, 98
changes to society, caused by technology, 212
Char, Jessica, 31
cheat sites, 364
chefvinod blog, 158
Chester French, 102–103, 104

children, socialization of, 175
Children's Internet Protection Act
 (CIPA), 368
Chiu, Dave, 183, 184
CIRP (Cooperative Institute for Research
 Program) study on Generation Y,
 134
citizen journalism, 235–236
Cizadlo, Dr. Gerald, 281–282
Club Penguin, 203
CNN, digital native-friendly features,
 243–244
Coding in Paradise (blog), 34
Cohn, David Pablo, 54–55
Coker, Dr. Brent, 11
collaboration, 22, 39–40
collaborative cloud-based real-time envi-
 ronments, 65
collaborative technologies with con-
 sumers, 50. *See also* Comcast
 Cares
college, social media as tool for getting
 into, 87–88
College of St. Scholastica, 279, 282–283
CollÉge Renaud-Barrault, 343–347
college students, 88, 156–157, 277,
 279–280, 281
Combes, Barbara, 338–339
Comcast cable television provider,
 50–51, 105–106
Comcast Cares, 43, 50, 105, 106, 157
Comcast Customer Connect, 106
ComcastMustDie.com, 105–107
commercials. *See* advertising
Common Sense Media, 154
communication, 9–10, 177, 281–282,
 334–335
communities, 39, 42–43, 52–53,
 161–162, 164, 176, 181–182
community boards, 164–165
community interactions, 115, 120
community-oriented policing, 68, 72, 73
Commute Trip reduction Program,
 Washington State, 27

companies
 brand, 88, 92
 consumers, interacting with, 44, 54,
  57, 111, 115–116, 119–121,
  145, 155–156, 175
 internal structure based on community contributions, 182
 leveling of playing field, 155, 157
 negative information about, 105–107,
  155, 197
 open source culture, 40–41, 58
 reputations, 178–179
 social media use, 43–44, 87, 91, 155,
  157–160, 170, 205
 typical innovation model, 42, 46, 48
competitor information, 51, 57
complexity, Stephen Hawking on, 296
compliance, 212
CompStat public accountability numbers
 system, 73
computer access, youth, 293
Cone Consumer Media Study, 120
Connect & Develop website, 47–48
"Connect and Develop, Inside Procter &
 Gamble's New Model for
 Innovation" (*Harvard Business
 Review*), 47, 48
connected state, as default, 117–118
connectivity, 12, 211–212, 335–336
consultants, 20, 88. *See also* freelancers
consumers
 collaborative technologies with, 43,
  50, 105, 106, 157
 community participation, 42–43
 companies' view of, 57, 175
 company interaction, 44, 54, 57, 111,
  115–116, 119–121, 145,
  155–156, 175
 content valued by, 167–168
 control of marketing information,
  123–124
 as creators, 50–51, 53
 digital natives as, 99–100
 expectations of, 111, 175, 177

consumers (*cont.*)
  feedback from, 111, 115, 120, 126–128, 144–146, 155–156, 196
  innovation, 50–51, 53
  interests, identifying, 122–123
  listening to, 110–111, 139, 161–162
  online information use, 42, 43–44
  trust, obtaining from, 111
content creation, 200–202, 233, 236, 292–293, 321–322, 355–356, 365–366
ContentNext Media, acquisition by Guardian News & Media, 234
content piracy, 219–220, 259–260, 261–262, 365, 367
contractors, 20
control of information/communication, 177
conversational content, 167
Conway, Kellyanne, 74
Cooperative Institute for Research Program (CIRP) study on Generation Y, 134
Cope, Bill, 293
copyright. *See* intellectual property
Cornille, Olivier, 343–347
coworking spaces, 20, 34–36
Coworking Visa program, 35
Creative Commons, 52, 55, 223, 323–324, 366
creative works, legal protection for. *See* intellectual property
creators, consumer, 50–51, 53
CREDOC (Centre de Recherche pour l'…tude et l'Observation des Conditions de Vie), 335
crime, fighting. *See* police officers
CRM (customer relationship management), 40, 99–103, 104, 105, 111–112. *See also* customer service
crowdsourcing, 42, 127–128, 168
crowdSPRING marketplace, 45–46
culture
  influence on technology, 250, 333–334

open source, 40–41, 58
remix, 49, 120
reputation-based, 178
technology, influence on, 333–334
workplace, needs of digital natives, 24–25
currency, reputation as, 182–185
Curtis, Mark, 128–129
Customer-Circus.com consumer website, 107
customer relationship management (CRM), 40, 99–103, 104, 105, 111–112. *See also* customer service
customer service, 25, 43, 50, 105, 106, 108–111, 157
customization, importance to digital natives, 24
cyberethics, 67

## D

daemons, mobile devices as, 128–129
Dailymotion, 345
damage control ethics, 141–142, 214, 218
dangerous online material, 363
database use, subscription, 361
Deezer music site, 258, 263
DeHart, Jacob, 99
Delicious, 165
Delicious Monster work environment, 31
*De l'Innovation* (Gaudin), 334–335
Dell Inc., customer responses, 160–161
Design by Design, 311
Dewaele, David and Stephen, 252
Digg, 165
Digidude, 51
digital breaks, 10–11. *See also* leisure activities
Digital Campus, 279–280
digital evidence gathering, 69–70
digital immigrants, 63, 352, 356, 369–371

digital literacy, importance, 329
"Digital Literacy in the Google
    Generation" (Yi), 326
*Digital Nation* (PBS), 240–241
"The Digital Native' Debate: A Critical
    review of the Evidence" (Bennet,
    Maton & Kerin), 338
digital natives
    characteristics, 72, 76–77, 134–135,
        175, 316, 356–360
    immigrants compared, 134, 141,
        149–150, 369–370
    technological knowledge/comfort, 7,
        134–135, 319, 351–353, 360,
        362
    term, 175, 353
"Digital Natives, Digital Immigrants,
    Part II: Do They Really *Think*
    Differently?" (Prensky), 63, 64,
    175
"Digital Natives' Lead Enterprise IT"
    (Gibson), 356
"Digital Natives or Digital Refugees?
    Why We Have Failed Gen Y?"
    (Combes), 338–339
digital storytelling, 326–327
Discovery School, 275–276
distributed networking technologies,
    effect on work practices, 11–12
Docstoc, 169
Doctorow, Cory, 180–181
doctors, training for, 64
Dolibarr open source software, 40
"Do They Really *Think* Differently?"
    (Prensky), 63, 64, 175
downtime, 66
*The Dreams of Reason: The Rise of the
    Sciences of Complexity* (Pagels), 296
*Dr. Horrible's Sing-Along Blog* (online
    series), 201
"Dr. Mashup; or, Why Educators Should
    Learn to Stop Worrying and Love
    the Remix" (Lamb), 355
dropout rates, school, 292, 293
Drummey, Max, 102
DVRs, ubiquity of, 198

**E**

ECAR Study of Undergraduate Students
    and Information Technology
    (EDUCAUSE), 156–157
education. *See also* Quest to Learn;
    "Writing and Research in the
    University: Writing in the Twenty-
    First Century"
    challenges to, 271
    college-level, 277, 279–280, 281
    digital literacy, 316–317, 322–324
    of digital natives, 338–339, 356–360
    dropout rates, 292, 293
    entertainment compared, 269
    evolution in, 338
    French system, 336–337, 339–345,
        346–348
    funding, 271–272
    goals, 368–369
    inclusive, 270
    key components, 286
    kindergarten through high school,
        271, 277–278, 280
    librarians' role, 318–319
    management systems, 276, 277,
        280–281
    online, 273–276, 278–279, 281–283,
        286
    outside of school, 270–271, 276,
        278–279
    plagiarism, avoiding, 365
    safety, 67
    in skills digital natives lack, 356–360
    skills needed, 315–316
    standards, 269, 271–273, 287
    technology, 270–271, 274–276,
        282–285, 293–294, 368
    tools for, 273–276, 353–354, 355
    trends, 286–287
    visual components, 281–282
EDUCAUSE, 156–157, 229–230
Eichler, Jeremy, 255–256
EIU (Economist Intelligence Unit), 139,
    140

Eliason, Frank, 43–44, 50, 105, 106, 157
Elliot, Missy, 253
email, 174
employees, 22, 24, 75–77, 88–90, 93–94
eMule P2P network, 263
Endless Love remix video, 221
entertainment. *See also* films/film industry; games/gaming
    branded, 199, 200–201, 202
    content creation, 200–202, 355–356
    digital natives' role as, 194–195, 202
    education compared, 269
    entertaining, requirement of, 197
    marketing as, 196–197, 208–209
    on multiple platforms, 192
    news as, 230–231
    for social media, 200–201
    traditional, fragmented compared, 192–193
    video, 192–193, 196–197
entitlement, digital natives' sense of, 49–50
entrepreneurs, 88, 98
environmental benefits of virtual work force, 26
The Equity Kicker (blog), 238
Erisman, Albert M., 225–226
Estèe Lauder, 200
ethics. *See also* intellectual property
    cyber-, 67
    damage control, 141–142, 214, 218
    decisions involving, examples, 216, 218–220
    described, 211, 212–215, 225
    law, relationship with, 212–214, 216–217
    legal changes and, 224
    mission control, 214–215, 218
    photographs, editing, 218–219
    plagiarism, 364–365
    remixed products, 221–223
    solving issues of, 215–216
    technology, effect of, 216–217, 218, 225

Etsy, 100–101, 104
Evans, Brynn, 17
Evans, Susan, 37
event sponsorships, 137
Excel, Microsoft, 358
"Executive Control of Cognitive Processes in Task Switching" (Rubinstein, Meyer, & Evans), 9
executive-level jobs, public advertisement of, 89
"Experts agree: Building, Tapping a Network Crucial to Finding New Job" (*Mercury News*), 83
extended enterprise communities, 181
"The Eyebrow Dance" video, 198–199

**F**

Faberge Shampoo marketing approach, 138
Facebook. *See also* social networks
    costs, 104
    described, 163–164
    friends, average number, 178
    history, 233
    multi-language interface, 251
    student use, 157, 324–325
    uses, 89–90, 155, 160, 195, 235, 244
"Facebook + Media" page, 235
Facebook Connect API, 242, 243
"fair use" concept of reuse, 222
fan community, Josh Groban, 161
Farley, Jim, 142
Fatty Spins (band), 196–197
FeedBurner, 170
file sharing, 174, 219–220, 259–262, 365, 367
films/film industry, 192–193, 196, 200–202
filters, internet, 367–368
Fisher, Steven, 159
*Five Strategies for Social Media Customer Service Excellence* (Petouhoff), 107, 108

Fleming, John, 147
Flickr, 165, 169
flip cams, 355
Flirtomatic social network, 118, 128
Flying Dewaele Brothers, 252
*Focusing the Digital Brain* (Sprenger), 347
force, online proliferation showing use of, 67
Ford Fiesta, marketing, 146–148
Forrester Research, 107, 108
forums, participating in, 164–165
France
    centralized structure, 336
    digital behavior, 335–336, 338
    educational system, 336–337,
        339–340, 342–345, 347–348
    integration model, 337
    internet access, 334–336, 343
    privacy concerns, 335
    technology skills, education for,
        202–203, 339–342, 346–348
*Free* (Anderson), 220, 221, 222
free content, 49–50
"Freedom to Surf: Workers More
    Productive if Allowed to Use the
    Internet for Leisure" (Coker), 11
freelancers, 20
freemium model, 203–204
FreePint, Ltd., 187, 246
"free" work, digital natives' view of,
    45–46
Friendster, 174
"From Narrative to Database:
    Multimedia Inquiry in a Cross-
    Classroom Scholarship of
    Teaching and Learning Study"
    (Coventry & Oppermann), 327
fun as corporate goal, 24
*The Future of Success: Working and Living
    in the New Economy* (Reich), 212

# G

Gallagher, Steve, 154
Galloway, Scott, 199–200
"Game Design and Learning: A
    Conjectural Analysis of How
    Massively Multiple Online Role-
    Playing Games (MMORPGs)
    Foster Intrinsic Motivation"
    (Dickey), 354
games/gaming
    communities, 52–53
    educational, 297, 302–303, 305,
        353–354
    as entertainment, 202–203
    police/military training, 64, 65
    role-playing, 174, 203, 354
    on social media, 202–203
    usage, 353
    video, 292, 354
    virtual world, 54–55, 64–65,
        203–204
Gamestar Mechanic (game), 295, 305
Gasser, Urs, 316, 321, 324, 325, 363
Gautschi, Heidi, 251, 265, 348
General Public License (GPL), 55
"Generation 2010" report (Pew Internet
    & American Life Project), 155
Generation X, 98, 228–229, 293
Generation Y
    blog readership, 229
    brand loyalty, lack of, 144
    entrepreneurs, 98
    financial influence, 98
    internet use, 136, 293
    life goals, 134
    marketing to, 133–134, 136–137
    numbers, 98, 141
    social network use, 98, 155
    technology use, 134–135
    traditional media use, 136, 228–229
"Generation 'Y Do I Have to Work From
    the Office?" (Conway), 74
"Gen Y Affluents: Media Survey" (L2),
    229

*Germinal* (Zola), 343
Gibbons, Susan, 316, 318
Global Web Index (Lightspeed Research), 126
Global Youth Lab research, 124
Godin, Seth, 141
*The Golden Compass* (Pullman), 128
Goodman, Michelle, 28
Goodwin, Larry, 279
Google, 22–23, 54–55, 56, 361
Google Alerts, 162
Google Analytics, 170
Google Doctype library, 54, 56
Google Generation, experience of, 325–326
Googleplex campus, 23
GPL (General Public License), 55
Graham, Paul, 8
Grant, Oscar, 67
"The Greatest Generation (of Networkers)" (Gallagher), 154
Griffith, Saul, 51, 52
Groundswell blog, 246
*Growing Up Online* (PBS), 240, 241
*Grown Up Digital: How the Net Generation is Changing Your World* (Tapscott), 21, 212, 218
*The Guardian*, 239–240
Guardian Club, 239–240
Guardian News & Media, acquisition of ContentNext Media, 234
guest posts, blog, 165
Guide for Educators (Schrock), 364
*The Guild* (online video series), 201

**H**

Hadopi law, 261–262
Hamilton Beach Slow Cooker, influence of ratings on sales, 44
Heidig, Lance J., 317, 329
Helio wireless network operator, 138, 139

Hemsoth, Nicole, 29
Henry, Shawn, 67
high-school students. *See* teens
îHigh Score Educationî (Gee), 354
Hillhorst, Didier, 183, 184
*His Dark Materials* (Pullman), 128
Hogan's Alley, 64
Hollywood, Mike, 121
home offices, 29–30
Howe, Jeff, 168
"How Executives Perceive The Net Generation" (Barzilai-Nahon & Mason), 356
"How I Work in Chunks" (Foster), 8
"How Social Computing Will Improve the Enterprise Value Chain: 8 Predictions" (*Social Computing Journal*), 181–182
"How Teens Use Media" (Nielsen), 135–136, 148
Howtoons, 52
http:// protocol, development, 39
Hubbard, Lieutenant David, 79
*The Huffington Post*, 242–243
Hull, Richard, 209–210
Hulu, 195
Hunt, Tara, 157, 158, 180–181
hybrid work spaces, 20, 30–32

**I**

ideas, 14–15, 54–55. *See also* intellectual property
"I Fell in Love at the Apple Store" (Fatty Spins), 196–197
Ignition Partners, 209
*I'm Having More Fun Than You* (Karo), 208
immediacy, digital natives' expectation of, 141, 143–144, 177
incentives, advertising, 125
Indeed.com job search engine, 82
Indique Heights, 158–159

Industrial Age, news in, 232
influencers, 177–178
information, ownership of, 54–55
"Information, Technology and
    Information Worker Productivity"
    (Aral, Brynjolfsson, & Van
    Alstyne), 9
Information Age, news in, 232
information discovery technology,
    195–196
information quality, assessing, 363–364
Ingenesist Project, 182–183
innovation
    commercial model, 42, 46, 48, 55–57
    consumer role, 50–51, 53
    crowdsourced, 46, 55–57
    digital native approach, 49, 50
    evolution, 41
    at Google, 54–55, 56
    by groups, 41–42
    internally driven, 42, 46, 48
    pace, 46
    promoting, 45
    re-mixing existing ideas, 46–47,
        221–223, 252–253, 355, 366
    rights to ideas/information, impor-
        tance to, 58
    social media as tool for, 45
    without inventors, 49
Innovation Bank, 183
Institute of Play, 301–303
Instructables forum/restaurant, 51–52
Intel, 48–49
intellectual property. See also Creative
    Commons
    digital natives' views on, 370
    laws protecting, 213, 216–217,
        221–223, 225, 365–366
    ownership, 366
    respect for, 365–366
    theft, 219–220, 259–262, 365, 367
intelligence software in police work, 77
International Society for Technology in
    Education (ISTE), 283–285

internet
    business, effect on, 97
    cell phone access, 148
    filters, 367–368
    France, access in, 335–336, 343
    information quality, 363–364
    invention, 39–40
    news presentation, 231–232
    safe use practices, 367–368
    use by generation, 40, 136
interoperability issues, avoiding, 56
intimacy, creating effect of, 13
inventor, view as hero, 41–42
iPad, accessing news on Apple, 237–238
Iranian elections in 2009, journalist cov-
    erage of, 236
iReport.com, 243
Israel, Shel, 168–169
ISTE (International Society for
    Technology in Education),
    283–285
Ito, Mizuko, 117
itsmy.com social network, 118
iTunes, 263

**J**

jobs-related services, 82–85, 88–91, 93
Jones, Glenn, f100
Jules Ferry law (1882), 336–337

**K**

Kalantzis, Mary, 293
Karo, Aaron, 208
Kaufman, Ben, 51
knowledge hoarding, 180
knowledge work, 7, 22
Kohlhaas, Karrie, 29–30
Kot, Greg, 260
Krok, Ray, 135
Krums, Janis, 236

## L

Lager, Marshall, 112
Lanier, Jaron, 222
LarrysWorld.com (blog), 72
Late of the Pier (band), 253
law, role in society, 212–214
law enforcement. *See* police officers
laws, outdated due to technology, 224–225
Leadbeater, Charles, 49, 53, 58
learning, 22, 63, 293–295. *See also* education
learning management system (LMS), 276, 277, 280–281
Leary, Brent, 155
leisure activities, 10–11, 17
*Le Monde de l'Education* (Baumard), 337
Lessig, Lawrence, 46, 213, 217, 221–223, 225, 252–253, 366
LGMobile Phones, competition sponsored by, 45–46
Li, Charlene, 246
LibGuides content management/publishing system, 318, 320
librarians, role in educating for digital literacy, 318–319
"Lifelong Readers: The Role of Teen Content" report (Newspaper Association of America), 228–229
*Life on the Screen* (Turkle), 323
Lille, France, 250
Lille Academy, information on B2i, 342
LinkedIn, 89, 90, 163, 165
LinkedIn Answers, 165
listening to consumers, recommendations, 110–111, 126–127, 139, 144, 161–162
listservs, history, 233
LMS (learning management system), 276, 277, 280–281
location-based services, 148–149
Loertscher, Dr. David, 359–360
loyalty, customer, 144

## M

"The Machine is Us/ing Us" (Wesch), 323
magazines, decline, 227
Magic Eraser, development, 47
Magid, Larry, 72
Maher, Sean, 46
"Major New Study Shatters Stereotypes About Teens and Video Games" (Lenhart), 353
maker's schedule, 8
"Maker's Schedule, Manager's Schedule" (Graham), 8
Manafy, Michelle, 187, 246–247
manager's schedule, 8
Man Machine Challenge, 127
Marc Ecko advertisement, 199
marketing. *See also* branding; mobile devices, marketing on
  to digital natives, 133–135, 139–142, 145–146, 150, 153–154, 206–209
  as entertainment, 196–197, 208–209
  event sponsorships, 137
  examples, 119–120, 122, 137–140, 142–143, 146–148, 157–159
  film industry, 192–193, 200
  information, consumer control of, 123–124
  interactive capabilities, 145
  listening to consumers, 110–111, 126–127, 139, 144, 161–162
  market, understanding, 138–139
  mass market approach, 135
  media, integrating, 145
  piecemeal, 193–194
  on social media, 42–43, 163–164, 168–169
  traditional, transforming to native, 193–194, 195
  via blogs, 144, 166–167
  via multiple channels, 146

via social media, 42–43, 144,
  154–155, 157–159, 163–164,
  168–169, 204
video messaging, 149
viral, 137–138, 144
"Marketing to the Millennial Generation:
  Beyond Howe and Strauss" (Hesel
  & Pryor), 134
Martin Luther King: A Historical
  Perspective (website), 363
mashes, 252. *See also* remixed products
mashup (term), 252. *See also* remixed
  products
massively multiplayer online role-playing
  games (MMORPH), 174, 354
mass media era, 233
math, teaching techniques, 273
"Maturing with the Millenials" (study by
  Economist Intelligence Unit), 139
Maycreate, 23–24
McDonald's in Japan, 122–123
McGee-Smith, Sheila, 102–103
media, 135–137, 145, 177, 232–233. *See
  also* individual media
mediabistro.com job board, 82–83
Mehserle, Johannes, 67
membership model, newspaper, 239–240
Menchaca, Lionel, 160–161
"Mental Exercising Through Simple
  Socializing: Social Interaction
  Promotes General Cognitive
  Functioning" (Ybarra et al), 15–16
Merlindia, 159
Metcalf, John Erik, 136, 137
*Metro Nordic*, 245
*Middlesbrough Evening Gazette*, 240
military training tools, 70
Millennials. *See* Generation Y
"Millennials Thrive on Choice, Instant
  Results" (Goodnow), 141
Miller, Christa M., 79
misleading online material, 363
mission control ethics, 214–215, 218
MMORPH (massively multiplayer online
  role-playing games), 174, 354

"Mobile Advertising" (Harris Interactive),
  149
*Mobile as 7th of the Mass Media: Cell
  Phone, Cameraphone, iPhone,
  Smartphone* (Ahonen), 118
mobile blogs, 118
mobile devices, 45–46, 118, 128–129,
  136. *See also* cell phones
mobile devices, marketing on
  acceptance, 137, 148
  advantages, 116, 126, 144
  applications for, 115–116, 149
  consumer control, 123–124
  dependence on, 128–129
  digital natives' views on, 116,
    117–119, 124, 137, 148
  effect, 115
  engagement, importance, 122–123
  evolution, 118, 148
  examples, 119, 121–123
  importance, 130
  relationships, effect on, 117
  rules, 125, 149
  use, 116–117, 119–120, 128–129
mobile phones. *See* cell phones
"Mobile Search & Content Discovery"
  (Salz), 130
mobile TV/video, 136
mobile work, 20, 25–26, 27–28
Mobile Youth project, 121–122
moblogging (mobile blogging), 118
Mochi Media online game network, 53
Monster Energy Drinks marketing campaign, 122
Monster job board, 82, 84
Moreau, Emilie, 251, 265
Motrin advertising, 204
mountain bike, invention, 49
Moveable Type, 233
movie entertainment marketing,
  192–193, 196, 200–202
"Moviegoers 2010" report (Stradella
  Road & Nielsen NRG), 196
MP3s, 250, 252, 257–259, 264

Mr. Clean Magic Eraser, development, 47
MSearchGroove, 130
MSNBC, acquisition of Newsvine, 234
MTV, 201–202, 236
multitasking, bursty work compared, 9
Mumbai terrorism, journalist coverage of, 236
Murdoch, Rupert, 236
music
  access to, 249–250, 254–255, 257, 262, 264, 355
  digital natives' relating to, 250
  downloading, 263
  Lille study, 250, 251, 263–264
  MP3 format, 250, 252, 257–259, 264
  natives as creators, 355
  ownership of, 257
  piracy, 215, 259–260, 261–262
  sales, 261, 263, 264–265
  sharing, 263, 365
  sources of knowledge on, 262–263
  vinyl format, 250, 252, 253–257, 264
myGamma social network, 118
Myspace, 104, 164, 195, 233, 236

**N**

NAA (Newspaper Association of America), 228–229
Nanna, Bob, 99–100
Napster, 174
National Educational Technology Standards (NETS), 284, 285
A Nation at Risk (National Commission on Excellence in Education), 271
Neopets, 203, 207
NetEase online game operator, 53
Net Geners (term), 316. See also digital natives
NETS (National Educational Technology Standards), 284, 285

Netsize Guide, 119–120
Network Solutions, 170–171
Neuberg, Brad, 34
new learning (term), 293–294
New Marketing Playbook (Microsoft), 142, 143
"The New Media Consortium" (Horizon), 328–329
New Media Survey (Economist, 2006), 233
"The New News Media-Scape" (Pew Internet & American Life Project), 232
news media
  citizen journalism, 235–236
  consumption by digital natives, 228, 229, 246
  content creation, 233
  expectations of digital natives, 232, 235–236
  Information Age/Industrial Age compared, 232
  participation, inviting user, 232
  paying for, 237–238, 239
  social media, linking to, 244
  survival strategies, 230, 233, 236–237, 238–239, 240, 246
  television, influence on, 230–231
  via social networks, 229–230, 246
Newspaper Association of America (NAA), 228–229
newspapers, 155–156, 227–231, 236–240, 244–246
Newstex, virtual work force in, 26–27
New Student Reading Project (Cornell), 329
Newsvine, 234
New York Times, 239, 240, 244
New York Times Knowledge Network, 239
niche social communities, 164
Nicholl, Jake, 99
Nieman Journalism Lab Blog, 239
nodal learning (term), 294–295

"norms of the net gen" (Tapscott), 21
Novell Pulse as training resource, 65
nursing training, 63
NYTimes.com, 244

## O

office environments, 19–25, 29–30,
    32–34, 36–37
Office Nomads, 35, 37–38
office pods, 30
online behavior, acceptable, 86
online education, 278–279
online media, digital native-friendly fea-
    tures, 242–243
"Online Product Research" (Pew Internet
    study), 43
openness in sharing ideas, 39, 40
Open Office Space site, 33
open source culture, 40–41, 58. *See also*
    openness in sharing ideas
open source enterprises, 51–52
Open Water Consulting LLC, 151
open web (term), 54
Oracle, 40
originality, digital natives' expectations,
    177
*Out in the Magic Kingdom* (Doctorow),
    180–181
*Outliers: The Story of Success* (Gladwell),
    277–278
ownership, 257. *See also* intellectual
    property

## P

P&G (Procter & Gamble), 47–48, 121,
    122
paidContent.org blog, 234
Paint, Microsoft, 358
Palfrey, John, 316, 321, 324, 325, 363
parents, digital natives' view of, 147

payment, shifting view of, 45–46
PBS television, digital native-friendly fea-
    tures, 240–241
peer influence, 177–178
people searching, 84–85
Pepsi, 122, 204
*Personal, Portable, Pedestrian* (Ito, Okabe
    & Matsuda), 117
personal branding, 81–82, 85–88,
    91–94, 144, 364–365. *See also*
    branding
Personal Branding Wiki, 85
Peters, Tom, 81
Petouhoff, Dr. Natalie, 107, 108
Phillips, Terry, 29
photo blogging, 166
Photobucket, 169
photographs, editing, 218–219
Pilgrim, Mark, 54
pirating, 219–220, 259–260, 261–262,
    365, 367
plagiarism, 364–365
podcasts, in education, 281–282
police departments, larger/smaller com-
    pared, 75–76
police officers
    branding, 76, 77, 78
    challenges, 62
    crowdsourcing, 73
    digital natives as, 62–63, 69–70,
        75–77, 78
    enforcement trends, 73
    information gathering, 69
    mentoring, 71–72, 75, 76, 78
    online conduct, 66–67, 68
    public, communications with, 68,
        73–74
    resource shortages, 62
    roles, 66
    technology use by, 61, 64–66, 69,
        71–72, 77–78
    television, misperceptions fostered by,
        62
    training, 63–64, 66, 68–69, 70–73
    workshifting, 74–75

political power, influence on communication, 334–335
Postman, Neil, 212, 230, 231, 232, 347
PowerCurl, 51
PowerPoint, Microsoft, 358
Prensky, Marc, 63, 64, 175, 179, 353, 354, 370
presentation software, digital natives' lack of skill with, 358
printing, indiscriminate, 360
print media, 227–228, 232, 238
printout mania, 360
privacy, 67–68, 124, 211–212, 335, 370
"'Procrastination' Tales of Mere Existence" (Yilmaz), 30
Procter & Gamble (P&G), 47–48, 121, 122
productivity, 9, 22
product reviews. See recommendations, consumer
products, 42, 43–44
professional contacts, social networking compared, 15
progress, linearity, 3–4
project-based work, 9–10
property rights and airplanes conflict, 217
Proudly Found Elsewhere program, 47
public accountability numbers systems, 73
Pullman, Philip, 128, 129

**Q**

Quest to Learn (Q2L)
    admission process, 292
    creation, 291
    curriculum, 295–298, 301–304, 309–311
    gaming in, 297, 302–303, 305
    goals, 291, 308
    knowledge domains, 299–301
    philosophy, 291–294
        resources on, 308
    teacher development, 305–307
    technology use, 304–305
Quirky, 51

**R**

Radian6 alert tool, 162
rallods currency, 182–183
Ralph Lauren, advertising success, 200
Rant & Rave, 127
Rapide Communication Ltd., 127
rating products/services, 42, 43–44
Ready Offices site, 33
reality-based training, 63–64
reality shows; role of trust in, 205–206
recommendations, consumer
    consumer use, 155
    on Facebook, 155
    films, effect on, 156, 196
    listening to, 110–111, 126–127, 139, 144, 161–162
    malcontents, influence of, 185–186
    positive, percentage, 186
    as social capital, 179
    in social media, 155, 161–164
recommendations of job seekers, 90–91
recording industry, 260–261
record labels, 260–261
recruiting employees, 75–77, 89–90
Reid, Carolina Madeleine, 58–59
Remix (Lessig), 213, 221–222
remix culture, 49, 120
remixed products, 46–47, 221–223, 252–253, 355, 366
Remix: Making Art and Commerce Thrive in the Hybrid Economy (Lessig), 46
Remote Revolution (blog), 29
remote work, 20, 25–26, 27–28
RentAThing, 183–184
reputation
    company, 178–179
    crowdsourcing, 185–186

as currency, 182–185
gaining on social networks, 178,
    179–180, 186–187
leveraging, 181–182
monitoring online, 87, 91, 159–160,
    170
personal, 173–174, 179
value, 180, 181
"Reputation as Property in Virtual
    Economies" (Blocher), 186–187
reputation-based culture, 178
research methodologies, training for,
    317–318
resumes, use in job searches, 83–84
Retweets, 159
reusing digital content, 213, 216. *See also*
    remixed products
reviews, product. *See* recommendations,
    consumer
Re-Vision Labs, 33, 34
rights to ideas/information, 54–55, 58.
    *See also* Creative Commons; GPL;
    intellectual property
*Ripped* (Kot), 260
Robles, Dan, 183
"The Rock Band and the Cloud"
    (McGee-Smith), 102–103
*Rocky Mountain News* (newspaper), 228
role-playing games, 174, 203, 354
Rowse, Darren, 165
Rufo-Tepper, Rebecca, 311–312
*Ruminations on College Life* (Karo), 208
*Ruminations on Twentysomething Life*
    (Karo), 208
Russell, Michael P., 151

**S**

Saba people management firm, 181, 182
safety education, 67
Sage North America, 108–111
Salen, Katie, 308
Salesforce.com, 102
Salva, Ryan, 31–32

Salz, Peggy Anne, 130
San Jose Model of field training, 68–69
Sarbanes-Oxley Act (2002), 213
Sarkozy, Nicolas, 261, 262
SBE (standards-based education), 269,
    271–272, 287
Schawbel, Dan, 94
Scheer, Gabriel, 33, 34
schools, alternative forms, 271–272. *See
    also* education
Schrock, Kathy, 364
Schwartz, Larry, 26–27
Scion cars, marketing, 142–143
Scribd, 169
search engines, 90, 359–360. *See also*
    Google
search skills, 360, 361–363
Search.Twitter, 162
*Seattle Post-Intelligencer* (newspaper), 228
Second Life, 54–55, 64–65, 203
Second Life Blog, 64–65
Seeking Alpha (blog), 46
Seesmic, 169
Segway, 140
selective hearing (term), 43
self-employment, 20, 28, 29–30, 32–36
senior adults, social network use, 155
Sentiment Engine, Rant & Rave, 127
services, feedback on, 42. *See also*
    products
Set 'n Forget slow cooker, Hamilton
    Beach, 44
Shanda Enterprises online game operator,
    52–53
Shapiro, Arana, 312–313
shared office environments, 20, 32–34
sharing content. *See also* intellectual
    property, theft
digital natives' attitudes, 67–68
files, 174
licensing, 52, 55, 223, 323–324, 366
music, 263, 365
ownership of, 54–55, 58, 67
sites for, 169
value, 169

sharing ideas, openness in, 39, 40
sharing knowledge, knowledge hoarding compared, 180
sharing personal status, 117–118
shifting work, 19
"The Silent Epidemic" report, 293
"Simultaneous Media Survey" (BIGresearch), 148
Siri, Santiago, 184–185
"Size, Structure and Growth of the U.S. Information Economy" (Apte & Nath), 7
Sleepycat Software, acquisition by Oracle, 40
SlideShare, 169
SMART Board, 274–275
smartphones, 129
Smith, Michael P., 245
social capital. *See* reputation
social gaming, 202–203
social interactions, 12–13, 15–16
socialization, employer focus on, 22
Socialize Mobilize (blog), 43
Social Mention, 162
social networks. *See also* specific networks
    alerts for detecting comments, 162
    benefits, 12, 14–15, 45
    as business tool, 99–102, 176–177
    checking, frequency of teens,' 154
    consumer expectations, 155
    costs, 104
    effects, 43–44, 72, 176–177
    evolution, 174
    games, 202–203
    goals, 174
    inappropriate content, 217–218
    as information resource, 195–196
    job search-related use, 84–85, 89–90
    made-for-mobile, 118
    marketing access, 144
    participating in, 42–43, 163–164, 168–169
    in police work, 77–78
    scope of influence, 177–178

term, 174
    as tool for innovation, 45
    tools for, 234
    use of, 117, 156–157, 195, 229–230
    using, purpose of, 196
    using, recommendations for, 161–163
    views, 13
social permeance, 12, 16
social tagging, 165–166
society, changes caused by technology, 212
Sons of Maxwell (band), 197
Sony, advertising successes, 119–120, 199–200
sound, increase in environment, 259. *See also* music
"Sound Studies: New Technology and Music" (Pinch & Bijsterveld), 259
speed, digital natives' expectation of, 141, 143–144
Spiral Muse coworking space, 34
sponsorships, event, 137
spreadsheet software, digital natives' lack of skill with, 358
standards-based education (SBE), 269, 271–272, 287
Starmind website, 45
startup companies, 99–101, 102–103, 104–105
state, sharing one's personal, 117–118
"State of Customer-Centric Retailing: A Best Practices Guide for Higher Sales, Customer Retention, and Satisfaction" (Aberdeen Group), 111
State of the Media Report (Pew Research Center's Project for Excellence in Journalism 2009), 228, 234–235
stealing, changing definition, 217
Stormfront, 363
storytelling, digital, 326–327
*Structural Holes: The Social Structure of Competition* (Burt), 14

Studio Q teacher development program, 305–307
Stumptown Coffee, Seattle, 31
*The Subtle Knife* (Pullman), 129
SuiteMatch site, 33
Sullivan, Jane, 274–275
Survey Monkey, 360–361
"A Survey of the Research on Human Factors Related to Lethal Force Encounters" (Law Enforcement Executive Forum), 64
Sutherland, Rory, 126
systems thinking, 291–292, 296–300, 309

## T

"Tagging Air Force One" video, 199
TalentZoo.com job board, 82–83
Tan, Rosemary, 120
task switching, 9
teacher development, 305–307, 369
*Teaching Every Student in the Digital Age* (Rose & Meyer), 277
"Technological Inertia in Economic History" (Mokyr), 334–335
technological knowledge/comfort, 351, 352–353
technology
    Baby Boomers, use by, 134–135
    cultural influence on, 250, 333–334
    digital natives, use of, 134–135
    digital natives' attitude toward, 7
    distributed networking, 11–12
    in education, 270–271, 274–275, 276, 283–285, 293–294
    education on, 339–342, 344–345, 346–348
    ethics, influence of, 216–217, 218, 225
    Generation Y, use by, 134–135
    information discovery, 195–196
    laws, inappropriate, 224–225
    networked lifestyle, support for, 7–8
    for police officers, 61, 65–66, 69, 71–72, 77–78
    in Quest to Learn, 304–305
    remixed products, 253
    social permeance, 12, 170
    society, changes caused to, 212
    technology-deprived people, education for, 368
*Technopoly: The Surrender of Culture to Technology* (Postman), 212
Technorati, 162
Teen Research Unlimited (TRU), 142
teens
    advertising to, 135–136, 148
    cell phone use, 116–117, 148
    challenges to, causes, 271
    computer access, 293
    French, digital behavior, 335–336
    gaming activity, 353
    media use, 135
    needs of, 121
    online presence, 293
    personal branding, 87–88
    social network use, 154, 155, 160
    spending, 142
    texting, 116, 154
"Teens and Social Media" (Pew Internet & American Life Project study), 365–366
telecommunications businesses, 138–139
*Télécommunications et Philosophie des Rèseaux* (Musso), 347
telecommuting, 20, 25–26, 27–28
tele-nesting, 117
television, 135–136, 195, 198, 230–231, 240–241, 243
Tencent online game operator, 52–53
testing methods, product, 57
texting, 116, 154, 217
Think27 (blog), 136
Thinkfinity, 275–276
Third Idea Consulting LLC, 112
Thompson, Clive, 13

Threadless T-shirt company, 99–100, 104
"Three Screen Nation: Marketing to Gen Y" (AOL), 142
TME Strategy Lab analysis (2007), 167–168
Torres, Connie, 124–125
Torres, Robert J., 311
traditional business culture, open source culture and, 40–41
transparency, 68
travel booking agents, virtual work force, 25
"Trends in Online Shopping" (Pew Internet study), 43
trespassing, changing definition, 217
Tribune Co., 228
TRU (Teen Research Unlimited), 142
TubeMogul, 169
Twitter
    alerts for detecting comments on, 162
    brand engagement, user, 204–205
    company use, 43, 50, 105–106, 157, 160–161, 205
    costs, 104
    described, 163
    influence of, 168
    as marketing tool, 204
    as news source, 235
    online ratings, 204–205
    personalization of responses, 161
    recruiting on, 89
    researching job candidates on, 90
    Retweet feature, 159
    usage statistics, 42, 160, 163, 195, 204
    uses, 163, 191, 195
"Twitter and Status Updating Fall 2009" report (Pew Internet), 160
"Twittering May Have Impact at Box Office" (Sragow), 156
Twitterville (Israel), 168–169
"2018: Digital Natives Grow Up and Rule the World" (Basso), 175–176
2Many DJs, 252

**U**

UBS, contest to promote innovation, 45
UDL (universal design for learning), 277
Understanding Media: The Extensions of Man (McLuhan), 323
unemployment figures, 83
United Airlines, Carroll conflict with, 197
universal design for learning (UDL), 277
URL protocol development, 39
U.S. Airways crash (January 2009), 236
USA TODAY, 231
"Using a Course Management System to Meet the Challenges of Large Lecture Classes" (Bongey, Cizadlo & Kalnbach), 280

**V**

Valemont video series, 201–202
Van Alen, Bas, 52
Vanasse, Diana, 273
Vanneck-Smith, Katie, 240
Vaynerchuk, Gary, 157–158
Viddler, 169
video, 149, 166, 192–193, 196–197, 323–324, 327–328, 355–356
video games, 292, 354
"Video Games: Why Kids Play and What They Learn" (Olthouse), 354
video remixes, 221
Vinod, K.N., 158–159
vinyl records, 250, 252, 253–257, 264
viral spread of online information, 67
Virgin Mobile U.S., 138
virtual reality tools, as training resource, 54–55, 64–65, 203
virtual work, 25
virtual world games, 203–204. See also Second Life
"Virtual Worlds for Kids, Tweens & Teens: 7 Must-Have Features" (interFuel), 203–204

# W

Wallach, D.A., 102, 103
Walt Disney Pictures, 200
Welch, Robyn, 35
*We Think: Mass Innovation, Not Mass Production* (Leadbeater), 49
*What Color is Your Parachute?* (Bolles), 83
"What Works with the Google Generation?" (Loertscher), 360
Whedon, Joss, 201
Whelan, Lisa, 43
*When in Rome* (Walt Disney Pictures), 200
"Who Tweets" (Pew Internet & American Life Project), 204
Whuffie (term), 180–181. See also reputation
Whuffie Bank, 184–185
*The Whuffie Factor* (Hunt), 157, 158, 181
wikis, learning to create/contribute to, 321–322
Wine Library TV, 157–158
wish fulfillment in digital role creation, 207
"Women's Activism" (Cornel course), 324
word processing applications, digital natives' lack of skill with, 357–358
work. *See also* office environments
anywhere-everywhere, 7, 9–12, 17
bursty, 8, 9, 10–11
of digital natives, 4, 5–7, 8, 16–17
evolution, 7
free, 45–46
information-based, 7, 22
location, 19
mobile, 20, 25–26, 27–28
project-based, 9–10
scheduling, 8, 19, 27
self-employment, 20, 28, 29–30, 32–36
setting, changes, 356

shifting, 74
understanding others,' importance, 4–5
virtual, 25
work environment, collaborative/socialization emphasis, 22. *See also* office environments
work force, preparing, 271
work-life balance, digital natives' changes to, 19, 74
work practice, defined, 4
workshifting, 74
WorkShifting blog, 74
*The World Is Flat: A Brief History of the Twenty-First Century* (Friedman et al), 271
World of Warcraft, 203
"The World That Changed the Machines" (Gautschi & Sabavala), 133, 141
World Wide Web invention, 39
writing, learning, 321–322, 328
"Writing and Research in the University: Writing in the Twenty-First Century" (Cornell seminar)
curriculum, 319–324, 326–328
goals, 317–319
overview, 328–329
student projects, 324–327

# Y

Yelp, 155, 156
Yi, Kun, 325, 326
Yilmaz, Lev, 30
*You Are Not a Gadget: A Manifesto* (Lanier), 222
"Youth Media DNA" (Newspaper Association of America), 229, 233
youths. *See* teens
YouTube, 104, 145, 169, 220, 233, 293, 355

## Z

Zarcorp (record label), 253
Zelenka, Anne, 8
Zuiker, Anton, 322